REDISCOVERING
HOMER

ALSO BY ANDREW DALBY

The Story of Venus

Flavours of Byzantium

Bacchus: A Biography

Food in the Ancient World from A to Z

Language in Danger

Dangerous Tastes

Empire of Pleasures:
Luxury and Indulgence in the Roman World

Dictionary of Languages

Cato on Farming

A Guide to World Language Dictionaries

The Classical Cookbook (with Sally Grainger)

REDISCOVERING HOMER

Inside the Origins of the Epic

ANDREW DALBY

W. W. NORTON & COMPANY
NEW YORK   LONDON

Copyright © 2006 by Andrew Dalby

For information about permission to reproduce selections from this book, write to
Permissions, W. W. Norton & Company, Inc., 500 Fifth Avenue, New York, NY 10110

Manufacturing by Quebecor, Fairfield
Book design by Soonyoung Kwaon
Production manager: Andrew Marasia

Library of Congress Cataloging-in-Publication Data

Dalby, Andrew, 1947–
Rediscovering Homer : inside the origins of the epic / Andrew Dalby. — 1st ed.
p. cm.
Includes bibliographical references and index.
ISBN-13: 978-0-393-05788-1 (hardcover)
ISBN-10: 0-393-05788-7 (hardcover)
1. Homer—Criticism and interpretation. 2. Homer. Iliad. 3. Homer. Odyssey.
4. Epic poetry, Greek—History and criticism—Theory, etc. 5. Folk poetry, Greek—
History and criticism. I. Title.
PA4037.D335 2006
883'.01—dc22

2005038011

ISBN 978-0-393-33019-9 pbk.

W. W. Norton & Company, Inc., 500 Fifth Avenue, New York, N.Y. 10110
www.wwnorton.com

W. W. Norton & Company Ltd., Castle House, 75/76 Wells Street, London W1T 3QT

1 2 3 4 5 6 7 8 9 0

CONTENTS

PART THREE

The Response

PREFACE

Some books will always be read. Among them are the two early Greek epics, *Iliad* and *Odyssey*, traditionally ascribed to Homer and now known to have emerged from a long tradition of oral poetry. No one challenges their place in the canon, and it's easy to become passionately involved with them, not only because we find more in them with each rereading, but because we demand an answer to the mysteries of who made them, how they came into existence, and how they came to be written down.

I am not alone in being convinced that the legendary poet Homer, forefather of the Greek oral tradition, must not be confused with the real poet who created the written *Iliad* and *Odyssey*. Why not? For two reasons: the ancient evidence that Homer worked orally, without access to writing, and modern proof that oral epics are ever created anew and become fixed only when written down. If we accept both the early evidence and the modern research, we cannot go on believing that Homer was the creator of the written *Iliad* and *Odyssey*.

There is an even better reason for holding to this conviction. It gives an advantage that I did not fully foresee when I began to work on the epics. It allows us to reconsider every detail about the unknown poet—even that poet's gender. The *Iliad* and the *Odyssey* were composed by one of the greatest representatives of the ancient Greek oral epic tradition, and it is possible, even probable, that this poet was a woman. As a working hypothesis, this helps to explain certain features in which these epics are better (more subtle, more complex, more universal) than most others.

Because the *Iliad* and the *Odyssey* are so important in our culture, everything about them is disputed. All imaginable views have been taken about every detail concerning the poems—their structure, purpose, original audience, and later transmission. Some positions taken in this book are controversial, but in general I have not argued them out against other opinions. Instead I have aimed to distinguish fact from conjecture and not to overinsist on arguable points.

In the Guide to Further Reading, I have listed some recent studies of the two epics and their contexts and pointed out a few crucial areas where their authors disagree with one another or with opinions expressed in this book. Here also is guidance to some recent translations of the epics and basic information about other early texts and other oral traditions that are mentioned here. Translations from the *Iliad* and the *Odyssey* are mine; translations from other ancient and medieval texts are also mine, except when credited in the notes.

I want to thank the teachers at Bristol and Cambridge who first made me read the *Iliad* and the *Odyssey*. Some of them would certainly have disagreed with some of what is said here, so I must thank them also for making me think for myself. For the insight that the poet's gender has to be reconsidered, I am grateful to the writers on oral tradition credited in Chapter 7, who have shown that women have often been the greatest makers of oral literature at the fateful moment in each tradition, the moment when these literatures are being turned into writing.

Finally, for making this book make sense, I thank Liz Duvall, the copy editor; and Maria Guarnaschelli of W. W. Norton. Maria and I first discussed Homer eight years ago in the best possible place for such discussions, on the island of Chios.

KEY WORDS

In this book, the words **singer** and **poet** mean almost the same thing. *Poet* is in origin the Greek word *poietes*, "maker" or "poet"; however, at the time when the *Iliad* and the *Odyssey* were made, poets more often called themselves *aoidoi*, "singers," because they were live entertainers, performing their work by singing it.

This was a rich culture, with many genres of song or poetry. The shorter forms can be conveniently grouped as **lyric**, a word of Greek origin meaning originally "sung to the music of the lyre." The *Iliad* and the *Odyssey*, however, are long narrative poems, or **epics**. They are in **hexameter** verse, a sequence of regular lines in six-beat rhythm, customarily chosen by early Greek narrative poets. Their structure relies on **formulas**, ready-made groups of words that fit this verse rhythm. These and other features help to demonstrate the existence in early Greece of an epic **tradition**. Verse rhythms vary, but formulas are a common feature of oral narrative poetry almost worldwide.

A skilled singer who specialized in epics was called in Greek *rhapsodos*, "singer of woven words." Such a singer used these features to build afresh at each performance a poem of any required length. Although not **oral poems** (because in fact they are written), the *Iliad* and the *Odyssey* come from an oral literary culture. They were surely composed by a skilled epic singer and written before that singer's eyes: composition and writing were simultaneous.

Oral epic traditions draw in historical material almost randomly, it seems, but their characters interact in a social framework that is convincing and consistent. This is particularly true of the *Iliad* and the *Odyssey*, whose imagined **Homeric society** tells us a great deal about lives and beliefs in archaic Greece.

We do not know the name of the singer who composed these epics. The singer's name is not incorporated in the poems; perhaps it was not considered important by those who wrote them down. Singers often ascribe their work to a predecessor, regarded as the first or greatest exponent of the tradition; perhaps the singer of the *Iliad* and the *Odyssey* would have done this. At any rate, 150 years after these epics were composed, it had become commonplace to attribute them, and several others, to a legendary singer named Homeros, or (in modern English) **Homer**. Assuming that Homer existed, nothing can now be known of him or his singing, if it is true that, as the sources say, his work was not recorded in writing. Some scholars, however, give the name Homer to the poet who dictated or wrote the poems.

In other books in English about Homeric poetry the singer is sometimes called a **bard** (which in early modern English meant a Gaelic praise-poet and vagabond), an **aoidos** (the Greek word for "singer"), a **rhapsode** (from the Greek word for "singer of woven words"), and occasionally a **minstrel** (the name for a singer in medieval England). These words carry baggage, partly because their earlier senses have been adjusted in modern use, partly because each modern writer endows them with overtones and assumptions. I prefer to use the everyday English equivalent **singer**.

GREEK NAMES

There are three ways of transliterating ancient Greek names into English. The traditional way is to convert them into Latin: this produces forms such as *Ajax, Aeschylus, Alcibiades, Demodocus, Dionysus, Hecuba, Calypso, Circe, Socrates*. It used to be done that way because in the past, ancient Greek was studied through the medium of Latin; but this is not always so nowadays. A second method, found in books printed in Greece, is to transcribe the modern Greek pronunciation into English. The method adopted in this book is to transfer names directly from the ancient Greek alphabet to ours: *Aias, Aischylos, Alkibiades, Demodokos, Dionysos, Hekabe, Kalypso, Kirke, Sokrates*. This method is also used in a growing number of modern reference books, including the *Cambridge Guide to Classical Civilization* and the six-volume *The Iliad: A Commentary*.[1]

Some names are so familiar in English that it makes sense to retain their traditional English form. This applies to the titles *Iliad* (Greek *Ilias*), *Odyssey* (Greek *Odysseia*), and *Aeneid* (Latin *Aeneis*) and to the personal names Helen (Greek *Helene*), Achilles (Greek *Achilleus*), Priam

(Greek *Priamos*), Homer (Greek *Homeros*), Pindar (Greek *Pindaros*), Plato (Greek *Platon*), Aristotle (*Aristoteles*); and Virgil (Latin *Vergilius*). It also applies to some well-known place-names: Troy (Greek *Troia* and *Ilion*), Athens (Greek *Athenai*, modern *Athine*), Corinth (Greek *Korinthos*), Thebes (Greek *Thebai*, modern *Thive*), Crete (Greek *Krete*, modern *Kriti*), Rhodes (Greek *Rhodos*). A few names are most familiar in Latin, so their Latin form is retained here. This applies to Aeneas (Greek *Aineias*) and Strabo (Greek *Strabon*).

INTRODUCTION

THE POEMS AND THEIR SETTING

The *Iliad* tells the story of a few adventurous weeks in the ten-year siege of Troy by a Greek army whose aim was to recapture the beautiful Helen. If the poem has a hero, that hero is Achilleus (traditionally called Achilles in English). The *Odyssey* tells the later adventures of one of the Greek warriors, the resourceful Odysseus (sometimes called Ulysses). Its climax is Odysseus's long-delayed return to Ithake, his island home.

Certainly composed before 600 B.C., these are among the earliest works of literature in Greek. They may even be the very earliest. In any case, they are among the oldest literary texts in any European language.

These poems contain no contemporary references (or scarcely any), and certainly no information about the poet. When exploring major works in Western literature, we expect that answers to some basic questions will be easy to find: Who wrote it? What was its purpose? Who was likely to read it? When was it written? What other literature was around? What else happened at that time? In the case of these two poems, nothing is known in advance. Only careful reading and skilled detective work will produce even the most tentative answers to these questions.

According to the earliest written sources of information (dating from about 500 to 300 B.C.), Homeros, a Greek singer of the distant past, composed the *Iliad* and the *Odyssey*, along with several other poems, most of which are now lost. To all the earliest writers who mention Homer, his is a name with scarcely any biography. He is the personification of epic, a *rhapsodos*, a "singer of woven words." He did not write down his poems; they were transmitted by word of mouth by his descendants and collected in writing many years later.

From modern research on oral traditions we know that if this is so, the poems we are reading are not Homer's. The only oral narrative poets whose work we can really experience are those who perform in our presence, write their poems down, or dictate them. In modern oral traditions, poets or singers often claim to be repeating word for word a composition by some famous, honored predecessor, but it has been shown by experiment and fully confirmed by research that this claim is not and can never be true in our terms. There is no possibility of exact transmission. Narratives in oral tradition are created anew every time they are performed.

Modern research shows that the *Iliad* and the *Odyssey* really do come from a tradition of oral poetry. In style and structure they are like oral narrative poems from other times and places. They are absolutely unlike the work of authors in literary traditions that depend on writing. In any case, writing was very new in Greece at this period; poetry was still something that you listened to, and the idea of reading poetry from a written text was unfamiliar. Yet the *Iliad* and the *Odyssey* were written down (they must have been; otherwise they would not exist now). They are so long that the writing must have taken weeks or months. These facts too present difficult questions, and we have to try to answer them before we can really understand the poems. Why did someone decide, on these two occasions, not to create a poem orally and earn food and applause for it but to write it? Why are these two poems so much longer than anything a poet would create for an audience? Who was the patron who fed the poet while this work was going on? Who supplied the ink and the many goatskins that had to be covered with writing?

Almost every reader has thought that these two poems are great works of art. Their makers spent time and effort on them and must surely have taken pride in the result. So why is there no record of the way they worked, and why are the poems themselves totally anonymous? Early written sources provide tantalizing clues, but no full and consistent story about where and when the writing took place—in other words, where and when the *Iliad* and the *Odyssey* were created. Here again are difficult questions, though we can draw on information from the history of early Greece to try to answer them. Who, poet or patron, was enough of a visionary to realize that the work would be worthwhile? How did that person think the written texts would be used? What readership did he or she envisage, and who in reality were the first readers? What reaction was expected from those readers? Finally, how are we to read, enjoy, and evaluate epic poetry of the distant past?

We can answer one question confidently: readers liked these poems. They have continued to do so ever since; the *Iliad* and the *Odyssey* have never been forgotten. The first major work of Roman poetry was a Latin translation of the *Odyssey*. Medieval European literature— English, French, German, even Icelandic—includes a whole succession of new versions of the *Iliad* story and the Trojan War; the romantic tale of Troilus and Cressida, told in English by Chaucer and afterward by Shakespeare, is among these popular retellings. Meanwhile, the original Greek texts were still in circulation in medieval Greece, during the Byzantine empire. When printing was introduced to Europe in the fifteenth century, the original *Iliad* and *Odyssey*, based on Byzantine manuscript copies, were among the first Greek texts to be printed. In modern times there have been more than fifty translations of the *Iliad* into English. *Troy* is only the latest in a series of films whose plots are drawn from the two epics.

By common consent, these are still among the greatest stories ever written. Every later epic and narrative poem looks back to them for inspiration: Virgil's *Aeneid*, telling the legendary origins of Rome;

Dante's *Divine Comedy;* Milton's *Paradise Lost.* Every adventure novel reflects back, in one way or another, to the *Odyssey.* Management studies, strategic studies, psychology, even the writing of history would take a different form if the *Iliad* and the *Odyssey* were not there in the background, a continuing example, a source of renewed inspiration.

Greece, the land from which these poems originate and whose legends they tell, is a region of mountains, valleys, and scattered islands. When the two epics were composed, Greeks grew vines (for wine), olive trees (for oil), and barley as their main cereal; they kept sheep, goats, pigs, and geese; they used oxen to pull plows and carts. They lived in cities of a few hundred or a few thousand inhabitants. They worshipped the twelve Olympian gods and some others.

Every city had an open space, an agora, where men conducted business and politics. There was no Greek nation-state; in principle, each city was totally independent. Their people shared the same language, ancient Greek; the same religion; and the same literature, which included familiar mythological tales about gods and heroes. Among these Greek cities democracy was born, a primitive democracy in which decisions depended on the vote or acclamation of adult male citizens.

Greek cities existed not only in European Greece and its surrounding islands but also along the coast of what is now western Turkey. It was in one of these cities, some people said, that Homer had lived.

Troy itself lies near this coastline. It was a very ancient and famous place. At the time when the poems were written down it was a ruin, but a shrine of Athene had recently been established there—possibly the earliest evidence that a legend of Troy was beginning to grow. Ithake, homeland of Odysseus, was a small and mountainous island with few inhabitants, west of the Greek mainland. Poets traveled, and the poet of the *Iliad* might conceivably have seen the ruins of Troy; few Greeks go to Ithake, however, and it would be surprising if the poet had done so.

THE STORY OF THE *ILIAD*

The story of Helen is the most famous in all of Greek mythology. Paris (who is usually called Alexandros in the *Iliad*; he is one of the sons of Priam, king of Troy) was invited to judge a beauty competition between three goddesses—the famous "judgment of Paris." He gave the prize to

Aphrodite, goddess of love, and she rewarded him (as she had secretly promised in advance) with the privilege of marrying the most beautiful of mortal women, Helen, who was already the wife of Menelaos, king of Sparta. So Paris visited Sparta and Helen fell in love with him, in accordance with Aphrodite's promise. They eloped to Troy. Menelaos's brother Agamemnon, king of Mykenai, gathered a Greek alliance to redress this affront to Menelaos. The Trojans were called on to return Helen, but they rejected the ultimatum. So the assembled Greek army sailed across the Aegean and camped outside the walls of Troy under Agamemnon's command. The ten-year siege began.

The *Iliad* does not tell the beginning of the story but narrates a series of incidents in the tenth year of the war, arising out of a dispute between Agamemnon and Achilles, the best of the Greek warriors. It depicts the death in battle of many heroes on both sides. The scene throughout is set in the battlefields outside the walls of Troy, in the city of Troy itself, and on Mount Olympos, where the gods live. What happened in Greece during these days, or during the whole ten years, is not told; it isn't part of the story.

The singer—the narrator—of the *Iliad* begins the story *when a quarrel arose between Agamemnon and Achilles* (see page xxiv for the opening passage). Chryses, the local priest of the god Apollo, offers Agamemnon a ransom for his daughter Chryseis, who has recently been captured in a raid and awarded to Agamemnon. He refuses to give her up. Apollo punishes him by sending a deadly plague to attack the Greek army. Agamemnon is persuaded to change his mind, but he refuses to be left without a prize; he saves face by seizing another captive woman, Briseis, who had been awarded to Achilles. Achilles is outraged, both because of Agamemnon's arbitrary use of power and because he loves Briseis. His mother, the sea goddess Thetis, visits and consoles him. Meanwhile the other gods, watching from Mount Olympos, begin to quarrel over this issue, but Apollo's music and the singing of the Muses help them to forget human affairs. Thetis, however, has persuaded Achilles to withdraw from fighting, and she now urges Zeus, king of the Olympian gods, to help the Trojans, because she wants the Greek army to suffer by Achilles' withdrawal.

Next day Agamemnon calls an assembly of the Greek troops. He intends to test their morale, and to his dismay he finds them ready to give up and return home, but Nestor and the wily Odysseus restore their courage. At this point in the poem the Greek leaders and their home cities are listed at full length (this section is known as the Catalogue of Ships), followed by a much shorter list of Trojan allies.

Paris, the first Trojan warrior to figure prominently in the *Iliad*, challenges his rival, Menelaos, to single combat to settle the ten-year dispute. A temporary truce is agreed upon, and Helen, standing on the wall of Troy, watches the duel between her two husbands. Paris is defeated, but his protector, the goddess Aphrodite, rescues him from the battlefield and forces Helen to go to bed with him, in spite of Helen's plainly expressed disgust for the relationship. The duel having ended inconclusively with Paris's disappearance from the battlefield, the Trojan Pandaros now breaks the truce by wounding Menelaos with an arrow, and a general battle ensues. The brave Diomedes features on the Greek side, daring even to aim weapons at the gods who participate in this mortal combat. Hektor, Paris's brother and the greatest warrior among the Trojans, is seen at home in Troy, with his wife, Andromache, and afterward in action on the battlefield. There follows a second day of fighting, which ends with the Trojans in the ascendant, still benefiting from Zeus's support, camped around their watch fires.

Agamemnon is at last persuaded to make overtures to Achilles. He now offers to give back Briseis and to make additional gifts to settle the quarrel. An "embassy" of Odysseus, Aias, and Phoinix goes to Achilles' tent. They find him with his constant companion, the warrior Patroklos; Achilles is sitting calmly, *singing of the fame of men*. They dine (Patroklos does the cooking; Achilles carves) and they negotiate, but in spite of Agamemnon's generous offer, Achilles will not give up his quarrel. He remains aloof from the fighting. That same night Diomedes and Odysseus set out to spy on the Trojans and eventually raid the camp of the Thracians, newly arrived Trojan allies.

In renewed fighting Agamemnon leads the Greeks to the walls of Troy, but then the tide turns: Agamemnon is wounded and the stubborn Aias is driven back; Nestor rescues the wounded Machaon from the battle; Achilles sees this and sends Patroklos to find out what is happening. Nestor's long reply includes a reminiscence of cattle-raiding in Greece in his younger days. Patroklos then encounters Eurypylos, who has also been wounded, and helps him to his hut. Led by the apparently unconquerable Hektor, the Trojans rush the Greek camp and drive the Greeks back among their ships.

Zeus, watching from Mount Olympos, is now distracted by his wife, Hera, who entices him into lovemaking. Afterward he sleeps, and his brother Poseidon, god of the sea, takes this opportunity to go into battle on the Greek side. Hektor is wounded. Zeus wakes and angrily restores Trojan fortunes: Hektor revives and pushes forward as far as the Greek ships. Patroklos now begs to be allowed to borrow Achilles' armor and lead their contingent, since Achilles himself still refuses to do so. Patroklos's intervention tips the balance: the Trojans turn to retreat, but with Apollo's help, Hektor manages to kill Patroklos. The Trojans strip the armor (Achilles' armor) from the body; the Greeks sadly carry back Patroklos's body and give Achilles the news of his friend's death.

Thetis asks the blacksmith god, Hephaistos, to make new armor for Achilles; this includes the famous "shield of Achilles," whose wonderful decoration is described at length in the poem. Strengthened by nectar and ambrosia, the food and drink of the gods, provided by the goddess Athene, Achilles now renounces his quarrel, and Agamemnon returns Briseis, swearing that he has not slept with her. Briseis and Achilles raise a lament over Patroklos's body. Achilles arms for battle. On this occasion the gods are encouraged by Zeus to take sides in the war; some even encounter one another on the battlefield, but unlike humans, they risk nothing. Aeneas and Hektor both stand against Achilles, but both are hastily withdrawn by their protector gods from a fight they cannot win. Achilles kills many Trojans and takes twelve youngsters alive to be butchered at the funeral of Patroklos; the remainder of the Trojans are driven behind their city walls. The brave Hektor, almost alone, remains outside. He is chased around the city wall by Achilles and is at last killed in single combat as his father, Priam, watches from the wall of Troy. Achilles gathers his warriors to sing a *paieon*, a chorus of triumph, as he drags Hektor's body behind his chariot in revenge for the death of Patroklos.

Achilles holds athletic games to mark the funeral of Patroklos; the games and the prizes are described in detail. He continues to spurn Hektor's body, dragging it daily around his friend's tomb. At last King Priam, guided by the god Hermes, goes in person to Achilles' tent at night to ask for his son's body. Achilles relents, grants Priam's request, and declares a truce. In a cart Priam takes Hektor's battered corpse home to Troy. The king's daughter, the prophet Kassandra, is the first to see them approach, and shouts the news to the Trojans. Hektor's widow, Andromache, and his mother, Hekabe, lead the lament. The poem ends with Hektor's funeral.

We can complete the Trojan War story with the help of flashbacks in the *Odyssey*, filled out with information from later Greek writings. Achilles was killed soon afterward, as is often foreshadowed in the *Iliad*. So was Paris. Helen was forced by the Trojans to marry Paris's brother Deiphobos.

The Greeks at last built a wooden horse and filled it with warriors. They then set fire to their camp and sailed away in their ships, pretending to abandon the siege but in fact preparing to return to Troy secretly after nightfall. The Trojans meanwhile dragged the horse inside their city, believing it to be a religious offering. That night the Greek warriors emerged from it to open the city gates for their comrades. Too late, the Trojans realized how they had been tricked. The men were mostly killed, the women and children enslaved. Menelaos mutilated and killed Deiphobos and recaptured Helen.[1] Agamemnon took Kassandra home as his concubine. The war was over.

THE STORY OF THE *ODYSSEY*

The victors had been absent from Greece for ten years, and their return home was not without incident. None of them wandered the seas for as long as the unlucky Odysseus. Telemachos, Odysseus's only son, was a baby when Odysseus left home to fight with the other Greeks at Troy. At the point where the *Odyssey* begins, Telemachos is about twenty and is sharing his absent father's house on the island of Ithake with his mother, Penelope, and a crowd of boisterous youngish men (always known as "the suitors") whose only aim in life is to persuade Penelope to accept her husband's disappearance as final and marry one of them.

The goddess Athene (who is Odysseus's protector) visits Telemachos, adopting a temporary disguise, to urge him to search for news of his father. He offers her food and drink. We see the suitors dining rowdily and the singer Phemios performing a narrative poem for them. Penelope appears and objects to Phemios's theme—the return from Troy—

because it reminds her of her missing husband, but Telemachos rebuts her objections.

Next morning Telemachos calls an assembly of citizens and demands a ship and crew. Still accompanied by Athene, who has now taken the shape of Telemachos's friend Mentor, he departs for the Greek mainland and the household of Nestor, the most venerable of the Greek warriors at Troy, who has long since returned home to Pylos. From there he rides overland to Sparta, where he finds Menelaos and Helen, fully reconciled. He gathers that they returned to Greece after a long voyage by way of Egypt; there, on the magical island of Pharos, Menelaos encountered the old sea god Proteus, who told him that Odysseus was a captive of the mysterious goddess Kalypso. In these visits Telemachos learns much about the aftermath of the Trojan War, including the fate of Menelaos's brother Agamemnon, murdered by his wife, Klytaimestra, and her lover, Aigisthos, on returning to Mykenai.[2]

Now the scene changes. Odysseus has indeed spent seven years in captivity on Kalypso's distant island. She is at last persuaded by the messenger god, Hermes, to release him: it is time for him to return to Penelope. Odysseus builds a raft. It is wrecked (the sea god Poseidon is his enemy), but he swims ashore on the island of Scherie, where, naked and exhausted, he falls asleep. Next morning, awakened by the laughter of girls, he sees the young Nausikaa, who has gone to the seashore with her maids to wash clothes. He emerges from hiding and appeals to her for help. She encourages him to seek the hospitality of her mother, Arete, and her father, Alkinoos. Odysseus is welcomed and well entertained; he is not at first asked for his name. He remains several days with Alkinoos, takes part in an athletic competition, and hears the blind singer Demodokos perform two narrative poems. The first is an otherwise obscure incident of the Trojan War, the "quarrel of Odysseus and Achilles"; the second is the amusing tale of a love affair between two Olympian gods, Ares and Aphrodite. Finally Odysseus asks Demodokos to return to the Trojan War theme and tell the story of the famous stratagem of the wooden horse—a story in which Odysseus played a leading role.

Unable to hide his emotion as he relives this episode, Odysseus at last reveals his identity. Naturally he does so, as Greeks traditionally did, by giving his own name, his father's name, and his home city. These are his words:

I am Odysseus, son of Laertes: for my cunning I am known
To all humankind, and my story has reached heaven.
I live in clear-seen Ithake. There is a mountain on it,
Neriton with swaying leaves, seen from afar. Around it islands,
Many of them, live very close to one another,
Doulichion and Same and wooded Zakynthos;
But Ithake lies land-bound, highest of all in the salt sea,
Toward the dark, the others further off toward the dawn and the sun;
Rough, but a good mother of children. I cannot
Imagine any other thing sweeter than that land.

(*Odyssey* 9.19–28)

He then begins to tell the amazing story of his return from Troy. After a piratical raid on Ismaros in the land of the Kikones, says Odysseus, he and his twelve ships were driven off course by storms. They visited the lazy Lotus-eaters and were captured by the fearsome one-eyed Kyklops Polyphemos, from whose cave they escaped by blinding him with a wooden stake. They stayed with Aiolos, the master of the winds; he gave Odysseus a leather bag containing all the winds, a gift that should have ensured them a safe return home, but the sailors foolishly opened the bag while Odysseus slept. All the winds flew out, and the resulting storm drove the ship back the way it had come.

After pleading in vain with Aiolos to help them further, they reembarked and encountered the cannibal Laistrygones. Odysseus's own ship was the only one to escape. He sailed on and visited the witch-goddess Kirke, whose magic potions turned most of his sailors into swine. Odysseus set out to rescue them and received from the god Hermes an antidote to her potion, a drug that is called *moly* in the language of the gods. Unaffected by her magic, he persuaded Kirke to release his men, and he himself slept with her. They stayed on Kirke's island for a year. Then, guided by her instructions, they crossed the Ocean and reached a harbor at the western edge of the world, where Odysseus sacrificed to the dead and summoned the spirit of the old prophet Teiresias to advise him. Here Odysseus learned for the first time news of his own household, threatened by the rapacity of the suitors. Here too he met the spirits of famous women and famous men; notably, he encountered the spirit of Agamemnon, whose murder he learned of for the first time.

Returning across the Ocean to Kirke's island, Odysseus and his men were advised by her on the remaining stages of the journey. Next they skirted the land of the sweet-singing Seirenes, passed safely between the many-headed monster Skylla and the whirlpool Charybdis, and landed on the Island of the Sun. There Odysseus's men, ignoring the warnings of Teiresias and Kirke, hunted and killed the Sun's sacred cattle. This sacrilege was punished by a shipwreck in which all but Odysseus were drowned. He was washed ashore on Kalypso's island, where she kept him as her unwilling lover. From that captivity he had only now escaped.

Having listened with rapt attention to his story, the Phaiekes, who are skilled mariners, agree to help Odysseus on his way home. They deliver him at night to a hidden harbor on his own island of Ithake, setting him ashore there while he is fast asleep. Next day he finds his way to the hut of one of his former slaves, the swineherd Eumaios. Here Odysseus plays the part of a wandering beggar in order to learn how things stand in his household. After dinner, maintaining his anonymity, he tells the farm laborers a fictitious tale about himself: he was born in Crete, had led a party of Cretans to fight alongside other Greeks in the Trojan War, and had then spent seven years at the court of the king of Egypt; finally he had been shipwrecked in Thesprotia, on the coast of mainland Greece, and crossed from there to Ithake.

Meanwhile Telemachos, whom we left at Sparta, sails home, evading an ambush set by the suitors. He disembarks on the coast of Ithake, leaving his friend Peiraios to see the ship home; Telemachos makes for Eumaios's hut. Father and son meet; Odysseus identifies himself, and they determine that the suitors must be killed. Telemachos gets home first, rejoins Peiraios, and eats. Accompanied by Eumaios, Odysseus now returns to his own house, still disguised as a beggar. He experiences the suitors' rowdy behavior at first hand and plans their death. He meets Penelope and tests her intentions with the invented story of his birth in Crete, where, he says, he once met Odysseus. Closely questioned, he adds that he has recently been in Thesprotia and has learned something there of Odysseus's recent wanderings.

Odysseus's identity is discovered by the housekeeper, Eurykleia, when he undresses for a bath and reveals an old thigh wound; he swears her to secrecy. Next day, at Athene's prompting, Penelope maneuvers the suitors into competing for her hand with an archery competition using Odysseus's bow. He takes part in the competition himself; he alone is strong enough to string the bow and therefore wins. Immediately he turns his arrows on the suitors and kills them all. Odysseus and Telemachos also kill twelve of their household maids, who had slept with the suitors, and mutilate the goatherd Melanthios, who had favored them. Now at last Odysseus identifies himself to Penelope. She is hesitant, but accepts him when he correctly describes to her the bed he built for her when they married.

Next day he and Telemachos visit the country farm of his old father, Laertes, who accepts his identity only when Odysseus correctly describes the orchard that Laertes once gave him.

The citizens of Ithake have followed Odysseus on the road, planning to avenge the deaths of Penelope's suitors, their sons. Their leader points out that Odysseus has now caused the deaths of two generations of the men of Ithake—his sailors, not one of whom survived, and the suitors, whom he has now executed. The goddess Athene intervenes and persuades both sides to give up the vendetta.

We never learn how long ago the Trojan War and the return of Odysseus took place. We are told only that it was "in the time of the heroes," when people were bigger, stronger, and healthier than they are now. We may wonder whether people of the poet's time—potential audiences for the poems—claimed to be directly descended from characters in the *Iliad* and the *Odyssey*. Some almost certainly did, but we would never know it from reading these poems.

READING AN ANCIENT EPIC

In the first lines of the *Iliad*, the poet calls upon a goddess and then outlines the story that is about to be told.

Sing, goddess, of the anger of Peleus's son Achilles—
Destructive anger that brought ten thousand troubles on the Achaioi
And dispatched to Hades many brave souls
Of heroes whose bodies became food for dogs
And carrion birds: thus Zeus's will was done.
Begin the story when a quarrel arose between those two,

> *Atreus's son, the ruler of men, and noble Achilles.*
> *So which of the gods set them to fighting?*
> *It was the son of Zeus and Leto.*
>
> (*Iliad* 1.1–9)

Behind these lines are some definite views about the gods, views that we do not share but that the poet took for granted—for example, that there is a community of gods (as we read on, we find that these gods live on Mount Olympos); that these gods act quite independently of one another (and we find that they sometimes quarrel, just as mortals do); that these gods have love affairs with one another and with mortals (we soon discover that Zeus, king of the gods, is married, and his wife is not the mortal woman Leto). Most important, we find that these gods cause mortals to make all kinds of decisions, about love and war and everything in between, with consequences that are sometimes good and sometimes disastrous. As we read on, we discover that the son of Zeus and Leto is the god Apollo; we find out why he took action against the Greek army, and against its leader in particular. We learn that the quarrel arising from Apollo's action was disastrous indeed.

In these lines also some factual information is assumed to be familiar to everyone, but it certainly is not familiar to modern readers: the identities of three individuals on whom these lines focus. Two of them, Atreus's son and Achilles, are mortal warriors; as signaled in the first line, Achilles will be the principal character of the poem. The third, as already explained, is the god Apollo. Two of the names are not even mentioned in these lines, because they did not happen to fit the rhythm and because surely everyone knew them anyway. Surely everyone knew that the leader of the Greek army at Troy, the son of Atreus who was about to quarrel with Achilles, was Agamemnon? Surely everyone knew that the only male child of the brief sexual liaison between Zeus and Leto was Apollo?

We have to take on board still more issues as we read these lines, reserving them for further exploration later. It seems that the souls of human beings (including the "heroes" who figure in this poem) go to Hades, the underworld, when they die; we will learn later that their bodies ought to be burned on a funeral pyre, but it is made clear in these

lines that this did not always happen when men died in battle. It seems
that the poet is addressing a goddess in line 1, but we do not know
which goddess, and we may not yet understand why she is asked to sing
when what is really happening is that we are beginning to read a written
poem by a human author. Finally, we accept that the warriors who are
fighting on one of the two sides in the Trojan War are not called Greeks,
as we might have expected, but Achaioi. We shall find that they have
several names, as the Trojans do. The poet's original audiences took
these multiple names for granted; in due course they will tell us something about the origins of the Trojan War legend.

In all these ways, it is no longer true, as it once was, that everyone
who encounters this poem will have nearly all the background information in advance. Even in classical Athens in Plato's time, 265 years after
the *Iliad* was written, readers were puzzled by some details. Now, after
2,650 years, it will take readers time to understand many matters, and
there are some issues that even scholars and specialists cannot resolve.
To read a text that was written so long ago, we have to open our minds.

Once we have made the initial leap, an epic narrative like the *Iliad*
and the *Odyssey*, even if it comes from a distant time and an unfamiliar
culture, is far more approachable than most other kinds of literature.
Although these two poems were written down, on all other occasions
the poet performed aloud, to audiences whose origin and reactions were
quite unpredictable. The stories were usually familiar to most of the
audience, but no poem was performed in the same way more than once,
so the audience had to be able to follow it at one hearing; those who
happened not to know the story beforehand had to be able to pick it up.
If they didn't care for it or couldn't understand it, they would stop listening. That's why the poems are easy to grasp and easy to get into. A
poet who made them any other way would have had no audiences.

Here is one particular way in which these poems are easy to
approach. Characters rapidly become familiar; we soon feel we know
something about them. In the few lines quoted above, Achilles is named
twice. On both occasions, he is not just named but characterized: once
as *Peleus's son* and once as *noble*. Those descriptions, along with others, will recur. Soon we can't forget Achilles; we remember his family
connections and link him with the range of attributes that are joined to

his name. Soon we will always think of Agamemnon as *leader of men.* We feel we can picture *white-armed Hera, red-haired Menelaos,* and *long-suffering noble Odysseus.* These phrases, usually called formulas, are the building blocks of epic. They are there because oral poets need them in order to construct a narrative fluently; they are also there to help the audience—any audience, including a modern reader—to make connections with the narrative.

TIMELINE FOR THE HOMERIC WORLD

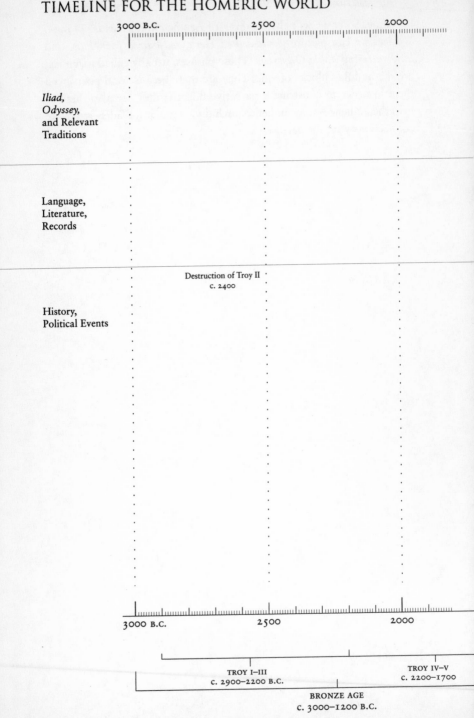

3000 B.C.   2500   2000

Iliad,
Odyssey,
and Relevant
Traditions

Language,
Literature,
Records

History,
Political Events

Destruction of Troy II
c. 2400

3000 B.C.   2500   2000

TROY I–III
c. 2900–2200 B.C.

TROY IV–V
c. 2200–1700

BRONZE AGE
c. 3000–1200 B.C.

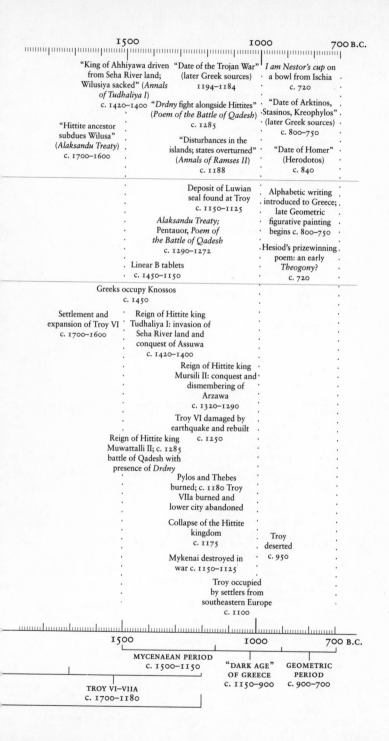

1500   1000   700 B.C.

"King of Ahhiyawa driven   "Date of the Trojan War"   *I am Nestor's cup* on
from Seha River land;   (later Greek sources)   a bowl from Ischia
Wilusiya sacked" (*Annals*   1194–1184   c. 720
of *Tudhaliya I*)
c. 1420–1400   *"Drdny* fight alongside Hittites"   "Date of Arktinos,
           (*Poem of the Battle of Qadesh*)   Stasinos, Kreophylos"
"Hittite ancestor   c. 1285   (later Greek sources)
subdues Wilusa"   c. 800–750
(*Alaksandu Treaty*)   "Disturbances in the
c. 1700–1600   islands; states overturned"   "Date of Homer"
             (*Annals of Ramses II*)   (Herodotos)
                c. 1188   c. 840

Deposit of Luwian   Alphabetic writing
seal found at Troy   introduced to Greece;
c. 1150–1125   late Geometric
Alaksandu Treaty;   figurative painting
Pentauor, *Poem of*   begins c. 800–750
the Battle of Qadesh
c. 1290–1272   Hesiod's prizewinning
Linear B tablets   poem: an early
c. 1450–1150   *Theogony?*
                    c. 720

Greeks occupy Knossos
c. 1450

Settlement and   Reign of Hittite king
expansion of Troy VI   Tudhaliya I: invasion of
c. 1700–1600   Seha River land and
            conquest of Assuwa
              c. 1420–1400

Reign of Hittite king
Mursili II: conquest and
dismembering of
Arzawa
c. 1320–1290

Troy VI damaged by
earthquake and rebuilt
Reign of Hittite king   c. 1250
Muwattalli II; c. 1285
battle of Qadesh with
presence of *Drdny*

Pylos and Thebes
burned; c. 1180 Troy
VIIa burned and
lower city abandoned

Collapse of the Hittite
kingdom   Troy
c. 1175   deserted
               c. 950

Mykenai destroyed in
war c. 1150–1125

Troy occupied
by settlers from
southeastern Europe
c. 1100

1500   1000   700 B.C.

MYCENAEAN PERIOD
c. 1500–1150   "DARK AGE"   GEOMETRIC
                OF GREECE   PERIOD
                c. 1150–900   c. 900–700

TROY VI–VIIA
c. 1700–1180

TIMELINE FOR THE HOMERIC WORLD

700 B.C.   200 B.C.   A.D.   500 A.D.

Iliad, Odyssey, and Relevant Traditions

Establishment of a sanctuary at Troy
c. 700

Blinding of Kyklops on a Lakonian cup

Kirke's magic potion on an Attic cup
c. 670

Writing of the *Iliad*? c. 650

Augustus visits Troy
20 B.C.

Writing of the *Odyssey*? c. 630

Anger of the sea-nymph's child (Alkaios), blinding of Kyklops on an Etruscan vase: earliest clear testimonia to *Iliad* and *Odyssey* c. 600

Roman scholarship
30 B.C.–476 A.D.

"Singers tell many lies" (Solon) c. 590

"Hipparchos brings the epics to Athens"
528–514

Byzantine scholarship
476–1453

"A man who is blind and lives in rocky Chios" (*Homeric Hymn to Apollo*) 522

"Kynaithos performs the epics in Syracuse" c. 504–501

Earliest references to Homer's name
c. 500

"Over Odysseus's lies and subterfuges something majestic extends" (Pindar)
c. 470

Alexander the Great visits Troy
c. 334

Alexandrian scholarship c. 305–30

Language, Literature, Records

Hesiod, *Works and Days* c. 700

Hesiod, *Theogony*
c. 690

Kallinos; Archilochos;
Tyrtaios c. 650

Alkman c. 630

Sappho; Alkaios c. 600

Strabo, *Geography*; Virgil, *Aeneid*
27 B.C.–14 A.D.

"Solon forbids written laments" (Plutarch) c. 590

Stesichoros c. 570

Homeric Hymn to Apollo 522

Kynaithos, "one of the Homeridai"; Hipponax c. 510

Xenophanes; Herakleitos; Simonides c. 500

Pausanias, *Guide to Greece*
c. 170

Pindar; Aischylos c. 470

Herodotos, *Histories* c. 445

Euripides, *Bakchai*; Thoukydides, *Histories*; Aristophanes, *Frogs* 410–405

Plato, *Symposion* c. 385

Aristotle c. 330

History, Political Events

Fall of Egyptian Thebes c. 663

Principate of Augustus
27 B.C. – 14 A.D.

Sack of Ismaros c. 650

Hipparchos rules Athens
528–514

Destruction of Mykenai by Argos 468/7

Byzantine Empire
476–1453

Peloponnesian War 431–405

Ptolemaic dynasty rules Egypt c. 305–30

Roman Empire
30 B.C. – 476 A.D.

Reign of Alexander the Great
336–323

700 B.C.   200 B.C.   A.D.   500 A.

ARCHAIC PERIOD c. 700–500

CLASSICAL PERIOD c. 500–300

HELLENISTIC PERIOD c. 300–30

ROMAN PERIOD c. 30 B.C.–476 A.D.

1000 A.D.   1500 A.D.   2000 A.D.

Schliemann excavates Troy and
Mykenai 1870–1890

Hrozny deciphers Hittite 1915

Blegen excavates Troy
1932–1938

Korfmann excavates Troy
1988 to date

Luwian seal found at Troy 1995

1000 A.D.   1500 A.D.   2000 A.D.

BYZANTINE PERIOD
c. 476 A.D.–1453 A.D.

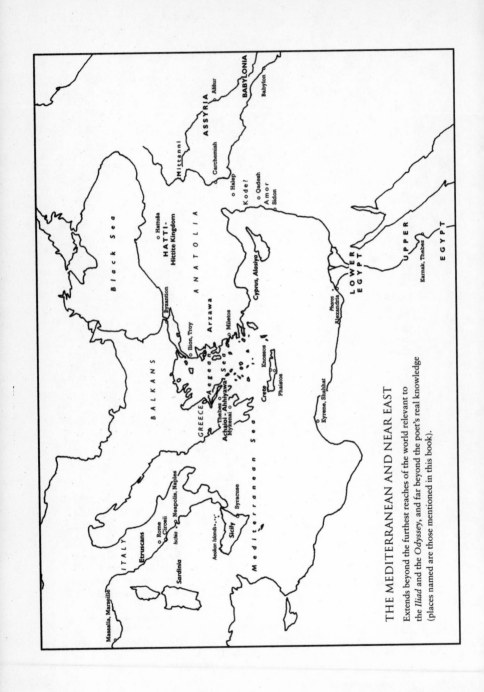

THE MEDITERRANEAN AND NEAR EAST

Extends beyond the furthest reaches of the world relevant to the *Iliad* and the *Odyssey*, and far beyond the poet's real knowledge (places named are those mentioned in this book).

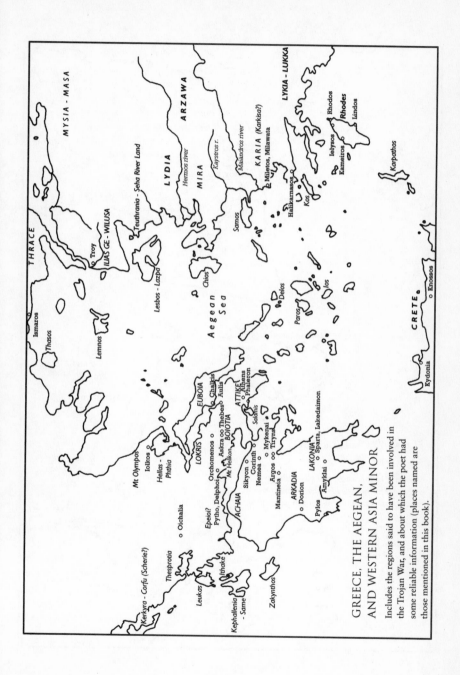

MYSIA - MASA

THRACE

ARZAWA

LYDIA

Hermos river

MIRA

Kaystros r.

Maiandros river

Teuthrania - Seha River Land

KARIA (Karkisa?)

LYKIA - LUKKA

Rhodos
Rhodos
Lindos
Ielysos
Kameiros

Miletos, Milawata

Halikarnasos

Kos

Karpathos

Ismaros

Thasos

Lemnos

Chios

Samos

Troy
ILIAS GE - WILUSA

Lesbos - Lazpa

Aegean
Sea

Delos

Paros

Ios

Kydonia

CRETE

Knossos

Mt Olympos

Iolkos

Hellas -
Phthia

EUBOIA

LOKRIS

Chalkis
Aulis
Askra oo Thebes
BOIOTIA
Mt Helikon,

Orchomenos

Pytho, Delphoi

Epeioi?

ACHAIA

Sikyon
Corinth
Nemea o
Argos oo Tiryns
Mantineia o

ATTIKE
Athens
Phaleron
Salamis

Mykenai

ARKADIA
o Dorion

LAKONIA
Amyklai o
Sparta, Lakedaimon

Pylos

Oichalia

Thesprotia

Kerkyra - Corfu (Scherie?)

Leukas

Ithake

Kephallenia
- Same

Zakynthos

GREECE, THE AEGEAN,
AND WESTERN ASIA MINOR

Includes the regions said to have been involved in
the Trojan War, and about which the poet had
some reliable information (places named are
those mentioned in this book).

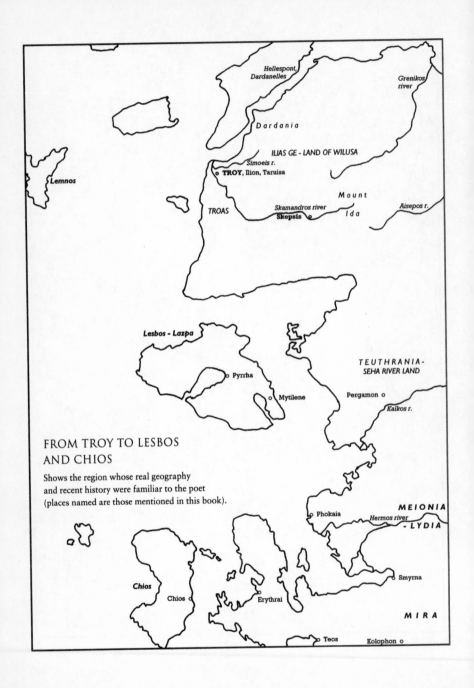

Hellespont,
Dardanelles

Grenikos
river

Dardania

ILIAS GE - LAND OF WILUSA

Simoeis r.

TROY, Ilion, Taruisa

Lemnos

Mount

TROAS

Skamandros river

I d a

Skepsis

Aisepos r.

Lesbos - Lazpa

TEUTHRANIA-
SEHA RIVER LAND

Pyrrha

Mytilene

Pergamon o

Kaikos r.

FROM TROY TO LESBOS
AND CHIOS

Shows the region whose real geography
and recent history were familiar to the poet
(places named are those mentioned in this book).

MEIONIA

Phokaia

Hermos river

- LYDIA

Smyrna

Chios

Chios

Erythrai

M I R A

Teos

Kolophon o

PART ONE

THE POEMS

I

Oral Poetry in Early Greece

I t's possible to begin to read the *Iliad* or the *Odyssey* without reading anything else in preparation. Many people do it.

It's possible to read them without knowing anything in advance about the culture from which they come, and without even thinking about the other poetry that was around at the time when they were composed. In fact, there is a common belief—even shared by some specialists—that no other poetry existed in Greece at that time, or none of much significance.

The *Iliad* and the *Odyssey* are the greatest surviving works of early Greek literature, and the first works in the Western canon as it is often defined. They carry a message that is timeless and depends on no specific cultural background. Yet much in them makes better sense when we know something of the literary culture from which they come.

It used to be assumed that the two great epics represent an earlier phase of Greek culture than the lyric poetry that began to be written down about 650 B.C. Some standard histories still say this: first there was epic, anonymous and impersonal; then there was lyric, personal and intimate. Personality had been invented; thus the early lyric poets mark a sudden break with the epic past. These broad generalizations are no longer acceptable. For one thing, the date at which the *Iliad* and the *Odyssey* were written is continually being recalculated. Some still place it in the mid-eighth century, almost immediately after the introduction of the alphabet to Greece, while others argue for the sixth century. These now appear to be extreme positions, and a consensus is slowly growing that the mid-seventh century (around 650 B.C.) will turn out to be right—exactly the same period when the first known lyric poets were at work. Meanwhile, study of oral traditions has shown ever more forcefully that the epics as written down must speak to us of their own time; we cannot expect to find in them an accurate picture of any earlier period.

This means that the epic world, when kings or aristocracies ruled unchallenged, and the world of the archaic lyric, when Greek cities were self-governing units, with trade and colonization and political faction, do not after all represent two different periods separated by a couple of generations of astonishingly rapid change. They are the same world.

LYRIC POETRY AND THE SHIELD OF ACHILLES

Just as modern novelists sometimes choose to write about novelists, oral poets include poets among their characters. Two thousand six hundred and fifty years ago, very little poetry had been put into writing (and scarcely any of it survives today). Poetry was oral, and thanks to the poet of the *Iliad* and the *Odyssey*, we can find out a great deal about contemporary poetic culture.

In book 18 of the *Iliad*, the blacksmith god, Hephaistos, makes a new set of armor for Achilles. The outstanding piece is the famous shield of Achilles. The poet imagines it freely and describes it at length.

The wonderful decoration worked into the face of this shield depicts the daily life of two Greek cities and of the Greek countryside, making a balance to the relentlessly warlike theme of the rest of the *Iliad*. Even on the shield there is war, because one of the cities is under siege; but there is also peace—a law case, a wedding, and the work of sowing and harvesting. In the center of it all are the sun, moon, and stars; around the rim of the shield flows the river of Ocean that surrounds the world.[1]

Many of the human activities depicted on the shield involve words and music. Let's begin with a vineyard, imagined at harvest time. Grape pickers are on their way in and youngsters are carrying the laden baskets out:

> *Maidens and young men with lively thoughts*
> *Carried away the honeyed fruit in wicker baskets*
> *And in the middle of them a child with a shrill lyre*
> *Played beautifully, singing to this music the lovely Linos*
> *In a high voice. Stamping their feet rhythmically*
> *And skipping, they all followed him with songs and shrieks.*
>
> (*Iliad* 18.567–572)

The shield of Achilles is a personal vision of the poet's rather than a conventional description adopted from the tradition, but it is still a picture of typical Greek cities and countryside. If it depicts *a child with a shrill lyre*, playing and singing along to the music, there must be nothing very unusual about that idea: there must have been many child singers. So is the performer just any child who happens to have picked up a lyre? No—if the other harvesters are stamping in time to the music, a real rhythm is being set up. This child is already a skilled performer.

Later Greek readers asked themselves another question at this point: What sort of song was the *Linos*, and why was it called that? To find an answer, they recalled and quoted four lines from a now-forgotten poem that was compiled perhaps fifty years after the *Iliad*, the so-called *Catalogue of Women*, a listing of the love affairs of gods and mortals.

> *Ouranie gave birth to a son, Linos the much-desired.*
> *Mortals who are singers and musicians*

All cry for him at festivals and dances,
Calling Linos *as they begin and as they end.*[2]

So the word *Linos* recurred in these songs as a kind of refrain, and the songs were understood, at least by some people, to be a lament for this mythical Linos, son of Ouranie.

One of the known genres of early Greek poetry, the dithyramb, a wild celebratory song, seems to fit this context. Early poems in this riotous genre were sung in honor of the wine god, Dionysos. Archilochos, a contemporary of the poet of the *Iliad* and the *Odyssey*, claimed that he would "lead the lovely song of King Dionysos, the dithyramb, when my mind is blown by the wine."[3] In what words he did this is not recorded—the dithyramb was still an oral genre—but soon after Archilochos's time, dithyrambs began to be recorded in writing. They had originally been rhythmical and had been constructed in regular, repeated verses, and that is why it had been possible and normal for ordinary people to sing along in chorus when celebrating the vintage with a dithyramb. After the dithyramb turned from oral to written composition, it became rhythmically more complex and nonrepeating. No longer a song sung spontaneously by returning harvesters, it now had to be performed by trained singers. This information comes from the Greek philosopher Aristotle; in his time, no one really understood the differing nature of oral and written composition and the reasons behind the difference, yet Aristotle is such an acute reporter that he gets very close to the truth. The later, written forms of dithyramb he describes as "imitative" (*mimetikos*), by which he means that performers were no longer expected to improvise—they "imitated" or repeated a written text word for word.[4]

Let's agree, then, that at this point in the description of the shield we are being shown a vignette of a young poet, a junior Homer or Archilochos, apprentice to a vocation that, in many traditional societies, you begin to learn when very young, as is the case with music in our own culture. One of the duties of the oral poet, at many times and places, has been to provide an accompaniment to agricultural work, and that is what is happening here.

We are still looking at the shield of Achilles. Elsewhere on its surface, the poet shows us a totally different kind of choral song. There is an image of an open-air dance floor, *choros*, a circular flat ground marked off by stones.

> *There young men and maidens worth many cows*
> *Were dancing, holding hands at the wrist.*
> *The girls wore fine linen gowns, the boys tunics*
> *Finely woven and still glossy with oil.*[5]
> *The girls wore lovely garlands, the boys daggers*
> *Of gold hanging from silver sword-belts . . .*
> *A large crowd stood around the lovely dance,*
> *Enjoying it; two tumblers among them,*
> *Leading the singing-dance, whirled in the middle.*
>
> (*Iliad* 19.593–606)

The girls are *worth many cows* because, like everything on the shield, they are beautiful and lucky; when they marry, their families will receive a bride price of many cows.

We are given no special reason that the boys and girls are singing and dancing; this *molpe*, or singing-dance, seems to take place for its own sake. An occasion very much like this one is described at length in the *Odyssey*. It takes place in the agora or marketplace of the Phaiekes, during Odysseus's brief stay on the island of Scherie, and it happens just because King Alkinoos wants to impress Odysseus with his people's skill in song and dance. The blind singer Demodokos goes to the center; adolescent boys skilled at dancing stand around him, and they *strike the divine dance floor with their feet*. Demodokos plays on his lyre and begins his singing. It is at this singing-dance in the marketplace that Demodokos sings the amusing story of the war god Ares and the love goddess Aphrodite, of their secret love affair and how her husband, Hephaistos, trapped them in bed together.[6]

Simpler and more informal than either of these occasions is the singing-dance (*molpe* again) in which Nausikaa leads her maids when they throw off their veils and play on the shore, observed by no one except the hidden Odysseus.[7]

The words *choros* and *molpe*, which belong to the realm of choral lyric, song accompanied by dance, are used in all three of these vignettes. Very soon after the writing of the *Iliad* and the *Odyssey*, this kind of song also began to be written down. Not many examples survive today, because by the Byzantine period, early Greek lyrics had already become very difficult for ordinary readers to understand, and therefore they were no longer being copied (we rely on copies made in that period for nearly all our surviving texts of classical Greek literature). Among the rare survivors is a beautiful choral song by the Spartan poet Alkman, who, like Archilochos, was a contemporary of the poet who composed the *Iliad* and the *Odyssey*. Unlike dithyrambs, choral songs continued to be composed in strophes with exactly repeated rhythms, even after the introduction of writing, and that made them easier for a chorus to learn. Later, until about 400 B.C., choral songs formed an integral part of Athenian tragedies and comedies.

Almost throughout this long period—at least from the fictional performance of Demodokos in the *Odyssey* and the "Maidens' Song" of Alkman, both written about 630 B.C., to the odes in Euripides' tragedy *Bakchai*, written about 407 B.C.—stories of the gods were one of the major subject areas for Greek choral songs. But choral lyric differed from epic in one very important feature. Epic poets told stories as narrative, which is why even the poet of the *Odyssey*, describing Demodokos's performance, tells the Ares and Aphrodite story as narrative; that is the natural way for an epic poet to handle it. But a choral poet's aim (from the very beginning of direct written records, with the "Maidens' Song") was actually different—not to tell stories but rather to allude to them, to suggest comparisons or to extract a moral from them.

The first poetic occasion that is depicted on the shield of Achilles is quite different from any of these. Here are the first lines of the description of the shield:

> *On it he made two cities of mortal men,*
> *Beautiful cities. In one, weddings and feastings were taking place*
> *And from their homes, under blazing torches, brides*
> *Were led in procession through the town, and a great wedding song*
> > *arose,*
> *And dancing boys whirled, and among them*
> *Pipes and lyres made their noise; and the women—*
> *Each stood and gazed from her own veranda.*
>
> > (*Iliad* 18.490–496)

Thus we learn that the wedding song (*hymenaios*) is another of the oldest genres of Greek song. This is not the only mention of a wedding song in the two epics. In the *Odyssey*, when Telemachos and Mentor (Athene in disguise) pay their visit to Sparta, a double wedding feast is taking place for the sons of Menelaos, and *a divine singer sang lyrics and played his lyre*. This scene takes place not in the streets of Sparta but in Menelaos's own great hall.[8]

Later in the *Odyssey*, when Odysseus is killing the suitors, the singer Phemios is told to strike up the music for a fictitious wedding song, so as to soothe the suspicions of neighbors and passers-by.

> *Meanwhile the divine singer with his shrill lyre*
> *Must conduct a playful dance for us,*
> *So that anyone hearing it would say it was a wedding.*
>   (*Odyssey* 23.133–135)

In these scenes we are learning of two kinds of wedding song: song in the city streets, accompanying the wedding procession, and song accompanying the feast. Fifty years after the writing of the *Iliad* and the *Odyssey*, these two kinds of songs were being recorded in writing. The earliest known to us are by Sappho, a contemporary of Alkaios's and one of the greatest of Greek poets. Sadly, they are now only brief fragments of poems, like the famous chorus

> *Up with the roofbeam,* ymenaon!
> *Lift it up, you joiners,* ymenaon!
> *Here comes the bridegroom, as big as Ares,*
> *Bigger than any tall man!*[9]

Ymenaon, in the dialect of Lesbos, used by Sappho, corresponds to the more familiar form *hymenaios*, and was the name for a wedding song because you shouted this word as a refrain. The riddle of how the bridegroom can be "bigger than any tall man" is not difficult to interpret, and shows that this is a song for late in the evening.

For performance earlier in the wedding festivities there were Sappho's songs of the marriage of Peleus and Thetis, the parents of Achilles, and of the wedding of Hektor and Andromache. This tale could well have been told by a singer of epic, but it is told differently by the poet of Lesbos. The story as she tells it ends, appropriately, with the songs that had been sung on that legendary occasion:

> The old women were shrieking, every one,
> And all the men were raising up a shout,
> Calling on Paon, far-shooting master of the lyre,
> And hymning the godlike couple Hektor and Andromache.[10]

Paon in Sappho's dialect is a title of the god Apollo. In other Greek dialects the word was usually *Paieon* (but it has many spellings), and its meaning was understood differently. It was a variant of the name of the country god Pan—an ancient god, though not a very respectable one, and not one of the twelve Olympians. Also it was a kind of song, and as such it is already mentioned in the *Iliad*, though not in the description of the shield. In book 22 Achilles gathers his warriors as he prepares to drag Hektor's body behind his chariot in barbaric triumph:

> Come on, you Achaian boys: singing a paieon
> We shall march back to our hollow ships, dragging this behind us.
> We have earned great honor! We have killed godlike Hektor.
> (*Iliad* 22.391–393)

How do we imagine this *paieon* of theirs? It has to be a choral song, sung by the young warriors in unison, and a song of praise to a god (Apollo or Pan or some other), because the word *paieon*, like *Linos* and *hymenaios*, is shouted before or after or during the song and becomes a divine name. Such songs were already familiar to Alkman, the earliest of the lyric poets. In Alkman's Sparta the men dined together in a longhouse called the *andreion*, "men's house," and one short fragment of his work, from an otherwise unknown poem, survives because a later scholarly author quoted it to exemplify Alkman's use of this important word: "At feasts and at revels, among the diners of the men's house, it is right to lead the *paian*."[11]

In a *Hymn to Apollo*, composed in Homeric verses not very long after the *Iliad* and the *Odyssey*, a story is told in which the god instructs his worshippers, after sacrifice, prayer, and feast, to return in procession to his temple singing *ie paieon*.

> *So they set out, and king Apollo, Zeus's son, led them*
> *Holding a lyre in his hands, playing sweetly,*
> *Stepping high and fair; and the Cretans followed him, stamping,*
> *To Pytho, and they sang the* ie paieon
> *Like the* paieon-*singers of Crete, and like those in whom the Muse,*
> *The goddess, has placed honey-voiced song.*[12]

In general, then, a *paieon* was a hymn of praise. But that is not the whole story. The particular *paieon* sung by the warriors as Hektor's body is ritually dishonored has to be a song of self-praise or of boasting, a song asserting that Achilles has avenged the death of Patroklos and that Hektor has paid for it. Such *paieones* used to be sung in chorus, it was later said, by the Greek warriors of Sparta after dinner on their military expeditions, followed by solo singing of the battle songs of Tyrtaios, and the best performer earned an extra portion of meat.[13] The boasting song reached its highest pitch of literary perfection 150 years after the making of the *Iliad* and the *Odyssey*, when the poet Pindar raised the genre to an entirely new level. Pindar's *epinikia*, or victory songs, each sponsored by a noble athlete or his family and composed in writing with extreme elaboration and complexity, were to be sung in chorus—once only, by professional performers—at feasts celebrating a victory at the games. Pindar also wrote *paieones* in the general sense; that genre continued to exist alongside the newer subgenre of victory songs. In due course, when Greeks began to worship their kings, *paieones* were addressed to them as well as to gods.[14]

Beyond the shield of Achilles, another form of oral literature is described several times in the *Iliad*. At the very end of the poem, when Hektor's battered corpse is brought home to Troy:

> *beside him they seated singers,*
> *Leaders of the laments: a mournful song*
> *They lamented. The women mourned after,*

> *And white-armed Andromache led their wailing,*
> *Holding the head of man-killing Hektor in her hands.*

Then we learn what was said by Andromache, his widow. After that, again:

> *the women mourned after,*
> *And next Hekabe led their bitter wailing . . .*

After his mother, Hekabe, has spoken, at last comes the woman whose abduction was the cause of all the killing: *Helen, third of all, led the wailing.*[15]

On another occasion for mourning in the *Iliad*, the death of Patroklos, there is no singer to take the lead, because this time we are among the Greek warriors, and the poet never says or implies that any specialized singers are in the Greek camp at Troy. Achilles first leads the lament for Patroklos, in which others join; then Briseis, newly sent back to Achilles' tent by Agamemnon, speaks a lament, and *the women mourned after;* after this Achilles again laments, and *the old men mourned after.* The old men must be the leaders of the Greek army—Agamemnon, Menelaos, Nestor, Idomeneus, Phoinix, and Odysseus.[16]

Then, in the last book of the *Odyssey*, the ghost of Agamemnon tells how at Achilles' death before the walls of Troy (after the end of the episodes narrated in the *Iliad*), the sea nymphs, his mother's companions, had lamented him and *the nine Muses all responding in their lovely voices lamented him,* and all the Greeks wept.[17]

There is consistency in all these passages, but there is also variation. In all cases women lament, and one or more women lead the lament; in some cases there are also men who lament or lead a lament, before or after the women. Even if no specialized singers are in the Greek camp, there are certainly women, prisoners of war who have become concubines and slaves, and we see that lamenting is among their proper duties. We know of at least two Greek cities, Sparta and Erythrai, where in later times people of an oppressed class were expected to join in laments for the deaths of their oppressors.[18]

We also know the kind of poetry that was made for these occasions, because a little later *threnoi,* or laments, were being composed, written down, and rehearsed before a formal funeral. It was said that the new-fangled practice of rehearsing laments was discouraged by Solon, law-giver and political poet of early Athens, around 590 B.C. If so, it must have been fashionable at that date. As lawgiver, Solon forbade "lamenting to a text," which has to mean that he wanted mourning at funerals to be an impromptu expression of grief; thus he forbade formally assembled choruses to practice and perform laments that had been composed for them in fixed words by a singer or poet. Here is the first evidence that another literary genre, the lament, was changing from oral to written composition not long after the time of the *Iliad* and the *Odyssey*. The anecdote does not say in so many words that the laments had begun to be written down, but it is natural to suppose that writing helped to produce a fixed text. Solon's decree surely made little difference. It is all very well to want things to be as they were in the old days, but many genres of Greek literature were making the oral-to-written crossover at this period, and even Solon could not stop it. Some fragments survive of laments written by Pindar and his contemporary Simonides, a hundred years after Solon. Simonides' laments are made up of extremely pessimistic philosophical poetry concerning the condition of humanity, and in a more complex and literary form they are exactly the kind of thing that the poet of the *Iliad* had imagined being said by Andromache, Hekabe, and Helen as they wailed over the body of Hektor.[19]

The singer Phemios, in book 1 of the *Odyssey*, is telling of the Trojan War. Distressed at having to listen to a narrative of her missing husband's adventures, Penelope interrupts him:

> *Phemios! After all, you know many other charms for mortals,*
> *The deeds of men and gods made famous by singers:*
> *So turn aside and sing one of those.*
>
> (*Odyssey* 1.337–340)

The *deeds of men and gods made famous by singers* are, quite simply, the whole range of narrative songs, all the stories that singers told. After all, what other subject for narrative could there be?

The poet is using this line as a longer and more complete version of the brief phrase *the fame of men*, which occurs in book 9 of the

Iliad at the moment when Achilles, sitting inactive in his tent, consoles himself with a song that is fated to be interrupted by the visit of Odysseus and Nestor.

> *They found him pleasing his mind with a shrill lyre,*
> *Beautiful and intricate and with a silver plectrum,*
> *Chosen from the spoils when he sacked Eetion's city:*
> *With this he was pleasing his mind and singing of the fame of men*
> *And Patroklos alone sat with him in silence,*
> *Awaiting the moment when Achilles should finish his singing.*
>
> (*Iliad* 9.186–191)

Incidentally, it is easy to overinterpret Homer, and there have been several overinterpretations of this short passage. Bryan Hainsworth assumes that *the fame of men* necessarily means "heroic poetry," an oral epic. He insists, correctly, that it takes skill and training to sing an oral epic and that warriors such as Achilles have no time for this, but rather than question his initial assumption, he questions whether the passage is unrealistic. Charles Segal highlights the fact that Patroklos is waiting for Achilles to finish; Segal draws the moral that the singing of someone such as a warrior, unlike that of a bard (a Celtic term used by some modern scholars for a Greek epic poet), "gives pleasure only to himself, not to others"; in other words, Achilles is a bad singer and Patroklos is bored. Gregory Nagy notes that in later Athens the *Iliad* and the *Odyssey* were performed at a quadrennial festival in a sort of relay by successive performers. Aiming to show that this tradition had a long history, Nagy argues that the poet has a relay performance in mind here, and that Patroklos is waiting to take a turn when Achilles is done.[20]

We will make no such bold assumptions. Instead we will ask one question: What is Achilles singing? Evidently that does not matter very much to Achilles himself. In a mood of calm meditation and with nothing to do, he is imagined *pleasing his mind* and singing more or less to himself. The scene is being set elaborately, so we get a description of Achilles' lyre; half a line remains, which leaves room for the poet to tell us that Achilles is *singing of the fame of men*. Many kinds of early Greek poetry were about this subject, including the praise poetry of Pindar, the allusive lyrics of Alkman and Sappho, and the narrative epics whose tradition culminated in the *Iliad* and the *Odyssey*. Later in book 9 the poet uses the phrase again, this time meaning simply "oral tradition."[21]

Thus we do not need to imagine an epic here. We can picture Achilles creating or recreating a brief lyric, possibly retelling the love affair of Paris and Helen—the ultimate reason that he is sitting in a tent outside the walls of Troy. If this guess happens to be right, his song would resemble one of the poems of Sappho's contemporary Alkaios:

> *He fluttered the heart of Argive Helen*
> *And deceived his host. Mad for the Trojan*
> *She followed him across the sea*
> *In his ship,*
> *Leaving her child behind at home*
> *And the bed that she rightly shared:*
> *The goddess conquered her mind*
> *With desire.*[22]

NARRATIVE POETRY AND THE TALES OF ODYSSEUS

So far the *Iliad* and the *Odyssey* have shown us the competition—the other kinds of poetry that were being made in Greece in their time. But what about oral narrative poetry, the tradition that led to the two great epics? The poet does indeed create for us, in both poems but particularly in the *Odyssey*, scenes that show a poet telling or singing a story before what looks like a typical epic audience.

To help us interpret these scenes better, and to begin to understand the poetic traditions from which the *Iliad* and the *Odyssey* emerged, we can again make comparisons with early Greek written texts that belong to the same traditions. First are two poems by Hesiod, much shorter than the Homeric epics and probably written down four or five decades earlier. I conjecturally place *Works and Days* at about 700 B.C. and *Theogony*, as now known, at 690 B.C. Then there are the *Homeric Hymns*, so called because some ancient readers believed that they were by Homer. Details of their language suggest that they were written at various dates about one to two hundred years after the *Iliad* and the *Odyssey*. Then there are the few remaining fragments of other epics that once existed in writing. Some of these were traditionally grouped as "the Cycle" because it was possible to arrange them in a logical sequence, incorporating the *Iliad* and the *Odyssey*, that told most of the major stories of Greek mythology. Others, including the *Catalogue of Women*, were grouped with the poems of Hesiod. All of these poems are composed in hexameter verse—in regular, rhythmical lines that always have six beats and thirteen to seventeen syllables—just like the *Iliad* and the *Odyssey*. Finally, nearly a century after the writing of the *Iliad*, another narrative poet was at the height of his powers: Stesichoros. Not one of his poems now survives complete, and he is unknown except to specialists. He told mythological stories at epic length and was thought by many ancient readers to be almost Homer's equal. One admirer (temporarily adopting Pythagoras's views on the afterlife) even described Stesichoros as the reincarnation of Homer.[23]

Stesichoros did not compose in hexameters, and for this reason modern scholars usually classify his work as lyric poetry. Such a distinction can tentatively be traced to the time of the *Iliad* and the *Odyssey*, when Greeks distinguished between prose (which was spoken) and verse (which was sung). A singer (*aoidos*) invoked the goddess, the Muse of poetry; a speaker—at a political assembly, for example—did not invoke the Muse. There may also have been a distinction between lyric (accompanied by a lyre, a stringed musical instrument) and narrative (accompanied by a stick, *skeptron*)—the stick was for beating the ground, whether to point up the emphases in prose or to mark the rhythm in regular verse. Thus we get what is potentially a three-way classification, between prose, spoken to the *skeptron*; regular verse, sung to the *skeptron*; and lyric, sung to the lyre. Keeping these variations in mind, what do the *Iliad* and the *Odyssey* tell us about oral narrative in their time?

To begin with, it is quite possible that when the singer Demodokos in the *Odyssey* plays his lyre and tells of the love affair of Ares and Aphrodite while children are dancing, he is not singing a choral lyric, as I have suggested, but singing a narrative. In that case it would have been something in the fashion of Stesichoros. Early Greek scholars asserted that Stesichoros was the inventor of his genre, but such statements are unlikely to be based on real knowledge. Certainly Demodokos's narrative would have been in a less learned style than any work of Stesichoros:

Demodokos is depicted as composing orally, while Stesichoros undoubtedly prepared his complex poetry in advance and probably used writing as an aid.

We have already heard about the *fame of men*, the *deeds of men and gods*, the whole tradition, the range of subjects about which the Muses will inspire a poet to sing. Stesichoros on one occasion invokes the Muse and proposes to her a more specific range of subjects:

> Muse, put wars aside and with me
> Sing the matings of the gods and the feasts of men
> And the joys of the blessed.[24]

Stesichoros is playing with our memories of the *Odyssey* here. He recalls Penelope and the *deeds of men and gods;* he hints at the adulterous love affair of Ares and Aphrodite, the "matings of the gods"; he recalls the "feasts of men" on Scherie and Ithake, and what's more, it was at those feasts that Phemios and Demodokos sang their narrative songs about episodes of the Trojan War.[25]

Not only is Stesichoros alluding to the *Odyssey* in this passage; he is also aligning himself with the two singers of the *Odyssey*. They sang to the lyre, and so does he. Are we really to imagine them singing in lyric verses like himself? Many scholars would completely rule out this idea. It has been commonly thought for at least 2,500 years that Demodokos is a self-portrait by the poet of the *Odyssey*, and the *Odyssey* is in hexameter verse. But epic poems, like other kinds of fiction, have a complex relationship with their creators. Oral poets are more versatile than is sometimes thought. From personal experience or from knowledge of the oral tradition, the poet of the *Iliad* and the *Odyssey* could imagine what it was like to be Demodokos, singing an amusing story to accompany a dance in the agora; what it was like to be Achilles, singing a lyric about his own troubles or those of the Greek army; what it was like to be Phemios, singing for the suitors *by compulsion* and afterward compelled by Odysseus to sing a wedding song to disguise the suitors' death cries; what it was like to be Nestor, boasting to Patroklos of his success long ago in a cattle raid (*"That's how I was, if ever I was, a man among men!"*), and what it was like to be Helen, telling Telemachos of her secret meeting with Odysseus in the days before Troy fell.[26]

Most of all, the poet knew what it was like to be Odysseus, telling his true or imaginary tales. In the *Odyssey* a *skeptron* is held by the soul of the seer Teiresias, who instructs Odysseus concerning his visit to the underworld; a *skeptron* is grasped by successive speakers at the agora in Ithake; and then Athene gives a *skeptron* to Odysseus when she disguises him as a beggar. Why? Of course he has a long walk ahead of him, and sticks are useful to walkers; but he also has a serious story to tell, a story that is important to him because if it satisfies its audience, it will earn him a warm cloak and a night's sleep near the fire.

Equipped with a *skeptron*, the wandering Odysseus resembles a seer, a public speaker, and a narrative poet. He tells four stories (and I must be honest and add that only two of these, the second and third, are told while Odysseus is disguised as a beggar and provided with a *skeptron*): first, his narrative to Alkinoos of his return from Troy (books 9 to 12); second, his lying tale to Eumaios of adventures in Egypt (book 14, lines 191–359); third, his false reminiscences of having met Odysseus, told in conversation to Penelope before he reveals his identity (book 19, lines 164–307); and fourth, his parallel lies to Laertes (book 24, lines 258–314).

Of course, these stories differ from hexameter epic. Odysseus does not sing them, and we have no special reason to imagine that he tells them in verse. The *Odyssey* itself is in hexameter verse from beginning to end, but we always have to make up our minds whether to imagine the quoted speakers using prose or some form of verse. Odysseus's stories do not belong to a narrative series, as the Trojan War tales of Phemios and Demodokos are said to do. And while Phemios and Demodokos are rewarded for their work with a secure living—they sing always at the same house or in the same town—Odysseus is an independent man and a wanderer. In this he resembles those who are said in later sources to have performed the Homeric poems, including Homer in person, which is why Odysseus's host Alkinoos compliments him with the words *You have told the tale sensibly, like a singer.*[27]

The Trojan War narratives of Phemios and Demodokos are told in the houses of *basileis*, which sometimes means "king" and sometimes no more than "landowner-farmer," even if some of these farmers (like Alkinoos and Odysseus) are more influential than others. The stories of Odysseus are told to his current hosts: Alkinoos and guests, Eumaios and the farmhands, Penelope. His storytelling skill is such that their reactions are exactly what he needs in each case: they sympathize and reward him with a warm cloak, a place near the fire, good food, and assistance in his eventual success.

Having looked at the after-dinner performances of Demodokos and Phemios, the two singers in the *Odyssey*, we need to give a warning. Whatever kinds of songs Demodokos and Phemios are performing, they are not fictional images of the *Iliad* and the *Odyssey*. The real epics are far too long to be presented in any such setting. Even if we can imagine an audience complaisant enough to listen to a serial *Iliad* created on consecutive evenings—it would take about twenty days—there would have been no way for anyone to write the text down, because it was impossible to write at that speed. Since oral narrative poetry is newly created on each occasion, the hypothesis of an *Iliad* first performed in the traditional way and afterward repeated to a scribe is also impossible. What the scribe wrote would be a new poem, different in many ways from what had previously been performed. Therefore, however sympathetic the real poet may be to Demodokos and Phemios, the real poet did not create the *Iliad* and the *Odyssey* as songs sung to aristocrats after dinner.

This is fortunate, because whether we are looking in ancient records or in modern anthropological reports, it is hard to find a monarch so lazy, and so placid, as to pay attention to a whole epic poem after dinner. It is hard to find a village headman so careless of his own reputation that he keeps a poet not to sing his own praises or those of his ancestors but to perform long narratives of heroic events far away and long ago.

Real traditional epics are *either* performed to an audience *or* written down. When they are performed, they are usually performed for popular audiences, not just for aristocrats. The *Iliad* and the *Odyssey*, however, were written down, and one of our aims is to understand when, how, and why this happened.

PLATO'S *SYMPOSION* AND THE WORKING OF ORAL TRADITION

Nearly three hundred years after the writing of the *Iliad* and the *Odyssey*, Sokrates was teaching philosophy and ethics at Athens. He did so by asking awkward questions, sometimes at a *symposion* (a drinking party), sometimes in chance conversations, sometimes because his followers and admirers needled him into a questioning mood. His student Plato was among the first to realize that Sokrates' teaching method might be just as effective if represented in writing.

Plato's short masterpiece, the *Symposion*, written about 385 B.C., is a philosophical discussion of the nature of love, cast as a report of a real conversation that took place at a celebratory drinking party hosted in 416 B.C. by the tragedian Agathon, whose play had just won a prize at an Athenian dramatic festival. Those participating in the discussion include Agathon himself, Sokrates, the comic playwright Aristophanes, and—a late arrival, drunk and boisterous after attending another party—the famous politician Alkibiades.

Here are the opening words of the *Symposion*, which I quote because they are the best evocation by any early writer of how texts are transmitted in oral tradition, without the use of writing. The reader eventually gathers that when the text begins abruptly, Apollodoros (a person previously unknown to us) has just been asked about the famous drinking party.

"As it happens, I'm well up on this question," said Apollodoros. "The day before yesterday I was on my way downtown from Phaleron when a friend caught sight of me from behind and shouted after me like a bailiff:

"'You there, man of Phaleron! Apollodoros! . . . Wait for me, can't you?'

"I stopped and waited.

"'I've been looking for you, Apollodoros,' he began. 'I want to ask you about this drinking party at Agathon's—the conversation between him and Sokrates and Alkibiades and the others, and what they said on the subject of love. I've heard about it from someone else, who said that you knew everything too. He had got it from Phoinix son of Philippos, but he couldn't give me a proper story. So you have to tell me. You're the right man to do it, since you're a friend of Sokrates. Now, first of all, were you at this party yourself?'

"'He certainly did not give you a proper story, if you think this party has only just happened, and that I was a guest.'

"'That's what I understood,' he said.

"'But Glaukon, surely you know that Agathon hasn't lived in Athens for many years! And it is only three years since I became a follower of Sokrates ... No, this happened when you and I were still boys, in the year that Agathon won the prize with his first tragedy, the day after he and the actors made their thanksgiving sacrifice.'

"'Oh, I see. A long time ago indeed. Who was it who told you about it, then? Socrates himself?'

"'No, no,' I said, 'it was a little fellow who always went about barefoot: he was called Aristodemos, and he was also the one who told Phoinix about it. This Aristodemos was at the party himself. In those days, if anyone was in love with Sokrates, he was, or so I gather. I've asked Sokrates about some of the details, and he's confirmed the version Aristodemos gave me.'"[28]

This passage depicts a multiple oral tradition, branching and recrossing, persisting over at least fifteen years. Aristodemos repeated the discussion to Phoinix and to Apollodoros. Phoinix told X ("someone else"); X was aware that Apollodoros also had the story. Apollodoros checked it with Sokrates. Now X has told Glaukon, and Apollodoros is about to give Glaukon a different version. How long ago the discussion originally happened is not necessarily part of the story; Glaukon has listened to Phoinix's version and has no idea. This would be true also of the *Iliad* and the *Odyssey*, which never tell us how many years ago Troy fell.

This passage has only one significant function in its context: it is a label of authenticity attached to the discussion of love that is at the heart of the *Symposion*. Plato uses it to persuade his readers to accept his narrative. It can only achieve this purpose if the picture it paints is realistic, and the picture is only realistic if people in Athens really did sometimes tell one another about drinking-party conversations of the past, transmitted such narratives at second hand, were aware that they were of varying reliability, and improved their knowledge of them by tracking down a second source of information—a different branch of the oral tradition.

So when Plato decided to write down the master's teachings and blend them with his own, he was making use of an existing, originally oral genre of literature—the reported drinking-party conversation, or "symposion."

He was making use of it—perhaps even subverting it, especially if by any chance he was the first person who used this genre to spread his own ideas while claiming to be transmitting a conversation faithfully. But others before Plato surely did the same, consciously or unconsciously (he was not even the first person to write dialogues featuring Sokrates).

More openly than most other texts that come out of oral tradition, the *Symposion* makes it clear that such texts have no simple origin, no single creator, and no easy relationship with historical truth. Generally treated by philosophers and literary scholars as "by Plato," the *Symposion* claims to report a conversation that took place thirty years earlier. In the course of this conversation, various speakers, like Sokrates, "report" things said and stories told at even earlier times. Plato did not attend the drinking party; the reader must assume that he heard about it at second hand, and I certainly will not argue that his record of the discussion is historically accurate. No one supposes that it is. Nor do I want to argue that versions of an original discussion back in 416 B.C. really had been reported by the particular people named in this quotation—Sokrates, Aristodemos, Phoinix, Apollodoros, and X; that may all be true or it may not be. It is quite likely that the drinking party really happened; the speakers were mostly real and well-known people, and if they were there, they really might have said some of the things attributed to them. Still, no one doubts that Plato has, at the very least, reshaped the conversation, and it is quite legitimate to believe that it is largely his invention.

In the *Symposion*, Plato includes a reminiscence by Sokrates of what the prophet Diotima said to him many years before (Plato is possibly hinting defensively that Sokrates used to report and adjust past conversations, just as he himself is now doing). One standard classical encyclopedia says: "There is no doubt that Diotima is a character invented by Plato." In fact, there has to be doubt. Sokrates may have invented her; Sokrates or Plato may have based her on a real person known to them; Diotima may really have existed. Sokrates, in introducing his reminiscence, says, "Before the plague, when the Athenians had been sacrificing to avert it, Diotima succeeded in postponing it for ten years." There was really a plague at Athens in Sokrates' lifetime, when the city was under siege during the Peloponnesian War, in 430 B.C. It looks very much as if this irrelevant detail is inserted in the *Symposion* to convince us of Diotima's existence.[29]

Plato also includes a reminiscence by Alkibiades of his early relations with Sokrates. This text seems to be telling us that although their relationship might have seemed sexual to outside observers, in fact it was not sexual. At the outset Alkibiades announces: "If I say anything untrue, interrupt, if you like, and tell me I'm lying: I won't lie intentionally. But if my memories are confused, don't be surprised." Alerted by this remark, we read on, noticing that in fact there are no interruptions, by Sokrates or anyone else. So are we to take it that this part of the *Symposion* is a true record of what Alkibiades said and that his memories are accurate? Or is it likely to be less accurate than the rest, because not many years after Agathon's party, Alkibiades' checkered Athenian career ended in permanent exile, after which he could no longer have any influence on the oral tradition about Agathon's drinking party? Or is this part of the dialogue really based not on a speech by Alkibiades, reported to Plato by others, but on Sokrates' own memories, told to Plato at some later period? In any case, has Plato reworked the story because he needed to deny the rumors of a sexual relationship between his revered teacher and the young and unreliable Alkibiades? I ask these questions not because there is much hope of answering them fully, but because they demonstrate some of the possible relationships between historical fact, oral tradition, and written literature that is based on oral tradition.[30]

Several myths are told in the *Symposion*. One of them forms part of Sokrates' reminiscence of the words of Diotima. She tells him how Eros, god of love, came to be born:

> """On the day that Aphrodite was born the gods were celebrating; Craft's son Resource was among them. While they were at dinner, Poverty came begging, as she naturally would when a feast was on, and hung about the door. Resource became drunk on nectar (wine did not yet exist), went into Zeus's garden and sank down to sleep; and Poverty, deciding in her resourcelessness to have a child by Resource, lay down beside him, and there she conceived Eros."'"[31]

The three sets of quotation marks around this translated paragraph are a reminder that this (in Plato's text) is what Apollodoros said that Sokrates said that Diotima said.

Now Diotima's story is quite different from all the other Greek myths (there are many) of the birth of Aphrodite and the parentage of Eros. Did Plato invent it and first record it in the *Symposion*? Or did Sokrates invent it? If so, was it Sokrates or Plato who first claimed that it was told by Diotima? Or, assuming that Diotima existed, did she really tell this story to Sokrates? Did she invent it, or had she been told it by someone else? Was it traditional in Mantineia, Diotima's city of origin?

Finally, therefore, no hearer or reader of the *Symposion* as we know it—the text written by Plato—is able to say with certainty what percentage of this text might best be attributed to Plato, what percentage had gradually developed during the thirty-year period when those who knew about the initial conversation were telling and retelling the story, what percentage is owed to the speakers of the initial conversation and what to the various earlier speakers reported by them.

The *Iliad* and the *Odyssey* too warn their audiences not to oversimplify the origins of traditional tales. First, the most obvious point: they are divinely inspired. The poet does not promise to sing but invites the goddess to sing. If we take this literally, the very words that the poet is writing or singing are not the poet's own. Yet it can be claimed that a poet is *self-taught* (this is said of Phemios in the *Odyssey*) and can speak with a very personal voice, as Hesiod does when addressing his brother severely in *Works and Days*. Beyond that issue, the real sources of this poetry, whether inspired by the goddess or picked up by the poet's native skill, are earlier singers and storytellers, and they in turn were inspired by even earlier ones. That tradition might theoretically go all the way back to actual observers and participants in the events of which the poems tell (events which, if they happened at all, happened five or six hundred years earlier). No wonder that the poet's own name appears nowhere.

Nothing is ever said openly about the tradition; it too is totally anonymous. Just once, however, we are made aware that such traditions last through many years. Helen, speaking bitterly of her elopement with Paris and its results, says, *We shall be themes of song for men of the future.* This is her way of saying that her reputation has been fixed for all time. Helen, as the poet imagines her, can know nothing about writing; for her no human communication can last longer than song, because song is transmitted from one singer to the next, from one generation of poets to the next.[32]

Three times we are given an indirect hint as to how this particular poetic tradition might have begun—the three occasions in the *Odyssey* when Phemios and Demodokos tell stories about the Trojan War, which had ended ten years earlier. On the last of these occasions Odysseus, himself a famous participant in the war but now an unknown wanderer, asks Demodokos to tell the last episode in the series:

> *Demodokos, I praise you above all mortals.*
> *Perhaps the Muse, child of Zeus, taught you; perhaps it was Apollo.*
> *You sing the fate of the Achaioi very properly,*
> *All that they did, all that they suffered, all of their groans,*
> *As if you were there yourself or heard it from another.*
> *So now move on and sing the Making of the Horse.*
>
> (*Odyssey* 8.487–492)

Fate in the translation stands for the Greek word *oitos;* here, clearly, it refers to the whole story of the *Achaioi,* "the Greeks who fought at Troy." *The fate of the Achaioi* is the Trojan War story as told in epic.

The poet is making us reflect that even within a few years of its origin, a story might be told properly or badly, and that the teller might have been present at the event or might have heard the story at second or third hand. Elsewhere the *Odyssey* even gives us a second version of part of the wooden horse story, a version that is told to Telemachos by Menelaos. Plato is making exactly the same point in the *Symposion* when he mentions the imperfect version given by Phoinix, now to be superseded by Apollodoros's version, the one that we are being persuaded to accept. In each case we are within a few years of the event, yet it already belongs to oral tradition and no longer to the world that we can see, touch, and measure. When exactly did the thing happen? Who was present? Certainty has vanished.

Already in the work of Plato, already in the *Iliad* and the *Odyssey,* we have the autonomous text and the unreliable narrator of twenty-first-century literary theory. Already in Plato and in the epics, we have the recognition of a divide between the real world and the oral tradition, a divide that takes place just as soon as a story is first reported. What we never find in these texts, or in ancient writings generally, is the idea that there is a cumulative, *increasing* difference between fact and tradition as time goes on, as one singer passes the story on to the next. From modern work on oral poetry it is clear that oral traditions will increasingly differ from their original, but this is a new idea, quite unfamiliar to singers in oral traditions, because they are never able to compare an original with its derivatives, and it did not occur to ancient scholars who studied Homer. Not even the most perceptive classical writer says that because Homer lived several hundred years after the Trojan War, Homer's story must differ extensively from what really happened. Most Greeks and Romans took it for granted that there are simply good reporters (like Apollodoros) and bad ones (like Phoinix), and nearly all of them were sure that Homer was one of the good reporters.

Therefore they accepted that the ten-year war really happened just as the poet describes it. As an example, Thoukydides, the greatest and the most critical of classical Greek historians, accepts without question the reality of the war and its ten-year course. He argues that if the Greeks had had adequate supplies, they would have captured Troy in a shorter time. He accepts without question that Agamemnon led the expedition, arguing that the Greeks backed him not because of family obligations but because he was the most powerful king of his time and possessed the best navy. To support this last point, Thoukydides cites the formulaic description of Agamemnon in the Catalogue of Ships in book 2 of the *Iliad*:

> Homer calls him *monarch of many islands and all Argos;* yet from the mainland he could not have ruled the *islands*—except the inshore ones, and they are not *many*—unless he had some sort of navy.[33]

This is the same kind of critical reading that we might give to reportage about the last war or the latest election. We accept facts as facts; we freely question interpretations and motives; we exploit every scrap of documentary evidence. Thoukydides' book really is about "the last war"—the initial twenty-one years (431–410 B.C.) of the Peloponnesian War, in which he himself fought on the Athenian side—and his critical use of evidence is generally very impressive. His introductory survey of earlier wars, including the siege of Troy, is weak because he approaches them in the same way. He is simply unaware that in an oral tradition separated from the original report by hundreds of years, not one detail can be assumed to be true.

THE SUCCESSION OF POETS

We are fortunate to have Plato's realistic sketch of an oral tradition at work. Luckily, the *Symposion* belongs to an oral literary genre that Plato, among others, was converting into written form; luckily, it suited Plato to show us how such texts had been transmitted thus far.

If we want to look into the oral transmission of epic poetry in early Greece, three centuries before Plato's time, we are not so lucky. No eye witness provides us with a report on how things happened, at least not in any detail. The poet of the *Odyssey* allows us no more than the lines just quoted, with two crucial but tantalizingly brief hints: there was an *oime*, or cycle, of the Trojan War (of which poets sang episodes), and no doubt there were other cycles too; some singers sang properly and others were less skilled.

When scholars of Alexandrian and Roman times attempted to reconstruct the tradition in which the poet of the *Iliad* and the *Odyssey* had worked, it was far too late. No comparable epic tradition now existed in Greek or Latin. This meant that they could not directly observe how singers constructed their narratives and transmitted them to other singers, so they never understood this important element of oral tradition. All that they could gather were a few stray facts, and the only framework in which they could interpret these facts was that of written literature, with its named authors, its fixed texts that are copied accurately or inaccurately, its plagiarisms, its interpolations (passages misleadingly inserted into a text by an editor or scribe), its forgeries (texts fraudulently ascribed to one author, actually written by another). But they did have the *Iliad* and the *Odyssey* and some other early poems. All too easily they assumed that the business of poetry at that early period had been the same as it was in their own time.

During the fifth century B.C., a strong tradition developed that a man named Homeros had composed at least some of the early narrative poetry. Around 470 B.C., the lyric poet Pindar asserted (according to a later, unreliable source) that the epic *Kypria*, which told of the judgment of Paris and the beginnings of the Trojan War, had been given by Homer as a dowry to his son-in-law, Stasinos of Cyprus. Whoever really said this first, it definitely became a common belief, as it served to explain neatly why both Homer and Stasinos were named in different sources as author of the *Kypria* (but, incidentally, two other names were sometimes given). Another story held that Homer had composed the *Capture of Oichalia*, an epic about the great hero Herakles, and given it to a certain Kreophylos of Samos in return for hospitality. By 440 B.C., when the historian Herodotos looked into the question, it was confidently said that this same Homer had composed the *Iliad* and the *Odyssey*, along with several other early poems; the full list, according to various sources, is *Phokais*, *Kypria*, *Thebais* and its sequel *Epigonoi*, *Little Iliad*, *Amazonia*, and *Return from Troy* (three sequels to the *Iliad*), plus several nonepic poems. Historians eventually reached some level of agreement that Homer had lived in the late ninth century B.C.

Gradually the names of several other early singers and writers of epic emerged from the darkness. Notably there was Syagros, apparently the earliest of all, the very first maker of an epic about the Trojan War and thus Homer's forerunner; then Arktinos of Miletos, Homer's pupil, who was said to have composed two sequels to the *Iliad* (the *Aithiopis* and the *Sack of Troy*) and an epic "about women," *Naupaktia*; and Antimachos of Teos, who possibly composed the *Epigonoi*, if Homer did not; and Eumelos of Korinthos, said to have composed the *Battle of the Titans* and also the *Return from Troy*, if Homer did not (others said that Agias of Troizen composed the *Return from Troy*). Then Lesches of Pyrrha, who composed the *Little Iliad*, if Homer did not, but three other names are also given, and perhaps after all it was Kinaithon of Lakedaimon, who might also have composed the *Oidipodeia*, the story of Oedipus, and the *Telegonia*, the story of the last years of Odysseus. Then Kyprias of Halikarnasos and Hegesinos of Salamis, either of whom might have composed the *Kypria*, if Homer and Stasinos did not; and Karkinos of Naupaktos, who might have composed the *Naupaktia*, if Arktinos did not. Then Prodikos of Phokaia, who perhaps composed the *Minyas*.

Later Greek scholars scarcely ever say that Homer or these other poets *wrote* these epics. Writing does not come into it. They understood clearly that Homer and the others were oral performers. They could hardly forget the fact, since the *Odyssey* gives such convincing descriptions of oral performances. What they say is that Homer (and the others) "made" or "composed" or sang their epics. Thereafter they pictured each poem as continuing to exist in transmission from poet to poet, more or less as it had been originally created. This view agrees with a common opinion among epic singers in many traditions. They believe they are transmitting poems accurately, and they often attribute their own work to singers of the past.

As for the various poems identified with the early singer Homer, it was natural for later Greek scholars to speculate about how these were transmitted and when they were written down. They could reach little agreement on this subject, however. It was said that the many epics of Homer were preserved orally by the family of Kreophylos of Samos; rumors about them spread, and gradually some partial and varying written texts were made. Then, some said, the legendary, mysterious, and undatable Spartan lawgiver Lykourgos heard and admired them, collected them in writing, and took them back to Sparta with him; as far as we know, this story was first recorded by Aristotle or his coworkers in their collection of constitutional histories of Greek cities. Others said that the *Iliad* and the *Odyssey* in particular had been gathered together from the early partial texts at Athens by the city's tyrant, or monarch, Peisistratos, about 540 B.C. But neither of these stories was well supported, and early authors who ought to have known of them somehow did not. Even less credible was the claim that Solon decreed that the poems of Homer be performed to a written text—Solon, the very ruler who forbade "lamenting to a text" and who warned that "singers tell many lies." There was still almost unanimous agreement that the early epics were transmitted orally for many years before they were written down.[34]

Various stories about the writing down of the more obscure epics exist. A certain writing master, Thestorides of Phokaia, was said to have written down the *Phokais* (with other epics, perhaps) from Homer's own performance and then pretended it was his own. The most likely origin for this story (which contradicts the consensus that writing was not available in Homer's circle) is that the city of Phokaia, subject of Thestorides' epic, preferred to claim that it was Homer's. Other stories involve theft or plagiarism, though they do not suggest a face-to-face meeting between poet and thief. Thus Eugammon of Kyrene was said to have stolen the epic *Telegonia* from the legendary semidivine poet

Mousaios, Peisandros of Kameiros was said to have stolen *Herakleia* from Peisinoos of Lindos, and Panyassis of Halikarnasos, a fifth-century writer, was said to have stolen the *Capture of Oichalia* from the eighth-century Kreophylos of Samos. This was just another way of saying that Panyassis's own carefully crafted masterpiece on the labors of Herakles was based on the tradition that Kreophylos had long ago shared. Similarly, the poem that Eugammon wrote stemmed from a long tradition in which Mousaios was said to have shared.

The gift story (Stasinos, Kreophylos) and the pupil story (Arktinos) are two alternative ways for later authors to deal with an issue that they honestly did not understand, the oral transmission of a poetic narrative tradition. The theft story (Panyassis, Eugammon) is a way of dealing with another issue that they did not understand, the different responsibilities of the poet who shares in an oral tradition and the poet who also writes or whose work is written down. No one grasped that an oral narrative poem is new and unique in each performance, or that the poem that is written down is the only one available to later readers—this is a twentieth-century realization, owed principally to Milman Parry. Therefore, no one understood that as far as later readers are concerned, the only crucial occasion in the case of each story or cycle was the occasion of writing, and the only creativity that can be recognized in later times is the creativity of the poet who participates in the occasion of writing.

We needed to go through these names of lost epics and shadowy poets in order to understand how distant and tenuous the links are between the legendary singer Homer, who is said to have contributed more than any other individual to the oral epic tradition, and the two great epics that we know. However unforgettable Syagros or Arktinos might have been as performers, their work was lost and could not be recoverable if it was not written down. However plagiaristic Panyassis and Eugammon were thought to be by unsympathetic contemporaries, they actually were the creators of their poems, because they were the ones who wrote them down. In just the same way, if Homer did not see his poems written down, his work is lost forever, as unrecoverable as that of the shadowy Syagros. Whatever poet was present at the writing of the *Iliad* and the *Odyssey* was the real creator of those poems.

2

The Iliad *and History*

I t's possible to read the *Iliad* without even thinking about whether the Trojan War really happened. In ancient times, nearly all readers assumed that it was history; in the eighteenth and nineteenth centuries, most readers took it to be fiction. The value of the *Iliad* to its audience—which means us—does not depend on such questions. And yet, quite reasonably, many people want to know the answers.

Is Troy a real place? Was there a ten-year siege of Troy at the same period when Mykenai was powerful, and did the siege end with the destruction of the city by an Achaian army? Were the opposing forces led by Hektor, son of King Priam, and Agamemnon? Was the war fought because Helen, the wife of Agamemnon's brother Menelaos, had eloped with the young Trojan Paris? Was Achilles the greatest warrior on the Achaian side?

With every new retelling of the Trojan War story, including the recent film *Troy*, these questions are asked again. Answers are always given—most recently in Joachim Latacz's *Troy and Homer*. The answers vary over time, depending partly on the gradual emergence of archaeological evidence and partly on current fashions among historians and archaeologists.

Classical Greeks and Romans believed that the *Iliad* was in essence history: an accurate oral tradition had transmitted this knowledge to Homer, who made it into a great poem, and this in turn was transmitted orally and eventually written down. Scholars of early modern Europe down to the mid-nineteenth century became more and more skeptical of this belief. They were aware of many conflicting legends of the origins of European peoples, including this one, and they were inclined to believe none of them. Then two big scientific advances set off the swings of fashion. First, beginning in 1870, Heinrich Schliemann's archaeological discoveries at Troy and Mykenai meant that flat skepticism had to give way to acceptance that these had been centers of power at the right time. Then, from the 1930s on, research into oral traditions showed that although historical events may be remembered for several centuries, details are not transmitted accurately and eventually become inextricably confused, and there can be no doubt that the *Iliad* was composed, purely on the basis of oral tradition, several centuries after the Trojan War would have taken place.

The answer to the basic questions is now known to be yes. Troy is identified with complete confidence; at the right period, its political links placed it in opposition to the Achaians of Greece. It was destroyed violently. However, we cannot say who carried out the destruction. There is archaeological support for many background details in the *Iliad*, but they turn out to belong to very different periods, as research into oral traditions would lead us to expect. As for a Trojan War and whether Achaians were the attackers, we have no evidence at all outside the *Iliad* itself.

THE TROJAN WAR IN ITS TRADITIONAL CONTEXT

In book 6 of the *Iliad*, when in conversation with Hektor and Paris (here called Alexandros), Helen recognizes that Hektor and the people of Troy are fighting because of her:

> *For the sake of myself, a bitch, and Alexandros's blind folly.*
> *On us two Zeus has set a sorry fate, so that afterward*
> *We shall be themes of song for men of the future.*
>
> (*Iliad* 6.356–358)

The poet makes Helen describe herself as a bitch because, though she is still married to Menelaos, she is living openly with another man; in this metaphor she equates her own apparent lack of shame with that proverbially attributed to dogs because they will mate in public view. On this rare occasion the poet of the *Iliad* gives in to the temptation, familiar to narrative poets, to allow characters to predict that songs will be made about them by later generations, and we, as audience, have to admire the skill with which Helen predicts the future. She's right, of course: these traditions would exist, the poet would make use of them, and the *Iliad* story would be told.

Here we have to work backward from the real *Iliad*. Is it possible to identify when and how the traditions that led to the poem really began?

To start with the most obvious point, the Trojan War was not a recent event. Unlike the singers Phemios and Demodokos in the *Odyssey*, who are shown to be narrating current affairs, the poet is telling of incidents that lie far beyond the reach of living memory. We can prove this on the basis of the quotation just given, because what is really happening in these lines is that Helen is predicting the Greek epic tradition. She is predicting the poet; therefore, as far as she is concerned, the poet is in the future. The matter is made clear elsewhere, in any case, because we are told four times that the heroes of the Trojan war belonged to a mighty generation of the past. Here is one example:

He seized a boulder in his hand,
Tydeus's son did, a big thing which even two men could not lift
Who were like mortals of today, but he hefted it easily on his own.

(Iliad 5.302–304)

In all four cases the half-line formula *who were like mortals of today* is included, as if to drive the point home to us.[1] This was a different epoch, an age of heroes.

But that's all. We are never told exactly how long ago the events of the *Iliad* took place. No lines of descent are given linking heroes of the Trojan War with the potential readership of the poems, or with any other people of the poet's own time—in fact, there is scarcely a hint that the heroes had any offspring. Later legends gradually filled the gap.

Other epics told of the later adventures of Telemachos and revealed that Odysseus had had a son by Kirke, named Telegonos (which means "fathered far away"), and that Telegonos eventually killed his father. Tragedians gave classic form to the legend of Agamemnon, which was completed with the story of his son, Orestes. Orestes avenged his father by killing his mother, Klytaimestra, along with her lover, Aigisthos, and was with difficulty cleansed of the pollution of the horrific act of matricide. Storytellers explored the adventures of certain Trojans who escaped death when their city fell and sought a new life in the west, notably Aeneas, a minor character in the *Iliad*. According to the legends crystallized in Virgil's *Aeneid*, Aeneas led a band of Trojans to Italy, where their descendants became the founders of Rome.

Genealogists and local historians, who soon abounded in Greece, traced the family lines from each of the heroes down to their own times. In due course, thanks to their work, Alexander the Great and Julius Caesar were both convinced of their "heroic" descent, the former from Andromache, the latter from Aeneas. Family trees spread luxuriantly; retrospectively, they filled the centuries that preceded the writing of the *Iliad* and the *Odyssey*.

Then came the chronologists. Their aim was to list the dates of historical events in the past, and where the sources provided no dates—as is the case with the *Iliad* and the *Odyssey*—they had to calculate them. This was generally done by counting generations in family trees or in lists of kings, working to an average of forty years between generations (between the father's birth and that of the son destined to succeed him). Similar methods were applied, with equally unreliable results, when Europeans began to investigate African and Polynesian historical traditions. In this way the precise date of the Trojan War was eventually worked out: converting from the ancient Greek calendar to our own, the accepted answer was that Troy was besieged in 1194 and fell in 1184 B.C. It has been argued that the calculation was faulty because the average generation should have been counted as thirty-three and not forty years. It has also been argued, rightly, that this does not matter, because the family lines and king lists were invented and unrealistic. Since there was no way to verify them, and since classical historians had no other method of determining the date of such ancient events, we have no reason to hope that the traditional date of the Trojan War corresponds to any kind of reality.[2]

Ancient readers accepted, as we have seen, that the ten-year war really happened. They accepted that its historical background was accurate, encouraged by the fact that its geography was detailed and convincing. True, the two most important places in the *Iliad* and the *Odyssey* narratives had no current significance by the date when the poems were written, yet their existence and even their location were not controversial. One of the two was Mykenai, a rich and powerful city, Agamemnon's homeland and apparently a metropolis of southern Greece. The other was Troy, which is called *Troie* and *Ilios* in the poems. Troy, the focus of the war, was a fortress near the mouth of the Hellespont or Dardanelles, in northwestern Asia Minor. These places could be confidently identified by classical Greeks who looked into the question.

A prominent hilltop fortress not far west of Argos had strong walls pierced with a narrow gate surmounted by two fine carved lions. This was Mykenai, a decayed city in which a few hundred people still lived, a place that the people of Argos would eventually feel strong enough to depopulate and partly to dismantle. Not only was it in the right place and not only did the name survive, but the elaborate burials in the neighborhood showed that it had once been the capital of a rich kingdom. People regularly made offerings at these burial mounds, as they did at others throughout Greece, to gain the favor of the semidivine "heroes," known or unknown, who must have been buried there in an earlier era. The classical geographical writers Strabo and Pausanias, both careful and critical readers of Homer, accept without question that the ruins are those of ancient Mykenai. Pausanias describes them:

> If we turn back toward Argos, the ruins of Mykenai will be on our left. The Greeks know that Perseus was the founder of Mykenai. . . . The gate survives, with lions standing over it, among other sections of the defensive wall, said to be the work of Kyklopes. . . . In the ruins of Mykenai . . . are the graves of those who came home from Troy with Agamemnon, to be murdered by Aigisthos over dinner: one grave is Kassandra's (but the Spartans at Amyklai claim that they have Kassandra's grave); one is Agamemnon's, another is Eurymedon the charioteer's; and one single grave holds Teledamos and Pelops, said to be the twin children of Kassandra, who were only babies when they were butchered by Aigisthos along with their parents.[3]

The story that Kassandra had already borne twins to Agamemnon is not in the epics. It must have been a local legend, invented to explain a double burial.

Then there was a big mound topped by a small and insignificant city on the plain near the mouth of the Skamandros River, which reaches the sea at the point where the Hellespont flows into the Aegean. The name of this place was Ilion—the usual name of Troy in the *Iliad*—and it was widely accepted as the site of Troy. Some skeptics had doubts about the location. Ilion stands at the end of a rocky ridge, and the Roman geographer Strabo insists that Achilles could never have dragged Hektor's body all around this city with his chariot. The alluvial plain between Ilion and the sea was a recent formation and could not have been the site of Greek-Trojan battles, said the female scholar Hestiaia of Alexandria. The historical geographer Demetrios of Skepsis concluded that the real Troy must have been further inland, and the battleground must have been an inland valley.

Still, no one doubted that ancient Troy was somewhere around here. The district was still known as Troas; other place-names (including the river, Skamandros) matched those of the *Iliad*; many local topographical features corresponded with the poet's descriptions. When Alexander the Great visited the site in 334 B.C., providing what would now be a photo opportunity after the first military victory of his Persian expedition, he was shown the "tomb of Achilles"—admittedly, not a real monument from the time of Achilles and Agamemnon, but a later memorial where visiting tourists and devotees could worship the hero. Not far away were shrines to Hektor, Paris, Hekabe, and the Greek heroes Aias and Patroklos.[4]

To sum up, later Greek readers were close enough to the heroes and their world to feel with absolute confidence that the story of the *Iliad* and the *Odyssey* was history. In fact, it was their own national history.

FROM NATIONAL MYTH TO ARCHAEOLOGY

Building on the *Iliad* and on later legends of Aeneas the Trojan refugee, Virgil's *Aeneid* adopts the Trojan War theme to provide a national mythology for the Romans. This inventive but high-handed literary use of what had been a Greek oral tradition set the pattern for the development in medieval times of a series of legends linking the peoples of various European countries with Troy. Geoffrey of Monmouth's twelfth-century *History of the Kings of Britain* for example, holds that the ancestor of the Britons was a certain Brutus, great-grandson of Aeneas. At least down to the Elizabethan period, many serious historians believed such tales. In the seventeenth and eighteenth centuries, critical historians at last perceived the fantasy that lay behind these legendary genealogies. Unfortunately, they did not see any difference between the literary inventions of Virgil and his imitators, on one side, and the oral tradition that had culminated in the *Iliad* and the *Odyssey*, on the other side. As a result, Geoffrey of Monmouth, Virgil, and Homer were all rejected as potential sources of history. Readers were no longer prepared to be taken in by the myth that there had been rich kingdoms and high culture in Greece and Asia Minor at the supposed date of the Trojan War.

Thus matters remained until Heinrich Schliemann, fired by his reading of the *Iliad*, excavated at the traditional sites of Troy and Mykenai. Schliemann, a successful businessman who applied his hard-earned wealth to his enthusiasm for Homer, was convinced that real history underlay the early Greek epics. Contradicting Strabo and many more recent doubters, he argued that the well-known mound of classical Ilion, then called Hissarlik, would in fact reveal the prehistoric city of

Troy. He began to dig there in 1870 and found a series of cities succeeding one another on the same site. In a deep layer (now called Troy II) he found spectacular golden jewelry which he called "the treasure of Priam"; it was modeled by Mrs. Schliemann in a famous photograph and then deposited in the Prussian State Museum in Berlin, but it was lost from sight at the end of World War II and has only recently been rediscovered in Russian custody.[5]

The remains of this very ancient city still showed signs that it had been destroyed by fire—one of the best possible archaeological indications of enemy action. Schliemann drew the natural conclusion that the Trojan War and the Greek victory were real historical events for which he had found the clinching evidence. He did not realize that Troy II is a thousand years older than any probable Greek siege of Troy.

His confidence bolstered by his finds at Troy, Schliemann dug at Mykenai, just inside the Lion Gate, and was lucky enough to rediscover several deep burial chambers, whose entrances had been carefully concealed. Some of them had been known to Pausanias; others had remained unknown and had never been plundered. In these chambers Schliemann found rich offerings that clearly originated from an unknown civilization many centuries older than the classical remains of Greece. The most celebrated item is probably the gold death mask of an aged man; "I have looked upon the face of Agamemnon," Schliemann announced.

In later excavations at Troy, in which Schliemann paid more attention to archaeological methods, it became clear that another of the eight successive cities (Troy VIIa), not very distant in date from the burial chambers of Mykenai, had also been destroyed by a catastrophic fire.

That is how Schliemann changed the agenda. Yes, we could test the *Iliad* archaeologically—he had begun to do exactly that. It was eventually clear beyond doubt that at around the same prehistoric period, Mykenai and Troy were rich, powerful, civilized cities and that both had been destroyed violently. A new era had opened in the study of the two epics. There was demonstrably some historical truth in them. Once more they could be looked on as potential historical sources, and they are still regarded in this light today.

Yet they result from an oral tradition that must have extended at least four hundred years, and probably much longer, without any written support, because writing was unknown in Greece between 1200 and

800 B.C. The real challenge, if we are to evaluate the *Iliad* as history, is to distinguish traditional from imagined, historical from fictional, early from late.

THE HISTORICAL GEOGRAPHY OF THE *ILIAD*

To face this challenge, we need to look beyond Mykenai and Troy to the other Greek and Aegean places and peoples named in the *Iliad*. Every name is a piece of historical information, indicating that this locality was known and worth naming at a certain date during the growth of the epic tradition and was retained in the story until the poet composed the *Iliad*. Can we obtain any consistent dating in this way for the historical information in the *Iliad*?

To begin to formulate an answer, we can focus on the Greek cities named in the Catalogue of Ships in book 2. This catalogue is presented as a list of the places of origin of the Greek contingents fighting at Troy in the last year of the war. However, any reader will soon see that the list actually has a different history—a history that turns out to be independent of the traditions from which the remainder of the *Iliad* was composed.

The catalogue evidently began simply as a list of Greek cities, which naturally went into hexameter verse because in an oral culture, versified lists are easier than prose lists to remember accurately. There was a vital tradition of versified lists and catalogues in early Greek literature, including Hesiod's *Theogony* and its sequel, the *Catalogue of Women*. The city list in the catalogue as we have it is incomplete. A few cities that were surely important are not there, and some regions of Greece are completely omitted, perhaps intentionally, for a reason unknown to us, or perhaps as a result of errors at some stage. The list has a geographical arrangement: a clockwise spiral around central and southern Greece; a counterclockwise spiral from Crete via Rhodes and Kos to Karpathos; a short counterclockwise spiral in part of northern Greece. This is why it is unlikely that the catalogue started out as a list of the contingents that sailed from Greece or that fought at Troy, because if it did, why would they be listed in geographical order of origin? The suggestion has been made that these were cities that would be visited by sacred ambassadors from a major shrine; such lists are known from later Greece.[6]

At a later date, numbers of ships or of men and names of military leaders were attached to this city list, turning it into a fictional poetic catalogue of the Greek military leaders and contingents who set out from Aulis in Boiotia to fight the Trojan War. However, some Greek heroes of the story as told in the remainder of the *Iliad*—Antilochos, Patroklos, Teukros, and others—are not in the catalogue at all. Some, such as Aias, appear to be squeezed in as afterthoughts. Others, including Achilles, Agamemnon, and Odysseus, are in the list but are affiliated with strange territories that are not consistent with what is said about them in the rest of the poem. Meanwhile, the Arkadians, though listed in the catalogue, never show up in the remainder of the *Iliad*, and the Boiotians play a very small part. Some of the leaders of catalogue contingents, including Nireus, Agapenor, and Gouneus, do nothing at all. Evidently, at the time when this catalogue was first adapted to the Trojan War story, the current local version of that story was significantly different from what was eventually adopted and developed in the *Iliad*.[7]

The poet of the *Iliad* clearly thought this version of the catalogue was important and relevant enough to be built into the new poem. Since the *Iliad* narrates only the tenth year of the war, the catalogue had to be introduced as a list of those who were present and fighting in the tenth year, but it was not adjusted all through to reflect this change. However, some essential adjustments were made—for example, to get Aias and Odysseus in.

Thus the catalogue is a serious, semi-independent document, a list of cities in many of the regions of Greece, claiming to show how many ships and how many men these places sent to Troy and who their leaders were. As a clue to its separateness, the poet begins with an invocation of the goddesses of poetry:

Tell me now, Muses whose homes are on Olympos—
For you are goddesses, you are everywhere and know all things
But we merely hear rumor and know nothing—
Who were the leaders and monarchs of the Danaoi?
I could not tell or name the whole army,
Not if I had ten tongues and ten mouths
And an unbreakable voice and a heart of bronze,
Unless the Olympian Muses, daughters of Zeus who holds the aigis,

Were to remind me how many went to fight under Ilion.
I shall list the shipmasters and all the ships.
The Boiotians were led by Peneleos and Leitos
And Arkesilaos and Prothoenor and Klonios:
Those who farmed Hyrie and rocky Aulis
And Schoinos and Skolos and Eteonos of many mountain spurs,
Thespeia and Graia and Mykalessos with broad dance floors,
Those who farmed around Harma and Eilesion and Erythrai,
Those who held Eleon and Hyle and Peteon . . .

(*Iliad* 2.484–500)

According to the usual story, it was from *rocky Aulis*, on the coast
of Boiotia, that the Greeks embarked on their voyage at the beginning
of the war, and it used to be guessed that this is why Boiotia comes first
in the catalogue. Recent discoveries have shown that there is a much
better reason. They include a major find at Thebes, the principal city of
Boiotia, of tablets in Linear B, the cuneiform script used in Mycenaean
Greece. They also include a newly interpreted letter of the mid-
thirteenth century B.C. to the king of the Hittites from the king of the
Achaioi, who names his ancestor Kadmos, a name familiar in later
mythology as the founder of Thebes. It is now clear that in Mycenaean
times, Thebes was the center of a major Achaian realm; it may even
have been the residence of the Great King.[8]

The *Iliad* as a whole takes no account of this fact and says very little about Thebes or the Boiotians. The story of Thebes was told in other
epics (*Thebais* and *Epigonoi*; see page 28), and the two story lines, perhaps once connected, had grown apart. However, one way in which the
catalogue displays its independence from the *Iliad* is that it takes full
account of the importance of Boiotia. Not only does it place Boiotia
first; it gives this region more space than any other (the entry is much
longer than I have quoted here), with a total of thirty cities and six
thousand warriors. The detail, in the Boiotia section and in the catalogue as a whole, is astonishing. It has posed many problems for readers
of the *Iliad* both ancient and modern, because so many of the places
named are highly obscure or completely unidentifiable.

Can the catalogue be dated? Naturally it lists some of the inhabited
cities of Greece at the period when the *Iliad* was compiled, in the sev-

enth century B.C., such as Aulis in the lines quoted above. But many cities of seventh-century Greece are left out (Lebadeia, Chaironeia, and Tanagra are among the well-known Boiotian cities that are not included), and it lists many places that were *not* inhabited in the seventh century. This is clear because there are simply too many names that classical readers could not identify, in spite of continuity of settlement and strong historical traditions running from that period into classical times. So the catalogue is definitely not current seventh-century information.

The catalogue lists many places that were inhabited in the four centuries that followed the collapse of Mycenaean culture in Greece; within the regions it covers and as far as our knowledge goes, not many major sites of this period are omitted. But archaeological evidence tells us that settlement in Greece in those centuries was rather sparse. A great many smaller Mycenaean towns fell into ruin at the end of the Mycenaean period or very soon after. If that is so, the catalogue has too many names to be a list of "dark age" cities.

Moving backward in time, it definitely includes many places that were inhabited in the Mycenaean period, when Troy fell; how many is uncertain, because we do not know the original names of all Mycenaean sites. It would be logical and satisfying if the catalogue turned out to be real Mycenaean information, from the period when a real Trojan War could have taken place. Evidence has been slowly accumulating in favor of this view, famously championed by Denys Page in 1959 and in general supported by the researches of Simpson and Lazenby in 1970. Scholars are excited that in the newly discovered Linear B tablets of Thebes, dated very close to the time of a possible Trojan War, no fewer than three of the places listed in the Boiotian entry in the Catalogue of Ships have turned up—the names Eleon, Hyle, and Peteon. All three were completely unknown to classical Greek writers, including Strabo, who worked very hard on the Catalogue of Ships, and all three had been given up as unidentifiable by modern scholars. Not only is this important evidence in itself; it strongly suggests that more names in the catalogue will turn out to be Mycenaean whenever more Mycenaean place-names happen to be rediscovered.

There is a puzzle here. If, as this new evidence seems to confirm, the catalogue lists many places that were inhabited over five hundred years before its time and were soon afterward abandoned, it is hard to understand how and why such names would have remained in the collective memory, in a purely oral tradition, through the centuries when they were uninhabited, down to the time when the *Iliad* was written. We could use this as an argument that the *Iliad* was created and put into writing earlier than is assumed, or that the catalogue had been recorded in writing in some separate form before it was incorporated in the *Iliad*, but these arguments would not help much. We cannot propose a date of writing earlier than about 800 B.C., because that is when the writing of Greek began, so there would still be a gap of nearly four hundred years to be bridged by oral tradition. Without claiming to have the final answer, I will say that in many cultures abandoned towns and villages continue to be centers of ritual or pilgrimage; in early historic Greece, worship was offered at prehistoric burial mounds that were identified vaguely as those of "heroes." So it is at least possible that the minor Mycenaean settlements of Greece, even as they fell into ruin, were still on a religious list.

Many minor names in the catalogue are Mycenaean. Unfortunately, this does not mean that we can really arrive at a firm dating for the catalogue as a whole. An exploration of some individual entries indicates that it would be better not to try. Here is one striking example from the same Boiotian part of the Catalogue of Ships:

> *Those who held Hypothebai, the well-built citadel . . .*
>
> (*Iliad* 2.505)

We must be talking about Thebai, or Thebes, the principal city of Boiotia in classical and modern times. The Mycenaean city and palace of Thebes were destroyed, according to archaeologists, at around 1200 B.C., not long before the fall of Troy VIIa, but suburbs were already clustering below the rock, and for a long time after the destruction these suburbs were all that existed of Thebes. Eventually the citadel was rebuilt and became once more the heart of the city. So the name given in the list, Hypothebai, or Under-Thebes, has a very precise sense. It carries a memory of the late Mycenaean period (say 1200 to 1100 B.C.), when the destruction of the upper city was still a recent event and people had not yet grown accustomed to using the simple name Thebai for the lower town. But now look at the descriptive phrase that ends the line. It suits Thebes very well at certain times, but definitely not at those times when the name Under-Thebes belongs in a list of Boiotian cities, because the lower town was not a *well-built citadel*. The citadel lay in ruins when the lower town represented Thebes. So this single line derives from two different periods of history, one of them about five hundred years before the date when the *Iliad* was written, the other even older or somewhat younger.[9]

Similar confusions of date can be found elsewhere in the *Iliad*, outside the catalogue. When Hektor seems invincible, the poet tells us that his progress could not be stopped by all the Greeks currently gathered against him,

> *The Boiotians and Iaones with trailing robes,*
> *The Lokrians and Phthians and brave Epeians . . .*
>
> (*Iliad* 13.685–686)

In this little catalogue of peoples of central Greece, it is the Iaones, or Ionians, who make us look twice. In the poet's time they had become one of the four major subdivisions of Greek peoples, and their dialect is the one that contributed most to the special poetic language of the epic tradition—to the language of the *Iliad* and the *Odyssey* themselves. By that time they occupied the Greek cities of the middle Asia Minor coast (founded long after the fall of Troy) and also some of the Aegean islands (but none of their islands are listed in the Catalogue of Ships). Now this little list in itself makes good sense. Later Greek writers said that the men of Athens and Euboia, Boiotia's neighbors, were ethnically Ionian, and the poet perhaps has one or both regions in mind here. The form of name in the *Iliad*, *Iaones*, is still very close to that used by the Mycenaeans and various Near Eastern peoples (Hebrew *Yawan*, for example), and all these people had learned to know the Ionians as fighters and traders long before the composition of the *Iliad*. So they are rightly included—but their epithet is anachronistic. The *Ionians with trailing robes* are not mercenaries or seamen; they are the luxury-loving citizens of western Asia Minor, at just the period when the *Iliad* was composed.

Now back to the Catalogue of Ships and to the island of Rhodes, a major center of Greek culture in prehistoric and classical times. No wonder it is mentioned several times in the *Iliad*. It is among the few Greek islands named in the catalogue, and it is named rather insistently:

Tlepolemos son of Herakles, big and brave,
Led from Rhodes nine ships of proud Rhodians
Who occupied Rhodes, arranged in three divisions,
Lindos and Ielysos and gleaming Kameiros.

(*Iliad* 2.653–656)

In other words, Rhodes and its inhabitants had been organized into three city-states, which are named in the last line. This listing (which is followed by a digression about the birth and adventures of Tlepolemos) fits Rhodian history accurately, but during one particular period. Formerly sharing in Mycenaean culture, Rhodes was afterward colonized by a second wave of Greek settlers, the Dorians, and classical Greek legend said that the Dorian settlements were led by the sons of Herakles, including Tlepolemos. Archaeologists place this colonization close to 900 B.C. In Mycenaean times there were several towns on the island, but it is thought that the newly arrived Dorians set up the three city-states named in the catalogue. These cities retained their importance until 408 B.C., when they united to found Rhodos (Rhodes Town), after which the island became a single state. Since the Rhodes entry in the catalogue names Tlepolemos and the three Dorian cities, our best guess must be that it originated after 900 B.C.

Let's now glance at the Trojan Battle Order with which book 2 of the *Iliad* ends. Clearly this section is inserted in order to balance the Catalogue of Ships; having had a list of the Greeks and their ships, we must have a list of Trojan and allied contingents also. It's a much shorter list, also in geographical order, dealing first with Troy and its neighborhood, then with allies from southeastern Europe, northwestern Asia Minor, and the western coast as far south as the people whom the Greeks called Lykioi. It's a frustrating list, because so far we do not have enough external evidence to date it. Yet it too stems from a tradition distinct from that of the *Iliad* in general, and some parts of it are very ancient. Greek cities on the Asia Minor coast, even the oldest, are not mentioned. This could be a planned omission, to avoid a glaring anachronism, since these cities were known to be more recent than the fall of Troy. But the major city of Miletos, believed from statements by two early Greek historians to have been Carian-speaking and then for a while bilingual before it became Greek, is here; it is said in this list to be the metropolis of the *Kares of foreign speech*. This listing again seems to take us back some hundreds of years, to the time when Miletos was a bilingual city and a buffer state independent of the Hittite empire of inland Anatolia, favoring the Achaioi of Mycenaean Greece.

Now, setting aside the catalogues, let's consider two formulaic descriptions of the peoples who took opposing sides in the Trojan War. Although horses were important to the peoples spoken of in the *Iliad*—in farming, in warfare, and in sports—only one ethnic group is described as *hippodamoi*, "horse-tamers," and that is the Trojans. On one occasion Agamemnon accuses Odysseus of laziness, and Odysseus replies hotly:

> *Son of Atreus, what a speech out of your teeth!*
> *How can you claim I avoid the fighting when the Achaioi*
> *Stir up fierce battle upon the horse-taming Trojans?*
> *Now watch, if you want to, if you care about it,*
> *As the father of Telemachos goes into the front line*
> *Against the horse-taming Trojans. Your words are wind.*
>
> *(Iliad 4.350–355)*

More than once the *horse-taming Trojans* are named alongside a comparable characterization of the Achaioi, *euknemides*, "well protected by greaves." When the goddess Athene suddenly appeared on the battlefield,

> *Astonishment gripped those who saw her,*
> *The horse-taming Trojans and the well-greaved Achaioi.*
>
> *(Iliad 4.79–80)*

Both of these formulaic adjectives carry real historical information. When the Trojans are singled out in this way from the many peoples in the *Iliad* who prized horses, and when Troy itself, elsewhere in the poem, appears as *Ilion of fine foals*, it is because the Trojans really did keep horses in large numbers—archaeologists confirm it. But these descriptions would make little sense after Troy was occupied by people from the Balkans and the Trojans ceased to exist as an identifiable people, around 1100 B.C.; they would make no sense at all after Troy was abandoned, around 950 B.C. When the Achaioi are distinguished in the *Iliad* by the leather greaves that protected their shins, it is because this really used to be a distinctive feature of their armor. Vase paintings and reliefs show that Egyptians and Near Easterners did not wear greaves, but Mycenaean Greeks did, and Mycenaean Greeks undoubtedly correspond to the Achaioi of the *Iliad*. The wearing of greaves cannot be traced beyond the decline of Mycenaean Greek civilization, soon after 1200 B.C.[10]

There is another description for the Achaioi, *kare komoontes*, "growing their hair long," or "long-haired." When Hektor taunts Paris in book 3, he exclaims:

> *How the long-haired Achaioi will be cackling,*
> *Saying that we made you our champion for your good looks,*
> *When there's no strength or valor in your heart.*
>
> (*Iliad* 3.43–45)

Cretan men of the ancient Minoan civilization are sometimes depicted in wall paintings with very long black hair, and Mycenaean men adopted this fashion, to judge by some Mycenaean vase paintings. Once the Minoan culture had disappeared and been forgotten—sometime around 1350 B.C.—the phrase *kare komoontes* might gradually be felt to be appropriate to the Mycenaean Greeks instead, because they kept up the fashion; but again, not after the decline of Mycenaean civilization, soon after 1200 B.C.

Thus three formulas characterizing the Trojans and the Achaioi almost certainly originated in the poetic tradition more than five hundred years before the creation of the *Iliad*. Although the Catalogue of Ships contains items that are easily recognizable as more recent, some other items are at least five hundred years old.

In the grand sweep of the *Iliad*, however, these are mere details. What can we say about the origins of the main story, the siege and destruction of Troy?

THE PREHISTORY OF TROY AND MYKENAI

Archaeology alone will never answer all the questions about the fall of Troy that historians and readers of the *Iliad* and the *Odyssey* want to ask. Archaeology practically never finds named persons. It is scarcely ever possible for archaeologists to trace the course of a journey by individuals, such as a naval expedition, or to ascribe the evidence of fire and destruction (such as what is visible at Troy) to identifiable and named attackers. It is fascinating to find signs of the flourishing and the destruction of two prehistoric cities separated by hundreds of miles, but dating the events concerned may be difficult or impossible, setting aside the even more difficult question of who or what caused the destruction. Yet archaeologists can tell us a great deal.

Let's begin with Greece. Mycenaean civilization in Greece seems to have flourished quite suddenly, around 1600 B.C. There was a great deal of mutual influence between it and the much older Minoan culture of Crete, though Minoans and Mycenaeans spoke different languages. Mycenaeans spoke an early form of Greek; they kept accounts and inventories on clay tablets, which were written in Greek in Linear B script, deciphered in the 1950s. In Crete people spoke a language unrelated to others in Europe, but we know little about it; it was written in Linear A script and is as yet undeciphered. Around 1450 B.C. the Mycenaeans took possession of central Crete. Mycenaean centers then included Knossos, Phaistos (Crete), Pylos, Sparta, Tiryns, Mykenai (southern Greece), and Thebes (central Greece), and at Knossos, as at the mainland sites, administrative records were henceforth kept in Greek, in Linear B.

All these places were destroyed violently, but not all at the same date. Pylos was burned around 1200 B.C. The fortified stronghold of Mykenai, with some others, lived on through the period at which Troy VIIa was burned, but for less than a hundred years. Many Cretan settlements were abandoned during this period, and people took to the hills. Archaeologists cannot identify the attackers. Once the Mycenaean administrative centers—the palaces—were destroyed, knowledge of Linear B writing was also forgotten. Greek became once more an unwritten language, the vehicle of a wholly oral culture.

Across the Aegean, Troy was further excavated in the twentieth century, and the excavations are continuing today. This later work has been much more scientific than Schliemann's was. The massive fortress called by the archaeologists Troy VI, built around 1700 B.C., stood for over four hundred years. It soon grew larger than the central hill, the mound of Hissarlik, could accommodate. The Lower City, outside the citadel walls and with its own defenses, might eventually have accommodated a population of several thousand; but the density of population is uncertain, because only small areas have yet been excavated. Troy VI collapsed in a great earthquake about 1250 B.C. It was rebuilt hastily and much less solidly. The new level, known as Troy VIIa, was a much less imposing fortress, which stood for perhaps as little as sixty years. Troy evidently had enemies, and maybe these enemies were aware that the city's defenses were no longer what they had been. At any rate, Troy VIIa was destroyed by violence sometime around 1180 B.C. All the buildings that can be identified were ruined by a devastating fire. Slingstones and other weapons found show that enemy attack brought about the end of Troy VIIa. People went on living at Troy even after that disaster; but the new and shrunken settlement, Troy VIIb, was of little interest to anyone except the insignificant few who had been untouched by whatever caused the fire. Around 1100 B.C. Troy was apparently occupied by people from across the Dardanelles, and about 950 B.C. it was abandoned altogether. All these dates are open to dispute, but the sequence of events is clear.[11]

The site lay unoccupied for at least two hundred years, until a Greek shrine was established there around 700 B.C. Later Greeks and then Romans, fully aware of the Troy legend, developed a new city on the site. It too was eventually abandoned.

In much of the rest of Anatolia in the second millennium B.C., the languages spoken and written belonged to the group now called Anatolian. All have been extinct since ancient times; the best known is Hittite, which was deciphered in 1915. Anatolian languages belonged to the Indo-European family, as does Greek. Hittite and the related Luwian were the two languages of record in the Hittite empire and its tributary states. Troy, as we shall see, was one of the latter; the find there in 1995 of a typical late Hittite seal with a short inscription in Hieroglyphic Luwian helps to demonstrate this link.[12]

Troy VI was no more than a small town by modern standards, but it was the capital city of a Hittite tributary state. Archaeological finds show that materials and works of art came there not only from Greece, Crete, and Hittite lands but from as far afield as central Europe and central Asia. The classicist Denys Page, recalling those equine formulas (the *horse-taming* Trojans and Troy *of fine foals*), long ago suggested that Troy exported horses to Greece, and if he had been equally aware of how the horses and chariots of Troy figure in Hittite documents, he might have hypothesized an export trade in horses in that direction also. Troy was in a remarkable and privileged geographical position, standing at a convenient crossing point between southwest Asia and Europe and guarding the only possible sea route between the Mediterranean and the Black Sea. Not only was the city a crossroads; it was also on the edge of the "developed world" of the second millennium B.C. Admittedly, there were cities of comparable size in southern Greece, but there were no long-distance land routes from them to the north. No cities existed anywhere else in Europe; no cities existed anywhere at all to the north or west of Troy. Whatever commodities from southwest Asia that people in southeastern Europe might want were likely to pass through Troy. Anything in southeastern Europe that attracted people in southwest Asia—and this might well include horses from the plains of the southern Balkans—was equally likely to pass through Troy. Though as yet very small in volume, long-distance trade of this kind continued and increased through the second millennium, although it was interrupted by the catastrophic events of around 1200 B.C. and after.[13]

Myths and legends naturally reduce history to personalities. If we look beyond Helen, Priam, Agamemnon, and Achilles, in terms of prehistoric geography Troy deserves its place in legend as a major city of the north, as a potential rival to Mykenai, as a crossroads, and as a center of trade in horses and other commodities.

THE MAJOR NAMES AND PLACES

As we look at the historical circumstances that might have surrounded a siege of Troy, we must keep in mind that the poet of the *Iliad* freely uses alternative names for places and peoples that are central to the story. Troy may be *Troia*, *Dardania*, or *Ilios*. The Greeks may be *Achaioi*, *Argeioi*, or *Danaoi*. Paris, the seducer of Helen, may be *Paris* or *Alexandros*. Let's explore these alternates and the possible reasons for them.

What we would really like to find, of course, is a detailed contemporary chronicle or inscription that we can identify as describing the burning of Troy VIIa soon after 1200 B.C. Then at last we would know who did it and maybe even why. It seems unlikely that any such text will ever come from Greece. Linear B script may well have been in use at the right time, but it survives only in accounts and inventories. If administrative and historical records were kept at Troy—and they surely were—they would have taken the form of clay tablets stored somewhere in the citadel. Some of them would have been baked hard by the fire that destroyed Troy VIIa, favoring their survival, but the whole center of the ruined citadel was cleared by later Greeks to make room for a temple of Athene, and any surviving written records would probably have been destroyed at that time. It seems unlikely, therefore, that a record of the crucial event will come from Troy. South of Troy lay the kingdoms of Arzawa and Mira and their dependencies. These were Hittite tributaries for a longer period than Troy was and had more direct links to the imperial capital, but as yet we have scarcely any historical records from them. So we must make the most of what records we have. They are meager records from peoples to whom Mykenai and Troy were obscure and close to the horizon, but they are much better than nothing. They tell us of events that lie in the background of the legends that eventually turned into the *Iliad* and the *Odyssey*. And they do mention a sack of Troy.

The Hittites ruled an extensive empire of inland Anatolia known to others as Hatti; it collapsed not long after the burning of Troy VIIa. The capital of this empire, which they called Hattuša, has been excavated at Boğazköy in Turkey. The Hittites had numerous allies and client states to their west, south, and southeast. They maintained regular contacts (sometimes peaceful, sometimes warlike) with rulers in Syria and even, further afield, with the monarchies of Assyria, Babylonia, and Egypt.

At the beginning of the thirteenth century, the Hittites and the Egyptians went to war for the domination of Syria, and in 1285 B.C. (by one current calculation) fought the battle of Qadesh in Syria. The battle is recorded in great detail in Egyptian sources. It did not go well for Egypt, but the Egyptian king Ramses II, proud of his military prowess, made sure that not only the dry official record but also the praise-song of the court poet Pentauor was inscribed for all to read. These records tell us that the Hittite king Muwattalli II (who ruled around 1290–1272 B.C.) had numerous allies fighting on his side, providing the excuse for a long preliminary list of peoples that the Egyptian king could claim to have defeated:

Here begins the victory of the King of Upper and Lower Egypt Usermare-Sotpenre, son of Re, Ramses II, beloved of Amun, endowed with eternal life; which he achieved over the land of Hatti, Naharina, the land of Arwad, Pidasa, the *Drdny*, Kashkash, the land of Masa, the land of Karkisha and Luka, Carchemish, Kode, the whole land of Nukhashse, the land of Qadesh, Ukeret, and Mushanet. . . .[14]

The name of one contingent of Hittite allies immediately strikes a chord with any reader of the *Iliad*. Those who appear in Egyptian script as *Drdny* surely ought to be the *Dardanoi*, one of the three names that the poet of the *Iliad* uses for the people of Troy and its hinterland. The list of Hittite allies is repeated, with variations, as they appear at Qadesh ("the wretched enemy from Hatti had arrived there, fetching together all the foreign lands as far as the end of the sea: the entire land of Hatti had come, that of Naharina . . .") and in the praise-song of the battle:

The wretched leader of Hatti stood among his infantry and chariotry,
Watching his majesty fight all alone
Without his infantry and chariotry . . .
Then he caused many leaders to come,
Each of them with his chariot
Equipped with weapons of war,
The leader of Arwad, of Luka,
Of Drdny, *of Carchemish,*
Of Karkisha, of Halep;
His brother leaders gathered together,
All of their thousand chariots rushing into the fire.[15]

These are lists of Hittite allies and tributaries "as far as the end of the sea," which, if it means anything, means the northern and eastern coasts of Anatolia. No other known place-name from the Near East appears to match *Drdny*. Is this a mere coincidence, or were Trojan infantry and chariots fighting for the Hittites at Qadesh in 1285?

It seems likely that they were, because just around this time, in 1290 or soon after, the same Hittite king, Muwattalli II, drew up an agreement with four states to the west of his own realm and adjacent to the better-known Hittite vassal kingdom Arzawa. One of these four, a new tributary ally of the Hittite empire, is *Wilusa*. Here we have a fairly close match, geographically and linguistically, to *Ilios*, the name used most commonly in the *Iliad* for Troy. In fact, it is a better match than we would think at first sight, because linguistic research has independently indicated that the prehistoric Greek form of the name was *Wilios* (the *w* sound disappeared from classical Greek).

The identification of place-names like this one in Hittite historical and diplomatic texts was the life work of John Garstang. Earlier scholars had taken some names out of context and linked them hypothetically with those known from later sources, and the link *Wilusa-Ilios* had already been made and had been the subject of fierce argument. Garstang's achievement was to set the work on a reliable basis by demonstrating, using all the historical texts and taking account of all records of journeys and campaigns, how each place must lie in relation to others. He made it clear that Arzawa (which had been placed far to the southeast by some earlier scholars) actually centered on the valleys of the Kaystros and Maiandros rivers in western Anatolia, and he showed that it was highly probable that Wilusa was in the neighborhood of Troy. Thanks to new documents, the identification of Wilusa with Troy was made a certainty in the late 1990s in work by J. D. Hawkins and Frank Starke.[16]

The introductory clauses of Muwattalli II's agreement make a specious claim that Hatti had established suzerainty over Wilusa 350 years earlier and had never lost it:

> Thus says the Sun, Muwattalli, Great King, King of the land of Hattuša, favorite of the Weather God, son of Mursili, Great King, Hero: In early times the *Labarna*, my forebear, subdued the whole land of Arzawa and the whole land of Wilusa. . . . I know of no subsequent secession by the land of Wilusa from any king of the land of Hattuša. Even if the land of Wilusa did secede from the land of Hattuša, friendship was maintained nonetheless with the kings of the land of Hattuša and envoys were exchanged regularly.[17]

In reality, the royal ancestor or *Labarna* probably went nowhere near Wilusa. When official documents claim to narrate events of the distant past, they are at least as unreliable as oral tradition. Reading between the lines, we can see that Muwattalli's archivist, instructed to find records of previous contacts with Wilusa, found evidence of relations between recent monarchs but nothing that would justify the new agreement, which these introductory clauses were required to do.

Moving on to its real purpose, the agreement binds the ruler of Wilusa to send troops in support of the Hittite king if the latter is attacked by certain enemies:

> If any of the kings who are equal in rank with the Sun (the kings of Egypt, Babylon, Mittanni, and Assyria) makes war, or if from within anyone stirs up rebellion against the Sun, and I write to demand infantry and chariotry from you, send infantry and chariotry at once to my aid. . . . If you obey these words, the thousand gods whom I, the Sun, the *Labarna*, Muwattalli, Great King, have convoked in assembly, gods of Hattuša and gods of Wilusa and the Weather God of myself the Sun, shall protect you and your wife, your sons, your grandsons, your towns, your threshing floor, your vineyard, your field, your heads of cattle and sheep; under the power of the Sun you shall prosper and grow old.[18]

The treaty therefore matches up neatly with the hypothesis that the *Drdny* at Qadesh were a contingent from Troy-Wilusa, because in accordance with the treaty, some contingent from Wilusa ought to have been there.

The treaty has more to tell us, however. The current ruler of the kingdom of Wilusa was *Alaksandu*, adopted son of his predecessor, Kukkunni. His name is clearly identical with one of the two names in the *Iliad* for the young prince who caused the Trojan War. Nowadays we call him Paris, but the poet of the *Iliad* more frequently uses the alternate name *Alexandros*. The making of the treaty took place a good sixty years earlier than the burning of Troy VIIa, so if that event happened to have been caused by Greeks in search of the abducted Helen, she certainly could not have been abducted by the Alaksandu of the treaty. Still, to find that name in a Hittite source as belonging to the royal family of Troy-Wilusa is a remarkable clue to the realities that might underlie the Trojan War story.

The Hittites were also in occasional contact with a state that lay offshore to the west of Arzawa, which they called *Ahhiyawa*. For a long time scholars have wanted to link this name with one of the names in the *Iliad* for the Greek warriors who fought at Troy, *Achaioi*, and they are clearly right. They really are the same name. According to Hittite records, contacts between the Hittites and Ahhiyawa were at their closest when both states were simultaneously involved, on the western coast of Asia Minor, with a place named *Milawata*, known in Greek as *Miletos* and according to the *Iliad* the chief city of the *Kares*.

Let's return to the challenging problem that arises with nearly all of these historical links—a problem that scholars almost forget to notice if they have a lifelong familiarity with European epic poetry, because all later poets, imitating Homer's handy example, have felt free to multiply names for their most important places and peoples. But why should there be three names for the Trojans and three for the Greeks? And why on earth should Paris have two names? It is an odd coincidence, when so few names out of Greek epic have matches in Egyptian and Hittite records, that no fewer than five of these matches belong to entities that have multiple names: *Wilusa-Ilios, Drdny-Dardanoi, Achaioi-Ahhiyawa, Alexandros-Alaksandu*, and *Tnyw-Danaoi*.

In the *Iliad* there are three groups of names for Troy and its people. First we have *Ilios* or *Ilion*, the city. Then there is *Troie*, the city; *Tros*, its founder, ancestor of Priam; *Troes*, the men of the city, and *Troiades*, the women. Third, we have *Dardanoi* and occasionally *Dardaniones*, the people; *Dardanos*, son of Zeus, founder of the kingdom; and *Dardania*, the country. The Dardanoi are sometimes (not always) explicitly distinguished from the Troes, as at the opening of speeches by Trojan leaders to their troops, *Listen to me, Troes and Dardanoi and allies!* and in a parallel listing of these troops, *Troes and Lykioi and Dardanoi fighting side by side*; these two formulaic lines occur four times and six times respectively in the course of the *Iliad*. The Lykioi are Trojan allies here, and *Lukka* is a tributary state (south of Arzawa) in Hittite records.[19]

We now have a sidelight on the possible implications of these names. The phrases *Ilias ge*, "land of Ilion," and *Troias ge*, "land of Troy," found in later Greek poetry, actually have precise equivalents in Hittite; the former corresponds to "the land of *Wilusa*," the official name in Hittite documents of the state that was ruled from Troy, while the latter corresponds to "the land of *Truisa*," named once in the *Annals of Tudhaliya* I. Hittites generally applied names in just this form to countries in their sphere of influence. *Dardanoi* is the precise equivalent of *Drdny*, the Egyptian name for a contingent of enemy soldiers at Qadesh. Egyptians often used names of peoples to designate attackers and enemy states; they must have learned this particular name from Hittite sources. We may now guess—though it can be no more than a guess—that the inhabitants of Troy, whatever language they spoke, used an equivalent of *Ilias ge* for the whole state ruled from Ilion, an equivalent of *Troie* for their capital city and *Troias ge* for the neighboring district, and an equivalent of *Dardanoi* for a division of their troops, perhaps levied not from the city but from an adjacent territory.[20]

Now to the three collective names for the Greek warriors. The most familiar is *Achaioi*, which, as already noted, corresponds to the Hittite name *Ahhiyawa*. In classical Greek, *Achaia* was a region on the northern coast of the Peloponnese, one bypassed by the later invasion of the Dorians. The second name for the Greeks is *Danaoi*, explained mythologically as "the descendents of Danaos" and apparently corresponding to the name *Tnyw* found in Egyptian documents. Less common is *Argeioi*, which means literally "men of Argos"; *Argos* itself, the name of a city near Mykenai, is sometimes mentioned in the *Iliad* as if it were the center of Greece and stood for the whole country. Least common of all are *Hellas* and *Hellenes*, the now familiar names for Greece and its people. In the Catalogue of Ships, *Hellas* is a district in northern Greece; elsewhere in the *Iliad* it seems that Achilles' own warriors, the Myrmidones, come from this district. But by the time the *Iliad* was composed, *Hellas* was also familiar as a name for all of northern Greece. This is reflected in a phrase in the catalogue, *Panellenas kai Achaious*, "all the Greeks and Achaioi"— that is, all the northern and southern Greeks—and likewise in the Odyssean formula *kath' Hellada kai meson Argos*, "throughout Hellas and middle Argos"—that is, throughout northern and southern Greece.[21]

We may guess that *Achaioi* was the name used for themselves by the people of a Mycenaean Greek kingdom of southern Greece; the related country name, in the form *Ahhiyawa*, was adopted in Hittite documents, in which the names of countries rather than peoples are preferred when listing foreign states. *Danaoi* perhaps had a more inclusive sense, encompassing Greek-speakers in general. Whatever its precise definition, it was adopted in Egyptian records because it was normal in Egyptian to use names of peoples in such contexts.

SIX POSSIBLE INGREDIENTS OF THE
TROJAN WAR LEGEND

But why does *Paris-Alexandros* have those two names? If the Hittite king did business with an *Alaksandu*, king of Wilusa, about a hundred years before the destruction of Troy VIIa, why do Greek legends make *Alexandros* not one of the ancestors of Priam but his son, destined never to be king of Troy? It isn't hard to find answers to these questions—similar inconsistencies and confusions are very common in royal genealogies preserved by oral tradition—but the answers are depressing to anyone who hopes to find proof that the Trojan War was fought in the way described and for the reasons stated in the *Iliad*. The double naming of Paris is a warning that the story of Troy, as it stands in the *Iliad* and the *Odyssey*, has complicated origins.

A quick tour of two other epic traditions will show us the kind of thing that can happen. The medieval French epics (*chansons de geste*), written between about A.D. 1080 and 1400, are explicitly set in the court of Charlemagne, crowned in 800, and his immediate successor, Louis the Pious. It is recorded that the oral traditions were in existence by 840, yet in the form in which we know them, these poems often incorporate episodes set in Constantinople and Jerusalem, inspired by the Crusades and by the east-west marriage alliances of the twelfth and thirteenth centuries. Epics and sagas in various languages of northern Europe—Anglo-Saxon, German, Icelandic, and medieval Latin—written between about 930 and 1300, deal with Ermanaric, king of the Ostrogoths; Attila, leader of the Huns; Theoderic, Gothic king of Italy; and their warriors. Ermanaric was powerful from 350 to 375; Attila ruled from 433 to 453, Theoderic from 493 to 526. In these narratives, which result from up to nine hundred years of development in oral tradition, the three heroes are treated as contemporaries.[22]

If oral narratives elsewhere combine historical characters of very different periods, then the *Iliad* and the *Odyssey* may certainly do the same. If we could follow the strands of the *Iliad* story back to their beginnings, they might involve a prince of Troy named Alexandros and a seducer named Paris—not the same person, not necessarily in the same place or at the same date.

Here are some known historical events of which there might be traces in the *Iliad* and related traditions: (1) the adoption by Kukkunni, a former ruler of Wilusa, of Alaksandu, who thus became his successor: (2) the presence of Trojans, and possibly of their ruler Alaksandu, at the battle of Qadesh; (3) the Hittite attack on the Seha River land; (4) the fall of Troy VIIa and the Hittite sack of Wilusiya; (5) the earthquake that destroyed Troy VI; (6) the raids on Egypt by the "Sea Peoples."

1. First let's look at the odd family history of Paris, said in later sources to have been abandoned at birth by King Priam and his wife, Hekabe, owing to a prophecy that he would bring destruction. The baby was found and brought up by a herdsman and afterward recognized and accepted into the royal family. There are many such stories in Greek legend and fiction, and we have no reason to take this one more seriously than most of the others—except that Alaksandu, who was king of Wilusa just after 1300 B.C., is said in the treaty to be not the natural son but the adopted son of his predecessor, Kukkunni. In legal terms, therefore, both Alaksandu and Paris-Alexandros entered the royal family not at birth but in later life. This is surely no coincidence—the Greek legend of Paris-Alexandros incorporates a real tradition concerning Alaksandu.

2. Now let's consider the hint in the *Iliad* that Paris, on returning to Troy with Helen, made a very long detour via the coast of Syria:

> *Hekabe herself went down into the sweet-smelling storeroom*
> *Where her robes were kept, intricate work by women*
> *Of Sidon, whom godlike Alexandros himself*
> *Had brought from Sidon, sailing the wide sea,*
> *On the voyage on which he had brought home noble Helen.*
>
> (*Iliad* 6.288–292)

These unexpected lines were a real puzzle to later commentators. If Paris and Helen were on the run, why did they not make immediately for the safety of the walls of Troy? And why did Paris have to bring the embroiderers home with him instead of just buying clothes for Helen? The story was flatly contradicted in other versions of the legend, including the lost epic *Kypria*, a narrative of the beginnings of the Trojan War that was composed somewhat later than the *Iliad* and the *Odyssey*. The

Kypria stated that Paris and Helen reached Troy three days after leaving Sparta, which means that they could not have taken a detour via Sidon. The historian Herodotos uses this conflict between the *Iliad* and the *Kypria* to demonstrate that the latter poem was not by Homer.[23]

There is obviously a chance that this odd detail in the *Iliad* is a real reminiscence of a similar journey made by Alaksandu of Wilusa, if he personally led the contingent of Drdny who fought alongside the Hittites at the battle of Qadesh in 1296. They had a leader, but the Egyptian source does not tell us his name. It is even possible, after the victory at Qadesh, that embroiderers from Sidon were among the booty allotted to Alaksandu.

3. Next we look at an odd episode at the beginning of the Trojan War. According to Greek legend, the first landfall of the Achaioi in Anatolia was *Teuthras pedion*, the lowlands of Teuthrania (this was the Greek name for the valley of the Kaikos River, now known as Bakir Çay). Led by Agamemnon, the Achaioi found themselves in conflict at once with a powerful enemy and were driven back to the sea in spite of the personal bravery of Achilles. The leader who opposed the landing at Teuthrania was Telephos. This story is not in the *Iliad* or the *Odyssey*, and Telephos does not appear in the *Iliad* at all, but his son, Eurypylos, is mentioned in the *Odyssey* as having been leader, in alliance with the Trojans, of a contingent of troops from the people called *Keteioi*. After the repulse at *Teuthras pedion*, the Greeks returned, set out once more from Aulis in Boiotia, and this time encamped before the walls of Troy.[24]

This story might correspond to a real occurrence recorded very briefly in the annals of the Hittite king Tudhaliya I, around 1410 B.C. The king advanced westward to subdue a vassal, King Manapadatta of the Seha River land. The kingdom known by this name to the Hittites lay north of Arzawa. It centered on the valley of the Hermos (modern Gediz) and probably extended northward to include the Kaikos valley; at any rate, it bordered on the kingdom of Wilusa, or Troy. Its territory corresponds with that of the people called *Meiones* in the *Iliad*. The annals record that as Tudhaliya approached, "the king of Ahhiyawa withdrew," implying perhaps that the latter had been involved in some resistance movement but did not wish to risk a direct confrontation with the Hittites. In their classic exploration of Hittite geography, John Garstang and O. R. Gurney suggested that the Seha River land included the Kaikos valley and noted the possible link between this occurrence and the Troy legend.[25]

The name of the troops whom Telephos's son led to Troy, *Keteioi*, was long ago conjecturally linked with the Hittites, known to the Egyptians as *Kheta*. This link has never been widely accepted, but it could be real. We do not as yet know what name the Mycenaean Greeks used to refer to the Hittite kingdom.

4. Now to the fall of Troy, sacked by the Achaioi after a ten-year war. Two quite separate events may stand in the background of this legend. The first is an archaeological landmark, the burning of Troy VIIa, dated to around 1180 B.C. The burning was the result of action by an enemy that used slingstones, but the archaeologists cannot yet say who the enemy was. The second event is one more incident from the annals of the eventful reign of Tudhaliya. After the intervention in the Seha River land, Arzawa revolted from Hittite domination, along with a long list of mostly unknown states. That revolt was suppressed. A more northerly polity, Assuwa, then opposed the Hittite monarchy in turn. *Wilusiya* (which must be substantially identical with Wilusa) was one of twenty-two "lands" included in Assuwa at this period, according to King Tudhaliya. He takes up the story:

> But when I turned back toward Hattuša, the following countries declared war against me: . . . the land of Kispuwa, the land of Unaliya, the land of Dura, the land of Halluwa, the land of Huwallusiya, the land of Karkisa, the land of Dunda, the land of Adadura, the land of Parista, the land of Warsiya, the land of Kuruppiya, the land of Alatra, the land of Mount Pahurina, the land of Pasuhalta, the land of Wilusiya, the land of Truisa. These countries with their fighting men assembled. They drew up their army facing me. I, Tudhaliya, brought up my forces at night. I surrounded the enemy army. The gods went before me. . . . I defeated the enemy army and entered every country that had sent an army to fight me. I stripped all the countries mentioned that had declared war against me. I brought to Hattuša the conquered people, the cattle, the sheep, and the equipment of the land. So when I had destroyed the land of Assuwa I came back home to Hattuša.[26]

The list is a curious one, because most of the names in it do not occur elsewhere in the Hittite records. Many cannot be identified; but alongside Wilusiya appears Truisa, which is certainly the Hittite equivalent of the name Troy. As noted above, Greek *Troias ge* corresponds directly to the Hittite term "land of Truisa" in this text.

Tudhaliya is evidently pleased with himself; his listing of Wilusiya and Truisa as two states, when we believe them to be one, would be pardonable exaggeration. The king's boast cannot be totally discounted. Ancient Near Eastern kings always recorded their successes and sometimes used them to paper over their failures (modern politicians do similar things), but Tudhaliya could hardly have made these assertions if he had not brought home at least some prisoners and sheep and oxen to sell in the markets of Hattuša.

Thus the annals of Tudhaliya claim that the city of Wilusiya and Truisa, that is, Troy, was conquered and stripped of its people and animals just before 1400 B.C. It is not difficult to believe that the Hittite sack of Troy contributed to the legend retold in the *Iliad* and the *Odyssey*.

5. In book 12 of the *Iliad* there is an unusual glimpse of the future. The Achaioi had built a wall around their camp on the plains of Troy. Immediately after the fall of the city, this wall was to be destroyed by the gods Apollo and Poseidon the Earthshaker:

> *When the city of Priam was destroyed in the tenth year,*
> *And the Argeioi went in their ships to their dear native land,*
> *Then Poseidon and Apollo devised a plan*
> *To overwhelm the wall, harnessing the force of rivers,*
> *All those that flow out to the sea from the mountains of Ida . . .*
> *Phoibos Apollo made all these rivers join at one mouth*
> *And for nine days hurled their waters at the wall, and Zeus rained*
> *Continuously, the sooner to wash the wall into the sea.*
> *The Earthshaker himself, his trident in his hands,*
> *Led them, and sent away in his waves all the foundations,*
> *Of logs and stones, over whose placing the Achaioi had groaned.*
>
> (*Iliad* 12.15–29)

The wall and its destruction might quite easily be fiction. They might, however, carry a reminiscence of a real natural disaster. If so, although flooding is the chief destructive force mentioned in this passage, we have to remember that Poseidon is the god of earthquakes and consider the earthquake that, according to the archaeologists, demolished the city of Troy VI around 1250 B.C. The destruction was not total, but it was so serious that the city had to be largely rebuilt; moreover, some archaeologists believe that fire, and perhaps enemy action, contributed to the destruction.

Incidentally, later poets depict the gods helping to destroy Troy with flood and earthquake as the Greeks overrun the city. This idea is not to be found in the *Iliad* and the *Odyssey*, and as far as we know it is not derived from early Greek legends.[27]

6. Now to the sixth recorded event. About 1188 B.C., the Egyptian ruler Ramses III included in his official annals a report of a fairly unusual occurrence for Egypt—a threatened invasion that somehow arose from disturbances far to the north. This is a free translation of the crucial words of his report:

> Year Eight . . . Certain foreign peoples created a disturbance in their islands. All at once, states were overturned and wiped out in the fighting. Not one state was able to stand against their arms: Hatti, Kode, Carchemish . . . and Alasiya [Cyprus] fell before them at the same moment. They camped at a location in Amor [in Palestine or Syria]: they destroyed the people there, and the land was in chaos. They moved forward toward Egypt.[28]

This describes the beginnings, as seen from Egypt, of the great upheaval caused by the wandering bands usually described as the Sea Peoples. They attacked Egypt itself, but Egypt stood against them; Egyptian rule in Syria and Palestine was ended, however.

It is far from clear where the Sea Peoples came from and whether they had any aims beyond looting and destruction. It seems likely, however, that the Mycenaean Greeks took part in these adventures. The stories told in the *Odyssey* by Menelaos and Odysseus of their adventures in Egypt around the time of the Trojan War, adventures that are completely irrelevant to the plot, may be pure fantasy. But they may contain small nuggets of historical fact, in the shape of reminiscences, transmitted by oral tradition, of Greek participation in the Sea Peoples' raids on Egypt in the early twelfth century.

In the second volume of his commentary on the *Iliad*, Geoffrey Kirk considers whether there is any historical basis for the *Iliad* story. In preparation, he asks whether it matters. This is a good question. We do not look to the *Iliad* for a historical narrative; what the epic has to tell us is timeless, and remains valid whether or not there happens to be any link with real events of the past. But we still want to know how traditions such as those of the Trojan War come into existence.[29]

We should not be surprised by conflicts of dates or contradictions of names. It's interesting, but not disturbing, that the adoption of Prince Alaksandu is to be dated a century earlier than the destruction of Troy VIIa; nor will it worry us if datings of that kind are suddenly altered by revisions in archaeological benchmarks or in the identification of documents. Whatever the dates of events 1 to 6, however inadequate their connections with one another, people remembered them and singers told of them. There were many other such events, equally tenuously linked, not identified here and in some cases never to be identified. Transformed in hundreds of years of oral tradition, these incidents survived in the repertoire. Thus they were available for their final transmutation, by a truly great poet, into the story of the written *Iliad*.

3

The Odyssey *and Society*

The *Iliad* and the *Odyssey* are many-layered, which is one of the reasons they have fascinated readers for so long. As we have just seen, they incorporate various historical details and incidents, nearly all of them hundreds of years earlier than the composition of the poems, all of them reshaped, once or many times, in the oral tradition that eventually conveyed them to the poet. At the same time, the two epics paint a picture of a human society in peace and at war. However disparate those historical incidents are, "Homeric society" is convincing and consistent. It hangs together. Paris, Agamemnon, Aias, and Odysseus may very well originate at quite different historical periods, but their thoughts, beliefs, and acts in the epics are those of people living in the same community at the same time.

After Schliemann, it used to be thought that this was a picture of life in Mycenaean Greece, but further excavations and the decipherment of the Linear B tablets showed that life and society at that period were utterly different from what is depicted in the epics. After long dispute, most scholars now agree that the living world of the *Odyssey* can relate only to the world in which the poet lived—the contemporary world of 700 B.C. and after, in which other epics in the same tradition were being sung by other poets to appreciative audiences. The ten-year war, the wooden horse, the visit to the Kyklops, and the competition with Odysseus's bow are, of course, unrealistic. They have nothing to do with Greece in the seventh century B.C.; they come from history and folklore by way of oral tradition. But we can indeed look for realism in the background to the stories and in small repeated incidents of everyday life.

In adopting this way of reading the poems, we are looking not at the plot but at the universals of the early Greek world. We will not necessarily find how life was for singers and their audiences, but how singers and audiences imagined life would be for heroes: very much like their own life, with identical problems and identical solutions, but slightly bigger and better. Thus we find patterns of behavior that were in the minds of singers and audiences, and of the poet of the *Iliad* and the *Odyssey* in particular, which is exactly what we want. We need to understand how this poet saw humans and gods, people and their cities, men and women and the balance of power between them—and that might be the most crucial issue if we are ever to understand these poems.

SIMILES, FORMULAS, AND REPEATED SCENES

Anyone who reads the epics in this way will be thankful that the description of the shield of Achilles, in book 18 of the *Iliad*, is as detailed as it is. We have already used it to explore the oral poetry of archaic Greece (pages 4–11), and we can use it equally well to sketch the social background to the epics. No real shield can have illustrated one tenth of these scenes, but they add up to a detailed vignette of Greek city life.

We are grateful too for the extended similes that the poet of the *Iliad* and the *Odyssey* uses to evoke everyday life in explaining some event in the plot. When Odysseus, shipwrecked on Scherie, tears off a branch to hide his nakedness and steps forward to appeal for Nausikaa's protection,

He advanced like a mountain-born lion, bold in his strength,
Who walks in rain and wind, with eyes that
Smolder, to meet with oxen or sheep
Or wild deer, because his hungry stomach drives him
To attack a solid house in the search for prey:
Just so Odysseus was ready to go among those maidens with lovely hair,
Naked though he was, because the need came to him.

$$(Odyssey\ 6.130\text{--}136)$$

This is reality. In those days lions lived in the mountains of southeastern Europe and Anatolia (a lion's lower jaw was found recently by the archaeologists at Troy), and they were indeed feared by hill farmers and their flocks.[1]

It may well be that such similes are a special contribution to the oral tradition by the poet of the *Iliad* and the *Odyssey*. In typical oral performances of Greek epic, such elaborate images were probably not used. Their composition takes time and requires careful thought. Time and thought are not readily available to an oral poet, but they must have been available when the two epics were composed.

In our aim of understanding the world of the poet, we relish two other specific features of the *Iliad* and the *Odyssey*, the formulas and the repeated scenes. These are typical of oral poetry across the world. They have two functions: first, to help a singer construct a narrative and keep up the momentum of a performance (see page 188), and second, to bring audiences—including modern readers—into the world of the epics.

A formula is a group of words carrying a single central idea, shaped to fit a whole line of verse or a part of one. For each name or idea that is likely to be used frequently, the singer has in mind a range of formulas, essentially synonymous, that fit different parts of a line. We have seen such formulas frequently in quotations thus far. For the idea "lyre," we have had, more than once, the phrase *shrill lyre;* for "ships," we have had *hollow ships;* for a "poet," we have had *a singer, a divine singer, the famous singer, our honorable singer;* for "themes of poetry," we have had *the fame of men* (a phrase that can be extended either into *the fame of men of the past, heroes,* or into a whole hexameter line, *the deeds of men and gods made famous by singers*). For the idea "virgin girls," in the passage just quoted, we have *maidens with lovely hair.*

Of course, we need to understand how the adjectives are used in these formulas. There will never be maidens with ugly hair, or a deep lyre in opposition to the shrill lyre, or an obscure or dishonorable singer in opposition to the famous and honorable ones; only Stesichoros in person, in humorous mood, dares to sing of the "feasts of men and the matings of the gods" as a variant on *the deeds of men and gods.* The formulas must be taken whole. They tell us not about the individuality of the world imagined by the poet but about its universals. All maidens had lovely hair. Ships were hollow, lyres were shrill, all singers achieved fame, and all singers bestowed fame on men and gods.

It's clear that the formulas must be central to any reading of the *Iliad* and the *Odyssey.* We have seen already that formulas built around proper names are helpful to any reader getting to know the main characters. Among examples already quoted are *thoughtful Telemachos, godlike Hektor, man-killing Hektor, Hektor the horse-tamer, Agamemnon lord of men.* Gods too are easy to get acquainted with: *Zeus who holds the aigis, Muses whose homes are on Olympos.*

Repeated scenes are extended formulas and are equally necessary to the oral poet's work. Whenever the poet wants to describe one of the landmarks of daily life, such as a sacrifice, the welcoming of a guest, a dinner, or the entertainment that follows dinner, the same words are available to be used (or they can be expanded or varied if the poet chooses to do so). Here is an example—the first that the reader of the *Odyssey* encounters. When Athene in male disguise visits Telemachos, in book 1, her host summons food and wine and shares it with her:

> *A maid bringing hand-water poured it from a jug*
> *Fair and golden, over a silver bowl,*
> *For them to wash, and drew up a carved table.*

A revered housekeeper brought and served bread,
Adding many relishes, giving supplies generously;
A waiter put out bronze trays of meats
Of all kinds, and put out gold goblets for them;
A squire often passed by, pouring wine for them.

(*Odyssey* 1.136–143)

This scene recurs five more times in the *Odyssey*. In the world imagined by the singers and audiences of Greek epics, this is the right way to show hospitality, so this is the way it is done each time: when Menelaos welcomes Telemachos and Peisistratos (book 4); when Alkinoos welcomes Odysseus (book 7); when Kirke has been persuaded or forced to welcome Odysseus (book 10); and when Telemachos returns home and rejoins Peiraios (book 17). The same words are used again when Telemachos eats with Menelaos just before departing from Sparta (book 15).[2]

Some scholars have found it difficult to deal with Homeric formulas and repeated scenes when looking at them from the reader's point of view. Older critics, as yet unaware of the necessity of these features in the structure of oral verse, tended to insist wherever possible that the repetitions were necessary in each specific context; in cases where this was simply incredible, they gave up and accused the poet of irrelevance. Even some modern critics apologize for the repetitions, and some translators camouflage them.

W. B. Stanford, one of those older critics, points to the Telemachos-Athene hospitality scene in his two-volume commentary on the *Odyssey* and writes: "Note [the] epithets: 'fair,' 'golden,' 'silver,' 'revered'; thus Homer emphasizes the beauty and dignity of the domestic things of which Odysseus has been deprived for nineteen years."[3] It cannot be so: Stanford is wrong here. The passage is repeated in just the same words whether the scene is Odysseus's house or not, and even when, in the course of Odysseus's wanderings, he himself is the guest and the goddess Kirke is his host. There is no reason to say that the poet is thinking about Odysseus's deprivation in one of these passages and not in the other five. The truth is that these words always go with the hospitality scene.

In the *Iliad*, Helen speaks of her brothers, Kastor and Polydeukes, unaware that they are already dead:

> But in fact the life-giving Earth already held them
> In Lakedaimon, in their beloved native land.

(Iliad 3.243–244)

Maurice Bowra, another of the older critics, insists that *life-giving Earth* is relevant to its context here, but he is wrong. The earth is being used as a burial ground; as such, it cannot be *life-giving*. Long ago the art critic John Ruskin thought about the same problem. His answer was completely opposed to Bowra's: "The poet has to speak of the earth in sadness; but he will not let that sadness affect or change his thought of it. No; though Castor and Pollux be dead, yet the earth is our mother still—fruitful, life-giving." Ruskin's contemporary Matthew Arnold ridiculed this idea: "It is not true that this kind of sentimentality, eminently modern, inspires Homer at all." Take out the sentimentality, though, and there is something to be said for Ruskin after all.[4]

The poet mentions the earth in a specific context irrelevant to its *life-giving* nature, but this does not change its nature. The formulas are universals. If we attach any special feeling to them in one particular context, we are misunderstanding them. Odysseus can be called *resourceful Odysseus* whether or not he knows what to do next. The sky is *starry* even when it is broad daylight. There is no contradiction in the line *the noisy dogs were silent*, and no tautology in *the noisy dogs barked*. Resourcefulness is part of Odysseus's nature; noise is part of the nature of dogs (certainly in rural Greece); the earth is always life-giving. And this is why the *Iliad* and the *Odyssey*, heavily formulaic as they are, are among the most compelling of all great poems. The reader can enjoy the poet's use of formulas that contribute nothing to the immediate narrative context, or even contradict it. The elements in the story—the elements of the world imagined by poet and audience—give the poem an added level, a second reading, one that we can read only *because* they are depicted in meaningful formulas. *The Earth* would be just the earth, *dogs* would be just dogs, just single words in the story, for us to notice or not notice. The *life-giving Earth* and *noisy dogs* are elements with their own meaning in a world-picture that we are gradually developing as we read the formulas, in parallel with the story that we are building as we read the narrative. When we have read the poems, we have not only followed the stories to their end but have also developed an image of the whole world and the human context in which those stories take place.[5]

This helps to explain why we feel the urge to elucidate and describe the world imagined in the epics so strongly. There is no better place to begin than with the poet's depiction of hospitality, which has charmed, impressed, and puzzled readers for well over two thousand years.

EPIC HOSPITALITY

Two unknown wanderers (actually they are Telemachos and the disguised Athene) are offered food and hospitality by King Nestor. After the first meal, their host begins the conversation thus:

> *Now it is fairer to turn and ask*
> *The strangers who they are, since we have satisfied them with food.*
> *Strangers, who are you? From where have you sailed the watery ways?*
> *Do you travel for trade, or have you ranged at random*
> *Like pirates on the salt sea, who wander,*
> *Risking their lives, and bringing evil to others?*
>
> (*Odyssey* 3.69–73)

Consider how Steve Reece, in a study of hospitality in the *Odyssey*, begins his discussion of this little speech: "Nestor's questions . . . may strike a modern reader as a blatant discourtesy. . . . Apparently the rituals of hospitality were so hallowed that a proper host like Nestor was obliged to offer hospitality to his guests regardless of who they were, even to pirates." But we have to read the *Odyssey* carefully. Nestor is not so discourteous as to ask Telemachos if he is a pirate. He asks whether the journey was on business or not; if not, he adds, it would be *like* that of a pirate. If this simile is the first that comes to Nestor's or the poet's mind, we are reminded—and it's worth remembering—that there were few tourists and many pirates in the world of the epics. Having got that out of the way, we can dismiss the idea that the grizzled warrior Nestor "was obliged to" offer hospitality to pirates. But we retain the basic rule, confirmed several times in the *Odyssey*, that in the world of the epics, wanderers who approach one's house are offered hospitality first and asked to identify themselves afterward.[6]

Hospitality is a general rule, but strangers can be dangerous. Nestor's little after-dinner speech reminds us that a ship coming into harbor may contain traders or pirates. The two can be hard to distinguish until it is too late (though you probably find out before you have given them lunch). When Odysseus, in the guise of a beggar, first approaches the swineherd Eumaios's house, he has to face an isolated farm's essential defense against raiders:

> *Suddenly the yelping dogs saw Odysseus*
> *And ran toward him, barking. Odysseus*
> *Sat down, prudently, and his stick fell from his hand.*
> *There—on his own land—he felt helpless fear.*
> *But the swineherd ran out hastily to the gate . . .*
> *Yelled at them, and scared them off this way and that*
> *With a hail of stones, and said to the king:*
> *"Another moment and my dogs would have savaged you,*
> *Old man, and you would have brought disgrace on me."*
>   (*Odyssey* 14.29–38)

Eumaios's dilemma, in the last two lines, follows logically from what Nestor has already taught us. In a largely lawless world, do you allow your dogs to deal with an unexpected intruder, or do you assume he is friendly and call them off? Disgrace or robbery and violent death may follow if you make the wrong choice.

Later during his visit to Nestor, Telemachos takes a bath:

> *Then Telemachos was bathed by fair Polykaste,*
> *Youngest daughter of Neleus' son Nestor.*
> *So when she had bathed him and rubbed him sleek with olive oil*
> *She put on him a tunic and a fair cloak*
> *And he stepped from the bathtub, a godlike figure,*
> *Went to Nestor's side and sat down there.*
>   (*Odyssey* 3.464–468)

At this point Steve Reece assures us that "it is very special treatment to have an unmarried daughter of a king bathe a stranger." Reece has gone wrong here, very much as Stanford went wrong. In the *Odyssey*, baths are an almost universal part of the picture of hospitality. It is always women who bathe male visitors. This passage is an example of a standard repeated scene without any elaboration, and within the imaginary world of the epics there is nothing special about it.[7]

And that imaginary world must somehow be very similar to the real world known to the poet. The Byzantine scholar Eustathios of Thessalonike, a remarkably perceptive reader of the *Odyssey*, can help us to understand this matter more clearly. He commented thus:

> Just as in the *Iliad* the goddess Hebe bathes someone, so here *fair Polykaste*, Nestor's youngest daughter, *bathed Telemachus and rubbed him sleek with olive oil*. . . . It was a woman's duty, and there was at the time no difficulty about it. Homer does not just describe urbane and polished and dignified ways, but also such as were common in those days: and, if on the rustic side, they stand as an object lesson to later times.[8]

As far as he goes, Eustathios is right. Hebe bathes the war god, Ares, after he has been wounded by Diomedes. Kirke, also a goddess (though an unusual one), bathes Odysseus. A bath is included by Alkinoos among the civilized amenities that Odysseus will enjoy among the Phaiekes; it is after he has bathed and dressed on this occasion that he and Nausikaa bid each other farewell. Newly returned to his own house, disguised as a beggar, Odysseus is bathed by the housekeeper Eurykleia, and has to silence her hastily when she recognizes his old thigh wound.[9] Penelope is present throughout; Athene clouds her eyes so that she does not notice the commotion, which must have been violent enough, since, in the aftermath,

> the old woman went out through the hall
> To fetch water for his feet, because the first lot was all spilled.
> So when she had bathed him and rubbed him sleek with olive oil
> Odysseus pulled his stool closer to the fire
> Boldly, hiding the wound again under his rags.
>   (*Odyssey* 19.503–507)

Thus in the world of the epics, it is normal and proper for women to bathe men. If we are surprised by the case of Telemachos and Polykaste,

it is our perspective that is at fault. In our world, perhaps, kings are different from householders, and princesses are different from other girls.
In the world imagined by the epic singers and their audiences, Nestor is
simply a householder. Some householders are richer than others, and
kings are among the richer ones. We shall see what difference this
makes, but in this imaginary world, it makes no difference to their daily
life or to that of their women.

One question comes back to puzzle us. In book 6, after Nausikaa
takes Odysseus into her protection, why does he react as he does when
she instructs her maids to bathe him?

> *They placed beside him a cloak and tunic to wear,*
> *And gave him olive oil in a golden flask,*
> *And urged him to bathe in the river water,*
> *But Odysseus replied to the maids:*
> *"Maids, stand over there, so that I by myself*
> *May wash the salt from my shoulders and rub myself*
> *With oil. My skin is unfamiliar with soaping,*
> *And I will not bathe in front of you. I am ashamed*
> *To stand naked before maidens with lovely hair."*
>
> (*Odyssey* 6.214–222)

Telemachos undressed to be bathed by Polykaste; Odysseus undressed
before Kirke; he would undress before Arete's slave women and before
Eurykleia and Penelope. He has already been seen almost naked by
Nausikaa and her maids, though at that point the poet says plainly
that he had no choice: like the hungry lion, *need came to him.* So why
does the poet decide that he should now refuse the maids' help in
bathing? Here, in contrast with every other case, the meeting has
taken place outdoors, in the country, far from the protection of any
household. Nausikaa, confident in her innocence, scarcely realizes it,
but in fact a different rule must exist in such surroundings. Odysseus,
no longer driven by necessity, must refuse this detail of Nausikaa's
generosity.

EPIC WEALTH AND EPIC REALITY

We have already seen how Odysseus is greeted by Eumaios's dogs when he first approaches his old servant's farm. Let's return to that scene and to what follows it. Eumaios is, of course, generous; he is the servant whom Odysseus trusts, and he repays that trust even before he has learned the secret that this is his master. In his generosity, he provides a meal that is very much like the meals that Telemachos enjoys when he visits the rich householders Nestor and Menelaos.

Yes, there is something unrealistic here. What's wrong is not the meal that Eumaios provides—we don't see what he eats every day, but we know that as a pig farmer he can easily kill a piglet on this occasion to provide food for a guest, and that's what he does. It is the meals among the rich that are unrealistic. They get too much meat.

This is the difference between ordinary life and the life of the rich in the *Odyssey*. The latter is more luxurious, more indigestible, built of more costly materials, and less real than the life that was actually familiar to the poet and to epic audiences. Just count the vast crowd of extras at Odysseus's house: there are fifty maids, and the house is temporarily home to a hundred and eight suitors, with squires to wait on them. There is Alkinoos's house on Scherie, made of bronze and gold. And there is the royal daily diet of roast meat, bread, and wine. Why meat? The really wealthy would soon tire of such a diet, or die of it, but to the poor of the poet's real world—to those who had to eat vegetables and bread and wine nearly all the time—the substitution of meat would make an epic meal.

Thus, as we make our way through the world of the epics, it gradually becomes easier to set aside the exaggeration and look for the ways in which life is simply real. This is when we notice that it isn't far from the bathtub to Nestor's table; we must picture Telemachos bathed and rubbed down in general view, in the same room in which he was soon to dine. This is when we notice the makeshift sleeping arrangements at Nestor's house:

> The Gerenian horseman Nestor put him to bed—
> Telemachos, dear son of divine Odysseus—
> On a wooden bedstead in the windy veranda,

And with him was ashen-speared Peisistratos, leader of men,
The one unmarried son remaining in Nestor's halls.
He himself slept in an alcove in his high house,
Where his noble wife made up bed and bedding for him.

(*Odyssey* 3.397–401)

Telemachos has been warmly invited to stay, and Nestor has carefully assured him in advance that there is plenty of bedding, but nonetheless he must sleep on the veranda. Nestor has no guest bedroom, no bedroom for his son, and possibly not even a bedroom for himself. Zenodotos, an Alexandrian editor of Homer, was so shocked by Nestor's implied poverty that he toned down this description by deleting the two lines about Peisistratos.[10]

This is when we notice that as Nausikaa advises the shipwrecked Odysseus about approaching her father's house, she can say just where her mother and father will be:

When you reach the buildings and the yard,
Go in quickly across the hall till you come to
My mother: she sits at the hearth in the glow of the fire,
Spinning her sea-purple wool, a wonder to see,
Leaning on a pillar, and slave girls sit behind her;
And there is my father's chair, leaning toward her,
Where he sits and drinks his wine like a god.

(*Odyssey* 6.303–309)

Translators like to call Alkinoos's chair a "throne" and to insert a second chair for Arete. In the text there is just one chair. Alkinoos himself may be *like a god*, his house may be made of bronze and gold, but it's not much of a palace. This is an imagined scene of everyday reality: a one-room household, the woman sitting at the hearth and spinning, the man occupying the only chair and drinking.

EARLY GREEK CITIES AND COLONIZATION

Greece is a land of steep and rocky mountains, enclosed valleys, and many islands, big and small. Until the past few years its roads have been rough and difficult. The sea is Greece's highway: there are numerous regular and familiar sea crossings, from island to mainland and from place to place on the mainland coast, and they are short, easy, and pre-dictable. Or rather, they would be predictable if not for the fact that Greek seas are subject to sudden and dangerous storms.

The unique geography of Greece has had a strong influence on the political and cultural development of the country. When the *Iliad* and the *Odyssey* were composed and for several centuries afterward, there was no unified government of Greece, although Greeks generally spoke a single language and were beginning to think of themselves as a single people, the Hellenes. In any case, the geography of what we call Greece only partly coincided with the lands where the Hellenes lived. They lived in the southern, central, and northeastern parts of the Greek main-land peninsula; in several islands to the west, one of which was Ithake; in the Aegean islands and in the big mountainous island of Crete; at many points along the western and southern coasts of Anatolia (mod-ern Turkey); and, intermingled with other peoples, in Cyprus.

In the center of this region—the middle Aegean islands and the coastal districts to east and west—archaeologists note big changes during a period that might roughly coincide with the poet's lifetime (say 700 to 625 B.C.). It seems likely that the population is steadily increasing. People are building houses with many rooms and an enclosed courtyard. Villages with no identifiable communal spaces are turning into or being supplanted by cities with a public open space and at least one major religious shrine. There may well be another shrine, at a distance from the city, on the borderlands (*eschatiai*). Gold, silver, and jewelry, formerly buried alongside the dead, are now more likely to be offered to gods at these shrines. On the fringes of this central region, in far northern and western Greece, there is less evi-dence of such changes.[11]

Fortunately, we can add to this strictly archaeological picture some nonarchaeological features, because the earliest Greek lyric poetry (of 650 to 550 B.C.) agrees with early traditions in historical texts (recorded 450 to 400 B.C.) in suggesting them.

Each city (Greek *polis*) had its own fiercely independent political system. These systems were developing separately, though with plenty of contact and cross-fertilization. They took quite different forms, from monarchy all the way to primitive democracy, but in many systems a big share of authority was accorded to "old men," who might be the heads of households or the leaders of wealthy and influential families. They met as a council and made decisions that did not need to be referred to any larger assembly of male citizens. Old men in early Greece *knew ten thousand things*, and they were required to contribute their knowledge.

A city's open space (*agora*) was the place where men gathered (*ageiro*) for the assembly (*agora* again) at which they made speeches (*agoreuo;* all these Greek words are related). Thus, at dawn, at the beginning of book 2 of the *Odyssey*, Odysseus's son Telemachos calls a meeting of the men of Ithake:

> *At once he told the clear-voiced criers*
> *To call the long-haired Achaioi to agora.*
> *This was done. They gathered very quickly.*
> *So when they were gathered all together*
> *He came to agora with a bronze spear in his hand,*
> *Not alone: two swift-footed dogs attended him! . . .*
> *He sat in his father's seat. The old men made way.*
> *Then the hero Aigyptios made the first speech:*
> *He was bent with age and knew ten thousand things.*
>
> (*Odyssey* 2.6–16)

The meeting must be called at dawn; otherwise, all but the wealthiest and the laziest would be out working in their fields.

This village on the remote island of Ithake at the time of the legendary Odysseus is imagined as a city like those of central Greece in the poet's own time. As it happens, that may be realistic enough. Although archaeologists do not find meeting places for settlements in the older period and on the periphery, as they do for central Greece in the seventh century, such places may have existed without leaving archaeological traces.

As we explore this living world, we must continue to question it. Some details are necessary to the plot; some are intended to surprise us or to make us laugh. Here, at the assembly on Ithake, our current hero, Telemachos, is allowed two special privileges. He summons the assembly—can he do that, a youngster still growing his first beard? The answer is that he has to do it, since, for the sake of the plot, the men of Ithake must allocate him a ship. He takes a seat in his missing father's place among the old men. Can he do this, when other young men no doubt have to stand around the outside of the circle? Possibly he can, if the seat represents Odysseus's property and power, because these currently devolve on Telemachos. Even so, it is not Telemachos but the oldest of the old men who must speak first. This, we had better understand, is a rule that cannot be set aside.

Democracies and assemblies are not the full story in any political system, and certainly not in this one. Does the unlucky Telemachos walk through town with no followers, with none of the hangers-on that we imagine attending the powerful Odysseus? Knowing that we will ask this question, and recalling that in a preceding scene Penelope came downstairs *not alone: two maids attended her*, the poet now smiles gently and adds a line to make clear the nature of Telemachos's predicament: *not alone: two swift-footed dogs attended him.*[12] Among humans Telemachos has no followers at all. He has utterly failed as yet to capture his father's power.

By the time when the *Odyssey* was composed—around 630 B.C.— new cities had been established by migrant Greek-speakers in western Sicily, in southern Italy, along the north coast of the Aegean, and at an increasing number of harbors around the Black Sea. Among the most famous of them are Byzantion, now Istanbul in Turkey; Kyrene, now Shahhat in Libya; Naples in Italy; and Syracuse in Sicily. Such settlements were always regarded as the outgrowth of an older, established city, which selected the "founder" (*oiketes*) who would personally guide the new city's first difficult years. These "Greek colonies," as historians now call them, were independent, but in spite of geographical distance, they retained political and religious links with the mother city. Archilochos, one of the earliest known Greek poets (c. 650 B.C.), was one of a party that set out from his native city, on the Aegean island of Paros, to fight for the new colony of Thasos in the north Aegean.

The island of the Phaiekes, the generous hosts who listen to Odysseus's narrative in the *Odyssey*, is in some ways a magical place. In other ways, as an island city newly established *far away from barley-eating men*, this Scherie is a Greek colony just like the ones that were really being founded when the *Odyssey* was composed.[13] The colony of Scherie was originally led, the poet tells us, by Alkinoos's father, Nausithoos:

Godlike Nausithoos led them away from there
And sat them in Scherie, far away from barley-eating men,
And drew a wall round the city and built houses
And made temples of gods and divided up fields.

(*Odyssey* 6.7–10)

Reading this quotation and the preceding one, we may well wonder how Moses Finley could possibly have said that neither the *Iliad* nor the *Odyssey* shows any trace of the *polis* (the classical Greek city). How could he have missed the city at war on the shield of Achilles, or the typical, primitive Greek democracy of Ithake, or the duties typical of the founders of Greek colonies that are here performed by Nausithoos for the new *polis* of the Phaiekes?[14]

Yet Finley is not alone. It has been a matter for controversy among classicists whether the *polis*, in the loving way in which Aristotle and modern political historians define it, exists at all in the two epics. We are facing a difference of perspective. Archilochos, an approximate contemporary of the poet, writes as a leading citizen, a participant in a Greek *polis*. Two generations later, Solon and Alkaios, approximate contemporaries of each other, were both active in party politics; for ten years Solon ruled Athens. The poet of the *Iliad* and the *Odyssey* has played no such role and sees city politics from the perspective of a nonparticipant. No wonder that the ancient poet and modern historians look at the *polis* very differently.

EXILE AND INHERITANCE

All too frequently Greek cities underwent traumatic political shifts accompanied by killings or mass exile. We know of such upheavals from the fiercely partisan lyrics of Alkaios. To judge from his words, he tried too hard to impose a government on his native Mytilene, one of the cities of Lesbos, and earned banishment as his reward.

I, poor wretch,
Live a rustic life,
Longing to hear the assembly
Summoned, Agesilaidas,
And the council. All that my father and my father's father

Possessed among those citizens
Who do evil to one another,
All this I have lost
In exile on the borderlands.
In this shrine of the happy gods,
Pacing the black earth . . .
. . . in their festivals. Here
I make a home, walking away from harm,
Where long-robed girls of Lesbos parade
To be judged for their beauty. One hears the echo
Of the sacred cry of women.[15]

Such festivals are for women and priests; Alkaios takes no pleasure in beauty competitions. He is plotting to be back there in the agora. This "rustic life" apparently forced on him is not so very different from the self-imposed political impotence of Odysseus's old father, Laertes, who is never seen throughout the *Odyssey*, until in the last book Odysseus goes out to the farm and makes himself known at last. Why wasn't Laertes ever in town meanwhile, to take his place among the old men and give moral support to his grandson, Telemachos? Because he has ceased to participate and has shut himself away at a country farm, where he works in his vineyard. Athene in disguise, speaking to Telemachos, mentions

Laertes, who, they say, never comes to the city
But suffers his sorrows far away on the farm
With an old servant woman, who prepares his food and wine
When exhaustion takes hold of his limbs
As he staggers across the ridge of his steep vineyard.

(*Odyssey* 1.189–193)

Laertes' position has to be stated explicitly in this way, at the beginning of the poem, because it is essential to the plot but would be very difficult for the poet's audience to comprehend. Here is one more way, incidentally, in which politics in early Greece differ from politics in a modern nation: you had to be there and take part in person; there was no election of representatives. In a Greek city-state, if you never went to the agora, you might as well not be a citizen at all.

Penelope is the personification of Odysseus's lands and wealth, the possessions on which his power must largely depend. She was also the source of many of these possessions, for she is described once, by Laertes, as *polydoros—accompanied by many gifts.*[16] An important man such as Odysseus would indeed have expected a generous dowry in land and wealth to come when he married. In this matter ancient Greek political life is not so different from ours. Real power, ancient and modern, often depends on wealth and family ties.

But the practical use and inheritance of wealth differ in many details between one culture and another. So do the ways in which families form alliances. The poet does not have to explain how these things worked in early Greece, because the poems' early audiences were all too familiar with property problems and everybody knew the rules perfectly well. We, however, need to know these facts. They are no longer familiar, and the logic of the *Odyssey* story depends on them.

We need to know at the beginning that when Odysseus went away, he gave Penelope a clear instruction as to what she should do if he did not return. Early audiences could wait until much later to be told this, because to them, there were no surprises here. It is only in book 18 that Penelope happens to tell the suitors of the words spoken by her missing husband on his departure:

> *"I cannot say whether a god will bring me home, or take my life*
> *At Troy. Everything here I leave to you to manage.*
> *Care for my father and mother here in my house*
> *As you do now—or more so, since I shall be gone.*
> *But when you see the boy's beard begin to grow*
> *You must marry the man you choose, leaving your house."*
> *That was his speech, and now it is all coming true.*
> *The fearful night of remarriage must come soon,*
> *To my sorrow. Zeus has taken my happiness away.*
>
> (*Odyssey* 18.265–273)

Yes, it is true. Having spent ten years at the siege of Troy, Odysseus has been missing for ten more years since Troy fell. In such a case, what will normally happen?

Question one: When a property owner is absent, who takes charge of his household and estate? That's easy. It will be managed by his wife, as Odysseus instructed. But since a woman has no political status, she needs to be represented in public business or in litigation by one of her husband's male relatives. The poet is careful to make it perfectly clear that this arrangement is now failing. Odysseus's father, Laertes, though still alive, has retired to his small farm and will not come back to town. There are no brothers and no uncles; both Laertes and Odysseus are only sons. These essential facts are set out in *Odyssey* 1.189–193 and 16.117–121. Therefore, Penelope has to do the best she can with no male support.

Question two: If the absence becomes permanent—if the property owner dies or is believed dead—what happens to his property and his widow? The answer is that a surviving son inherits the property, and a male relative manages the estate temporarily if the son is too young to do so; but if there is no son or the son dies without offspring, the widow must marry one of her husband's male relatives.

In anthropology, the question "Why?" is sometimes easier to ask than to answer, but since this remarriage rule is unusual, I must try to explain its logic. In ancient Greek thinking, a childless, widowed wife must remarry in her husband's family, because that will provide a new opportunity to produce a son in that family, so the alliance and property exchange between families established by the original marriage negotiation survives. But in this case, Odysseus has no male relatives competent either to manage his property or (if Telemachos dies) to marry Penelope. Theoretically, Laertes would be the one to do so, and as a widower, he is free to marry; but every description of Laertes' behavior and way of life tends to reinforce the audience's impression (supported by his usual epithet, *geron*, "old") that Laertes is no longer capable of remarrying and fathering children, although this is never said overtly. Finally, if no son and no competent male relative exists, that's it. The property owner's line ends, and his widow returns to her own family, who negotiate a new marriage for her—although as a woman of property and experience, she will be in a good position to seize the initiative and make her own choice.[17]

The interplay of rules and customs ensures, as it would in some other societies, that the interests of Penelope and Telemachos differ very sharply. Telemachos is just reaching maturity, and there are no older males to look after him. His life is threatened if the suitors form a conspiracy to enable one of them to reunite Odysseus's wealth and power, an aim that could easily be achieved if Telemachos dies before Penelope remarries. No wonder Penelope is horrified to learn that he has set out, without consulting her, across stormy seas to visit Menelaos at Sparta. No wonder the suitors plot to kill him on his return. No wonder the young man cannot altogether trust his mother. He signals this in an opening scene with the unexpected words

> *My mother tells me that I am Odysseus's son. Myself*
> *I don't know: no one can know what seed he comes of.*
> (*Odyssey* 1.215–216)

Several times the poet plays on the potential for conflict between Telemachos and his mother. During a sleepless night, while visiting Menelaos, Telemachos hears the voice of the goddess Athene saying to him:

> *No, you must immediately urge loud-voiced Menelaos*
> *To send you home, if you want to find your mother still there.*
> *Her father and brothers are telling her right now*
> *To marry Eurymachos, because he outdoes all*
> *The suitors with his gifts, and bids the highest bride-price.*
> *And beware she does not take some of your inheritance from the house.*
> (*Odyssey* 15.14–19)

Notice the hint in these lines that a bride-price (*eedna*) will be paid by Penelope's supposed new husband to her father and brothers, therefore passing in the opposite direction to a dowry. It is quite natural to expect such a payment to be made if an heiress remarries, since her dowry was fixed many years ago and the only question that now arises is who will get it. A substantial gift may help her male relatives make the right decision.

In spite of such rumors and innuendos, Penelope has in fact managed extremely well during Odysseus's long absence—until now. From her viewpoint, the longer Telemachus's maturity can be postponed and his beard overlooked, the better, because while he is beardless, Odysseus's final instruction will not take effect. She has been preparing to obey it, as slowly as she can. Time has now run out. The suitors' plans now depend not on Odysseus's last instruction but on Greek customary law. They know that marriage with Penelope will pay better if Telemachos is out of the way. They also know, as Penelope herself knows and as Odysseus predicted, that she can in practice take the man she chooses, with her father's acquiescence, once she has come to an end of her excuses for procrastination.

To the audience of the *Odyssey*, the poem's depiction of a typical Greek *polis* will have an additional resonance, one set up by the suitors themselves. As readers of the *Odyssey*, we hate the suitors, of course. Athene tells us what is wrong with them in book 1, and every ancient and modern commentator reminds us of their defects. They eat too much. They plot to kill Telemachos. They pester Penelope and screw the servant girls. They are rude to Eumaios, whom we like, and they are unkind to the disguised Odysseus. In short, they are bad men and they will come to grief.

Setting aside these personal feelings, we ought to reflect that Ithake at the end of book 23 of the *Odyssey*, now that it has the townsmen on one side and Telemachos and Odysseus on the other, is not so different from any little Greek city undergoing one of its regular political upheavals.

> *Yes, this is the land that you longed to find*
> *But it is held by unruly and wicked men,*
>   (*Odyssey* 24.281–282)

says Laertes, who has withdrawn from his ancestral possessions to his country farm. Alkaios said very similar things of those who had deprived him of "all that my father and my father's father possessed." Meanwhile, on the other side, the townspeople are encouraged to avenge upon Odysseus the killing of their sons:

Friends, look at all that Odysseus has done to the Achaioi.
He took one lot of us, numerous and brave, in his ships
And he lost the ships and he lost every one of the men.
Now he returns and has killed another lot, the best of the Kephallenes! . . .

It is shame to us and will be shame to those who come after
If we fail to avenge the murder of our sons and brothers.

(*Odyssey* 24.426–435)

The Kephallenes must be the people of Ithake and neighboring Same, the island that was later called Kephallenia.

Both of these speeches are perfectly justified. On one side, the suitors really are *unruly* and, we may well agree, *wicked;* on the other side, Odysseus really has lost every one of the young Ithacans who went to war with him and really has wiped out a second generation on his return. At the very end of the *Odyssey*, the new round of killing that is about to follow these rousing words is stopped by the goddess Athene and her father, Zeus. That's good; many Greek wars did not end so quickly, and it might be (if, as some scholars think, book 24 was added to the *Odyssey* by a later editor) that the realistic imagination of the poet who composed books 1 to 23 was unable to envisage such a quick and comfortable end to the conflict in Ithake.

The narrator in an early Greek epic does not take sides. People say and do what they say and do, and it is for the gods and the audience to decide among them. The war in which Odysseus and the long-suffering people of Ithake are about to engage is called by the poet *homoiios*, a difficult word that might mean "leveling" (that is, it cuts everyone down to size—no one gains from it). But the same word is used of other wars too; there is no hint that this civil war, as we would now call it, would be any better or worse than other wars. The poet never comes nearer to giving a judgment than when speaking of the suitors, calling them *hyperenoreontes*, a term that describes characters who are strong, supremely confident, and about to fall. All too human, the suitors are characterized by this word as "aiming above humanity."

But the suitors themselves, like other speakers in the epic, certainly can take sides, so it is no coincidence that the same word, *eschatie*, "borderland," arises in Alkaios's depiction of an exile's frustration on the Mytilenean borderlands and in what the suitors' spokesman says of the political conspiracy that was to bring about their deaths:

Then an evil spirit somehow brought Odysseus
To a farm on the borderland where the swineherd lived,

And divine Odysseus's dear son went there too
On returning from sandy Pylos in his black ship.
And so those two, plotting an evil death for the suitors,
Came back to our town.

(*Odyssey* 24.149–154)

There is no irony here, incidentally—in Homeric formulas, any hero can be *divine* and any son can be a *dear son*, even if they are the speaker's enemies.

WOMEN AND POLITICS

Women had no political status in early Greek society. Penelope, Odysseus's wife, is nowhere to be seen when the citizens of Ithake meet in their agora. *Basileia*, the feminine equivalent to the masculine *basileus*, "king" or "headman," is a rare word, and as far as the *Iliad* and the *Odyssey* are concerned, the wife of a *basileus* is usually just a wife and has no public role corresponding to her husband's. Yet politics are not everything. Penelope's role is crucial in the story that is told in the *Odyssey*. She is the anchor for Odysseus, the wife to whom he longs to return and the manager of his household. Elsewhere, Arete and her daughter, Nausikaa, preside over the household of Alkinoos on the island of Scherie. In the *Iliad*, Zeus's wife, Hera, and his daughters, Aphrodite and Athene, have similar power, which sometimes even outweighs the power of Zeus himself.

At the very opening of the *Iliad*, an issue is set before us and, as it were, left for us to reflect on. We are faced immediately with the disputes over women prisoners: first Chryseis, daughter of Chryses, and then (more central to the plot) Briseis. We have no excuse to suppose that Agamemnon had any good reason for refusing to accept Chryses' generous ransom for his daughter, nor that he had any good reason for seizing Briseis from Achilles; we simply learn that these apparently minor issues set the Greek leaders at loggerheads. Then, in book 3, we meet Helen, who, before the single combat between her husbands, stands high on the wall of Troy with King Priam, telling him of Agamemnon and Odysseus, whom they see below. In book 6,

Andromache, Hektor's wife, appears. In the words given to these two powerful and contrasting figures we may realize at last that we have a commentary from women's viewpoints on the war that men have been fighting, a commentary no less illuminating for its brevity. It is not the last; toward the end of the poem we read Andromache's two laments for Hektor, in the first of which she gives voice to her fears for their child, Astyanax, now to suffer the fate of an orphan, deprived of fine foods and spurned by ordinary people (a theme of women's traditional laments in many cultures):[18]

> *The day of orphaning renders a child wholly without friends.*
> *His eyes are hollow, his cheeks are wet with tears*
> *As the child in need runs to his father's companions,*
> *Tugging at the cloak of one and the tunic of another,*
> *And one of them, pitying him, holds out a cup for a moment,*
> *Enough to wet his lips but not to wet his throat.*
> *Then a child with two living parents chases him from the feast,*
> *Beating him with his fists, attacking him with insults:*
> *"Yes, go! I don't see your father dining with us."*
> *So the child tearfully runs to his widowed mother—*
> *My Astyanax—who till now, sitting on his father's knee,*
> *Used to eat nothing but marrow and rich mutton fat.*
>
> (*Iliad* 22.490–501)

Finally, in the last forty lines of the *Iliad* comes Helen's lament, a brief reminder of the terrible events that she has been the cause of. No woman in the *Iliad*, not even Helen, expresses a wish to supplant men's role in society; men are and will continue to be the decisionmakers. Whether or not the poet was conscious of the fact, Helen demonstrates by her place in the story and her words in the poem that in human affairs there is a deeper level at which women decide and men are left to face the consequences.

The poet never says so, but the *Odyssey* has two heroes, Odysseus and Penelope, and their reunion is the achievement of both. They act, of course, in utterly different ways. Odysseus is the most adventurous and weatherbeaten of all heroes. Penelope is almost motionless, as some twentieth-century male readers noted with satisfaction, entering the living room of Odysseus's house only "when she is in the mood" (G. M. Calhoun) and "for the most part [keeping] to a private room because it was natural to do so in her situation" (W. B. Stanford).[19] Effortlessly she keeps her household together. As Eumaios tells Odysseus, her servants and slaves enjoy

> *Chatting in front of the mistress and finding things out*
> *And eating and drinking—and then taking a little back*
> *To the farm.*
>
> (*Odyssey* 15.377–379)

Just as effortlessly she controls the suitors. Telemachos, though headstrong and lacking in respect, has caused her no real problem. She even succeeds in avoiding Odysseus's final instruction until he at last returns—and then takes her own time about accepting his identity. Playing a far stronger role than Helen's, Penelope also makes the decisions, at a different level from the decisionmaking of men. In this remarkable portrait we may well wonder to what extent the traditional story has been subverted by an inventive, thoughtful, and mature poet.[20]

PART TWO

THE POET

4

The Making of the Iliad

In Part Two of this book we are searching for the maker of the *Iliad* and the *Odyssey*. We have to try to find a personality that has been hidden in obscurity for 2,650 years. We have no direct clues; only circumstantial evidence can help us, and this means exploring the motivation of singers and audiences, of writers and readers. In Part One we looked at the poems, but we now turn our attention to their creators. Why did they sing? Why did the audiences attend? Why did someone decide that oral performance was not enough and that the new medium of writing would serve better? If this decision had not been made, these poems would not exist today.

We need to try to understand the very different choices that were made for the subject of the first poem, which became the *Iliad*, and of the second poem, the *Odyssey*, which followed after twenty or more years. The differences between the two epics have been variously interpreted. Here I argue that they are the work of the same poet, who rethought, with greater self-confidence, the views on human society and morality that underlie the *Iliad*. From these admittedly speculative explorations we move on to a reconsideration of the identity of this unknown poet.

THE SINGERS

When we first encounter the singer Phemios, in book 1 of the *Odyssey*, he is performing to the suitors after their dinner in the house of the absent Odysseus.

> *When they had had their fill of drink and food,*
> *Those suitors, they thought of something different,*
> *Of song and dance: these are the ornaments of a feast.*
> *A squire placed a beautiful lyre in the hands*
> *Of Phemios, who under compulsion sang for the suitors,*
> *And he plucked the strings and began to sing finely.*
>
> (*Odyssey* 1.150–155)

At this point Telemachos withdraws for a private conversation with the disguised Athene. A little later he returns:

> *The famous singer was singing to them; in silence*
> *They sat listening. He sang the return of the Achaioi,*
> *The painful return from Troy that Pallas Athene allotted them.*
> *From upstairs the divine song was heard*
> *By the daughter of Ikarios, wise Penelope,*
> *And she came down the long stairs from her room . . .*
> *Then, weeping, she addressed the divine singer:*
> *"Phemios! After all, you know many other charms for mortals."*
>
> (*Odyssey* 1.325–337)

Penelope goes on to demand a different choice of theme, one that will not remind her of her long-lost husband. Telemachos overrules her (his words are partly quoted on page 98), and we must take it that the song of *the painful return from Troy* continues.

This is always the setting in the *Odyssey* for songs about *the fame of men:* they are performed in the hall, after dinner. The audience always consists of the male diners and everyone else within range, including anyone in the women's quarters, which are upstairs but well within earshot. As we already know, the setting in which the *Iliad* and the *Odyssey* were created must have been utterly different, but this does not change the fact that in the performances of Phemios and Demodokos —and Achilles, and the child who sings the *Linos* song—the poet is showing us the nature of oral poetic traditions in the very same culture to which the two great epics belong, and telling us something about the singers and others who shared in the tradition.

We might imagine that oral poets or singers (*aoidoi*), from the child on the shield of Achilles to the two performers in the *Odyssey*, had a special, high social status. Demodokos is regularly sent for by Alkinoos, it seems, and there is always someone to help the blind singer to his seat and place the lyre in his hands. Odysseus rewards Demodokos for one of his performances with a fine cut of roast meat. No doubt the poet likes to emphasize the status of poets and the rightness of rewarding them generously, but is this realistic? Exploring further, we find that in this culture, singers are grouped among independent tradesmen. Not long before the writing of the *Iliad* and the *Odyssey*, Hesiod includes a list of four trades in his famous poem of advice on life and husbandry, *Works and Days*. This list was probably proverbial already (the Greek hexameter was one of the most popular formats for proverbs), but if not, it became proverbial afterward, for these are two of Hesiod's most quotable lines. He is warning us, as usual, that there is fierce competition for limited resources, resulting in deadly rivalries and jealousies:

> *Potter hates potter and joiner hates joiner;*
> *Beggar is jealous of beggar, singer of singer.*[1]

Who are these four sets of colleagues? A joiner or constructor made things in wood and stone and metal; a potter worked in clay, and sometimes decorated the result with paint; a singer worked with words and music. What all four have in common is that they demand a living—

resources, food and drink, even money if money exists—from other people. Hesiod, himself a singer, knew well the value of the work he did, but we notice that he is not boasting about it here. From this neutral standpoint, singers are in competition for attention and payment on the same footing as the others.

The *Odyssey* too gives a list of tradesmen, and this list also gives the impression of being proverbial. Here the swineherd Eumaios is denying that he guided the mysterious beggar—Odysseus in disguise—to the house of Odysseus.

> *Who, when himself just arriving, calls in a stranger from elsewhere,*
> *Another, unless it be one of those who are public workers,*
> *A seer or a healer of sicknesses or a constructor of shields,*
> *Or again an inspired singer, who pleases with his song?*
> *These are welcomed by mortals across the boundless earth.*
> *No one would call in a beggar to wear him down.*
>
> (*Odyssey* 17.382–387)

We know Eumaios is lying (he *did* bring Odysseus), but we don't care about that, because he is lying to the suitors.

Hesiod's "joiner" is the same word as the *Odyssey*'s "constructor" (*tekton*), but the poet of the *Odyssey* fills the line with an example: among other things, such a craftsman made shields. Thus the *Odyssey* gives us a more complicated sequence than Hesiod's. We have five trades, of which the first three, at least, are *public workers;* singers are not that, since they produce nothing practical, but their trade still makes them welcome. This time beggars are placed separately from the rest. All five demand a living, but beggars, unlike the others, are unwelcome because they have nothing to offer. The poet of the *Odyssey* does not assert, as Hesiod does, that "singer is jealous of singer" but would probably have agreed that it was true. In the early twentieth century, a Bosnian singer told the Slovene scholar Matija Murko, "We are enemies of one another. It is torture for me when I see another singer who knows more than I."[2]

As in nearly all lists in the two epics, more space is automatically given to the last item—in this case, the fourth tradesman. This does not mean that the singer is more important than the other three; it is simply that the last item in a list earns a formula. The chosen adjective is *thespis*, a rare word that is applied elsewhere in Greek poetry to songs and storms, for these, like singers, are filled with a divine breath—they are inspired. Epic poets in many traditions are considered to be divinely inspired; they are often called "seers," those who can see, because unlike ordinary people, they are permitted by inspiration to see the past and the future as well as the present. The claim was put into clear words by Hesiod:

> *The Muses once taught Hesiod the lovely art of song*
> *As he watched his lambs under sacred Mount Helicon.*
> *They made this speech to me first of all, those goddesses,*
> *Muses of Olympos, virgin daughters of Zeus:*
> *"You shepherds of the bad lands, things of shame, ravening bellies!*
> *We can tell many lies that are as if true*
> *And, when we want, we can speak the truth,"*
> *Said the smooth-spoken daughters of great Zeus;*
> *And they broke off a stick, stem of a sturdy bay tree,*
> *And gave it to me, a magical thing; they breathed into me a voice*
> *Divine, for me to tell what will be and what has been.*[3]

The stick is the *skeptron* (in this case, a stem or branch of bay), wielded not only by narrative singers but also by seers and heralds and speakers at a public assembly. The words of a speaker who holds a *skeptron* are invested with authority.

Hesiod's poems are much more outspoken than the *Iliad* and the *Odyssey* on the subject of the poet's work and inspiration, perhaps because Hesiod is making a slightly different kind of poetry or perhaps because he is personally less reticent. The *Odyssey*, however, does remind its audience that singers are inspired by a Muse, both in its very first line (quoted on page 179) and again, in one of the songs within the song, when Demodokos first performs for the Phaiekes:

> *The Muse reached out to the singer to make him sing the fame of men*
> *From the cycle whose fame had even then reached the wide heaven,*
> *The quarrel of Odysseus and of Peleus's son Achilles.*
>
> (Odyssey 8.73–75)

The poets of epic speak of divine inspiration only occasionally. There was no need to insist on it, as someone able to produce a long narrative poem on demand obviously had a gift not shared by everybody. In the worldview of early Greeks, such skills and knowledge were literally *divine*: they belonged to and were bestowed by gods, and in a random-seeming aside in the Catalogue of Ships, the *Iliad* offers a hint of the full power of the Muses. What they give, they can also take away. The last of the places from which Nestor's contingent comes is

> *Dorion, where once the Muses,*
> *Encountering Thamyris the Thracian, stopped his song . . .*
> *For he had boasted that he would win even if the Muses*
> *Themselves should compete, the virgin daughters of Zeus;*
> *And they were angry and paralyzed him, and took away*
> *Heavenly song from him, and made him forget his lyre-playing.*
>   (*Iliad* 2.594–600)

According to later legend, Thamyris had named as prize, if he defeated the Muses, the privilege of having sex with them all (in one version) or of marrying one of them (in another). Whatever his precise demand, he was punished in life and his punishment continued in the underworld.[4]

THE AUDIENCES

Having sketched what we would call the source of his inspiration, Hesiod continues his deceptively simple poem with an outline of what the Muses themselves sing on Mount Olympos:

> *They in their immortal voices*
> *First sing the unspoken births of the gods*
> *From the beginning, the children of Gaia and broad Ouranos,*
> *And the gods who were born from these, givers of good things.*
> *Second, of Zeus the father of gods and men*
> *They sing at the outset and as they end their song,*

> *How he is the best of the gods and the greatest in strength.*
> *Then the birth of humans and of strong Giants.*[5]

This is in fact an outline of what Hesiod himself, inspired by the Muses, intends to sing, so we can imagine that the Muses on this occasion are singing in hexameter and not in lyric verse to accompany the melodic lyre of Apollo.

In an aside in the *Works and Days*, Hesiod says proudly that he attended the funeral games of Amphidamas on the island of Euboia— the only time he ever crossed the sea—and at these games he won a prize for song. Some believe that his prizewinning song was the *Theogony*. Whatever it was, Hesiod is telling us that games and festivals were a likely setting for the performance of hexameter poems, and that poets sometimes competed formally against one another (just as the authors of tragedy and comedy competed later) for public acclaim and prizes. These prizes were similar to those awarded to athletes. Hesiod's was a thoroughly traditional one, a bronze tripod or three-legged caldron, and his response was equally proper and traditional: he dedicated it at the shrine of the Muses on Mount Helikon.[6]

Poets sing what they are inspired to sing, and if asked to give a non-divine reason that they do it, they simply explain that they sing *to give pleasure* (which was why a singer's harp, in Old English poetry, was called "pleasure-wood"). According to Odysseus, speaking to Alkinoos, it is the finest of all pleasures:

> *I believe there is no more delightful satisfaction*
> *Than when there is happiness among all the people;*
> *When feasters in the house can listen to a singer,*
> *All seated in rows, while beside them tables are full*
> *Of bread and meat, and wine in brimming bowls*
> *Is brought by a waiter and poured into their cups:*
> *This seems to me in my heart to be best of all.*

> (*Odyssey* 9.2–11)

But oral singers need an audience. No matter what inspiration may come from the gods, oral poetry in practice is built on audience response, and poets make no secret of the fact. In all the scenes of oral poetry in the *Iliad* and the *Odyssey*, we know who the audience was and what it was doing, as well as who was performing and what was sung. Certain scenes in the *Odyssey* show us quite explicitly how oral poems depended on interaction between singer and audience.

In the *Odyssey*, the singer Phemios is telling of the return of the heroes from Troy and Penelope asks him for a different story, as noted. Telemachos interrupts to oppose her request. He ends his speech roughly (see page 125), but he begins it reflectively:

> *Mother, why do you blame our honorable singer*
> *For giving pleasure as his mind moves him?*
> *The singers are not to blame: Zeus is to blame, who allots*
> *Among barley-eating men whatever he wishes to each.*
> *For Phemios to sing the fate of the Achaioi is no evil act:*
> *Humans give more applause to any song*
> *That comes newest to their hearing.*
>
> (*Odyssey* 1.346–352)

Penelope, fictional participant and critic, is as entitled as anyone else to tell Phemios what subject to choose, and the dispute with her son is a neat picture of the painful tensions that exist in the three-way relationship between Penelope, Telemachos, and the suitors, the male audience to whom he is awarding the right to choose Phemios's topic. Some male commentators line up with Telemachos here (W. B. Stanford, for example, talks of "the rapidly developing Telemachos and his rather vain and inert mother"), but as they read further they are reminded by the poet that any of the singer's audience who feel strongly on the matter may intervene, just as Penelope did.[7]

Odysseus himself, incognito, still separated from his wife by many miles of sea, causes a similar upset while being entertained among the Phaiekes. Demodokos is about to perform, and Odysseus asks for the story of the Trojan horse. But he has already been distressed by the preceding story of his quarrel with Achilles, and now his evident grief as he listens to the painful details of his own adventures impels his host, Alkinoos, to demand a change of topic.

> *Listen, leaders and counselors of the Phaiekes:*
> *Demodokos must now hold silent his shrill lyre,*
> *For somehow in his singing he does not please everyone.*
>
> (*Odyssey* 8.536–538)

It is not always easy *to give pleasure.* Both of Demodokos's songs of
current events, like Phemios's, cause distress to one member of the audience. The only narrative song that pleases everyone is Demodokos's
choral lyric telling the love affair of Ares and Aphrodite.

> *This was the story that the famous singer sang. Odysseus*
> *Was pleased in his heart as he heard it, and so were all the others,*
> *The long-oared Phaiekes, famed for their ships.*
>
> (*Odyssey* 8.367–369)

Pleasure is the audience reaction that the singer has to aim for first
and foremost, because if listeners are not pleased, they will demand a
different song or a different singer. The fullest expression of this aim is
given by Hesiod in the *Theogony*:

> *Even if a man lives with sorrow in his troubled spirit*
> *And grief in his heart, still, a singer,*
> *Servant of the Muses, sings the fame of earlier people*
> *And the happy gods who possess Olympos,*
> *Then his gloom is forgotten and his cares*
> *Not recalled: the gifts of the goddesses soon distract him.*[8]

It's true even of the *Iliad* and the *Odyssey*, and this is part of the magic
of these two epics. We can read them for no other reasons than those
ascribed to the fictional Phaiekes and acknowledged by Hesiod—for
pleasure and as distraction.

WRITING IN THE *ILIAD*

Five thousand years after the invention of writing, it is difficult for us, in a culture that depends absolutely on the written word, to imagine how writing might appear to people who encounter it for the first time—difficult, but not impossible. The *Iliad* comes from the time when writing was getting established in Europe.

The epic tells an anecdote about King Proitos, who wrongly suspected that Bellerophontes had tried to seduce his wife. Proitos sent the young man on a journey to the king of Lykia,

> *And with him he sent fearful symbols;*
> *He scratched many deadly marks on a folded tablet*
> *And told him to show them to his host. (And that would destroy him.)*
> (*Iliad* 6.168–170)

Those *symbols* evidently instructed the king of Lykia to kill Bellerophontes. The messenger who unsuspectingly carries a message that is intended to kill him has become a familiar folktale theme. Most later readers of the *Iliad* have immediately understood that the *fearful symbols*, the *deadly marks* scratched on the sealed tablet, are writing; it's easy if you know. In modern times, archaeologists have found pairs of tablets with waxed surfaces on which private messages could be scratched with a stylus before the tablets (already sewn together along one edge) were folded shut and sealed. One such tablet was carried on a merchant ship that sank off southern Turkey, on its way to or from Greece, sometime around the date of the siege of Troy. Similar tablets were used in the Near East, and eventually in Greece, around the time when the *Iliad* and the *Odyssey* were written down.

The poet knew what writing was, and therefore knew that the alphabetic or pictographic *symbols* that people wrote on a waxed tablet were not in themselves *fearful* or *deadly*. Most of the expected audience, even for a written poem, could not read or write and as yet understood little of this. The poet speaks as one who knows about writing, and makes clear, even to those who do not know, the deadly meaning that those innocuous symbols can carry. (For the controversies on this point, see page 231.)

Around 700 B.C., writing had begun to be used in recording Greek poetry. The first literary text so recorded was probably a wisdom poem, naturally enough, because wisdom texts were already commonly put in writing in the Near East and Egypt. They were excellent practice for apprentice scribes, who already half knew the proverbial lines and could concentrate on the letter forms and the spelling. Finally, one intelligent person who had learned to read in the Near East decided to record a similar text in Greek, Hesiod's *Works and Days*. Soon afterward, around 690 B.C., someone decided to record a version of the older composition, *Theogony*, with which Hesiod had won a prize in his youth. What was now written down could not possibly be identical to the poem that Hesiod composed as a young man; it would be a new *Theogony*, a theme reshaped in many intervening performances and in his maturing mind. He himself would never know how much it had changed, since in what was as yet a wholly oral literary culture, the materials for answering that question did not exist.

Among the next to be written were numerous relatively short poems by Archilochos, Kallinos, and others. Once the idea of literary writing had occurred to Hesiod or those who admired him, it is not hard to imagine that other poets, such as these two, decided it was a good idea. As for Alkman, the earliest Greek choral poet of whose work we know anything, he may have followed this example. He may equally have been aware that choral poems were among the texts that were frequently written down in the Near East, because somehow choruses have to keep to an agreed text from first practice to public performance, and it helps if an author, prompter, or chorus leader holds a written copy. This is exactly why laments for the dead began to be written, at the time of Solon (about 600 B.C.) if not before, because laments were sung by groups of women acting as a chorus with a leader. But Solon, as we have seen, forbade "lamenting to a text."

What about oral narrative poetry? For oral poets there can be no measure of success other than the audience's pleasure; the greatest poets may attract the largest and most attentive audiences, but none is great enough to ignore the audience's response. Successful oral poets respond to each audience afresh. Therefore, as long as Greek epic poetry was recognized merely as a source of pleasure and distraction for live audiences, and as long as skilled oral singers existed who could go on giving that pleasure, there was no need to write down their work. The singers could go on singing it and the audiences could go on taking pleasure from it. They continued to do so for another 250 years, and for most of that period it did not matter, to singers or audiences, whether a written text existed or not. It would be slightly surprising if, as some argue, the epics were the *first* Greek poems to be written down—why would anyone do this? Still, it is a fact that someone, not long after writing first began to be used by Greek poets, decided that a specimen or sample of the oral epic tradition deserved to be recorded in this way. The written poem that resulted is the *Iliad*.

HOW AND WHY THE *ILIAD* WAS MADE

Let's set out the facts we are certain of.

The *Iliad* was composed by a poet who performed in an oral tradition. From study of oral literature we know that such poems have a long history, yet they are made only once. Each performance is a new poem, because a poem can be made only from the materials the poet has to work with and because each poem has a different audience.

There were many poems in the tradition that preceded the *Iliad*, but none of them was a proto-*Iliad*. We must absolutely reject any assertion that the poem existed in some form that we can recover or reimagine before the act of composition that resulted in the *Iliad* that we know. Each poem performed in an oral narrative tradition is new, and the *Iliad* was doubly new, because there is not the slightest evidence or the smallest probability that a poem of anything like this length could have been performed in any normal circumstances in the Greek tradition of the eighth and seventh centuries B.C. There is no way around this. What did exist beforehand was a great repertoire of themes, episodes, and characters, which were continually being embodied in epic performances (of similar length to the *Works and Days*) by many singers. Part of this repertoire formed a cycle around the story of the Greeks at Troy and their return home. The poet of the *Iliad* was—must have been—an expert in this repertoire.

The *Iliad* exists in writing, and it cannot have been recorded from normal performances. Therefore it was composed to be written, and the acts of composition and writing took place simultaneously.[9]

It is not too daunting to think of writing down the *Works and Days* and the *Theogony*, poems of 828 and 962 lines respectively, a length that we might imagine to be no more than normal for one evening's oral performance. Greeks at this period wrote on leather, and a couple of cured goatskins would provide enough leather for such short texts. Again, it would be no marathon task for Archilochos to write down one of his poems, typically less than 200 lines in length. But it was an extremely daunting project to think of creating and writing down a text the length of the *Iliad*. A great many goats would have to be killed and skinned, and the chosen singer and the scribe would have to set aside many weeks, if a poem of nearly 16,000 lines were to be created.

This is why we must imagine a powerful backer for the process of writing. In our terms, the making of the *Iliad* would take a lot of money. (Money did not yet exist, but its absence does not change the facts.) Cured leather was a valuable commodity. The singer and the scribe had to be free of other concerns in order to perform their laborious task, and they had to be persuaded to undertake it. Oral narrative poets are not rich or leisured people. They need the warmth, shelter, food, and drink that only an appreciative audience will usually supply. For this project, there could be no appreciative audience. The singer and the scribe must have been persuaded that the backer would supply those necessities instead.

Because it was to be written, the *Iliad* can have had scarcely any audience in the oral sense—perhaps only a scribe, who was kept too busy copying the text to respond to it. And yet in working with the new medium of writing, each early Greek poet, including the poet who made the *Iliad*, was evidently aware that the newly created work would transmit itself, not only in meaning but also in its precise words, to other poets and other audiences unknown to them. They probably saw no further than this. The first Greek poet who literally claims to be transmitting ideas to later times and who is therefore certainly conscious that a text can survive in fixed form after the author's death is Xenophanes, whose long working life extended from about 540 to 480 B.C.[10] Unlike Xenophanes, the poet of the *Iliad* could hardly have imagined that people might go on reading and hearing the same text in the identical words even after the death of the person who had spoken them, and certainly did not guess that these words would be a textbook for the next millennium, destined to be read and recited by hundreds of thousands of students. Although aware that texts pass easily from language to language, the poet certainly did not foresee that speakers of dozens of languages around the world would still be reading this *Iliad* 2,650 years later.

We have assumed that a scribe wrote down the *Iliad* from the poet's words, but even this detail is uncertain and controversial. The poet of the *Iliad* knew *something* about writing, a fact we know from the Bellerophontes story, which, as it happens, is the only clear mention of writing in the work of any of the earliest Greek poets. So did this poet know how to write?

The argument can go either way. Some oral performers have certainly been literate, yet some scholars of oral tradition believe that oral poets who learn to write lose their oral skills. Our answer may finally depend on how we view the small inconsistencies, typical of oral narrative, that are frequently found in the *Iliad*. Unwise details supplied early in the text are, when necessary, freely contradicted later. Loose ends are not always cleared up. What helped Odysseus to withstand Kirke's enchantment? Was it the herb *moly* that Hermes gave him, or threatening her with his drawn sword, or his *undaunted mind* (as Kirke herself says to him in bed)? As Jasper Griffin observes, these three options seem to represent three layers, from folktale via heroic legend to psychological drama, here visible in successive scenes of a single episode.[11]

The telling point is that whenever such things happen in the *Iliad* and the *Odyssey*, the earlier passages are left as they are; they are not adjusted to agree with what the poet decided later, as usually happens in written composition. A poet who customarily worked in writing, having finally decided that Odysseus's *undaunted mind* would conquer Kirke, would then backtrack to cut out the herb *moly* and Odysseus's drawn sword, details that seemed right at the time but turned out to be red herrings. By contrast, what we see in the epics corresponds perfectly with the nature of orality. In oral performance, if you require a character to be alive at line 800 but you killed him at line 200, you cannot go back and change line 200; you spoke it an hour ago, and what's said is said. You just have to bring him to life again. If you have drawn the performance to a close and realize that you have omitted to tie up the fate of a minor character, that's it. Your audience has dispersed. They may hear what becomes of the character in your *next* poem, but they can never hear it in *this* poem, because this poem, once sung, is gone forever.

Admittedly, this evidence is not quite conclusive. Even if composing in writing on this one occasion, the poet may have been too familiar with oral composition to think of backtracking to make minor corrections. It is more likely, however, that the poet was dictating, was personally unfamiliar with writing, and did not even think of editing the dictated text.

Meanwhile, we can now begin to see *why* the *Iliad* was made. The writing of the *Works and Days* had been a natural extension from one of the uses of writing in the Near East. The written *Theogony* demonstrated that an epic catalogue could be put into written form. Although modern readers rightly see big differences between the *Theogony* and the *Iliad*, both poems satisfy some of the same desires. As audiences we need to know about gods and the extent to which they control human life. We want stories that explain the way we are now, and we will readily listen to such stories more than once. We like lists, especially lists of traditional things we partly know already, especially lists that offer titillating new morsels of information; anyone who enjoys the lists of nymphs in the *Theogony* will love the lists of cities in the Catalogue of Ships and the list of rivers near Troy (quoted on page 116).

The two poems by Hesiod began to reach new audiences. Meanwhile, the earliest choral lyrics were being written down—perhaps to solve rehearsal problems, but these poems too would attract new audiences. It would be anachronistic to imagine any conscious nationalism or pan-Hellenism,[12] but it is no coincidence that at this very time the potential audience for Greek poetry had grown rapidly and spread around the Mediterranean. This was happening both because Greek-speakers were founding colonies and because others, notably Lydians, Etruscans, and other Italians, had become interested in Greek culture. We remember that Homer was said by Xenophanes and Herakleitos to sing "to the peoples," meaning that Greek epic poetry of their time was reaching a multilingual audience. Thus the new medium of writing, when applied to literature, filled a new need. Suddenly there were too many potential audiences, too widely scattered, for the available supply of oral poets.

THE CHOICE OF SUBJECT

In oral narrative poetry, the choice of subject is sometimes the poet's, sometimes the audience's (as Odysseus demands of Demodokos, *now move on and sing the Making of the Horse*). Audiences sometimes want novelty (as Telemachos says to Penelope, *Humans give more applause to any song that comes newest to their hearing*), but they are often pleased with a familiar story well told (as Odysseus says to Demodokos, *You sing the saga of the Achaioi very properly, all that they did, all that they suffered*). That being so, a new poem may of course adopt a plot, episodes, and even words and formulas that have pleased audiences before, but even if it does, it is likely to vary considerably from any previous performance. The episodes might be taken in a different order; one main character may be replaced by another; depending on time and place and the patience of the audience, the poem might be twice as long as before, or it may be suddenly curtailed, as when Alkinoos says, *Demodokos must now hold silent his shrill lyre, for somehow in his singing he does not please everyone*.

Just as a singer and an audience might do, the singer and the backer had to decide on a plot, taken from the traditional repertoire, which must have been familiar to both. In choosing the story of the Trojan War, they chose a cycle of stories that had become remarkably popular in Greece in the preceding 150 years—something we know from the frequency with which Trojan War themes are found as painted illustrations on ceramics.

Many centuries before the making of the *Iliad* and the *Odyssey*, when people of the Minoan culture in Crete and Greece built vast palaces and complex houses, they painted elaborate and beautiful scenes on the plaster walls, known to us now from excavations at the palace of Knossos and at the ruined town called Akrotiri, on the south coast of Thera (Santorini), which was wiped out by a catastrophic volcanic eruption in the seventeenth century B.C. After the Minoan collapse there was a gap of several hundred years during which practically no figurative art was produced in Greece. But in the three or four generations before the writing of the *Iliad* and the *Odyssey*, Greeks found themselves once more looking at narrative pictures produced by local artists, this time in the form of vignettes decorating ceramics of the Geometric style.

Geometric pictures seem almost totally different in purpose and in style from those of the Minoans. The earliest examples are almost as formal as the abstract shapes that surround them. Typically they depict a dead figure, lying on a couch and surrounded by lines of standing or seated mourners. All the figures make the identical gesture, raising both hands to their head as if tugging at their hair. These scenes confirm what the archaeologists knew anyway: such vases were used to mark a grave. And then, at about the same time that the poet of the *Iliad* might have been learning the epic art, figurative painting on ceramics gained the upper hand and abstract lines and shapes were abandoned. Larger human and semihuman figures appear, doing identifiable things and making more interesting gestures. There are gods and goddesses, and mythical creatures such as centaurs and gorgons. Anthony Snodgrass has shown that of all the surviving pictures that have to do with mythology or legend, about one fourth, over three hundred in total, show some incident of the Trojan War, its causes, or its aftermath. Considering the wide potential range of Greek myth and legend, that is an astonishingly high proportion. It demonstrates that the story of Troy fascinated Greeks during this period. And at least a third of these Trojan cycle images—one hundred, if not more—show an episode narrated in the *Iliad* and the *Odyssey*. Thus the *Iliad* theme would be the best and most obvious choice when it was at last decided to create and write down a long epic poem from the tradition.

Here is a famous example. Around 735 B.C. someone made a large four-handled goblet (a strange and impractical design) and inscribed on it three verses: one iambic line, such as Archilochos uses, and two hexameters, as used in the epics:

> *I am the cup of Nestor, good to drink from.*
> *Whoever drinks this cup, he immediately*
> *Will be seized by desire of fair-crowned Aphrodite.*

There can be little doubt what this goblet is meant to be. It is an imitation of Nestor's cup as described in book 11 of the *Iliad*:

> *a very beautiful cup that the old man brought from home,*
> *Studded with gold rivets, and its handles*
> *Were four, and a pair of doves around each,*
> *Of gold, were feeding, and there were two supports below.*
> *Any other would strain to lift it from the table*
> *When full, but old Nestor lifted it without strain.*
>
> (*Iliad* 11.632–637)

The cup was found in a grave dated to about 720 B.C. on the island of Pithekousai (modern Ischia), a very early Greek settlement off the coast of southern Italy. Now, if you want to believe that the *Iliad* had already been written down by 720 B.C., you will use this cup as evidence. But it cannot really prove that the *Iliad* existed, or even that the owner was thinking about the siege of Troy; clearly Nestor belongs to an independent story line, brought in when the *Iliad* was composed and engaging enough to feature in the *Odyssey* as well. It does prove that Nestor's legend, complete with four-handled cup, was already popular in 720 B.C.[13]

Other examples from eighth- and seventh-century Greek painted vases can be cited just as easily, including lively scenes of the blinding of the Kyklops and of how Kirke turned Odysseus's sailors into swine. The details of these picture-stories differ from one another and, of course, from the versions told in the *Iliad* and the *Odyssey*, which did not yet exist. They confirm what excellent choices were made by those who planned and created the epics that we know, because the stories they tell were already highly popular.

In planning the *Iliad*, the poet and backer actually selected a limited sequence of incidents from the Trojan War cycle. In one sense, the poem makes them appear more limited than they really are, by fitting them into just a few days near the end of the war and linking them to a single theme, the anger of Achilles. Yet at the same time, the incidents are skillfully expanded and endowed with more general interest; flashbacks and premonitions are included, and thus a full and very long narrative is created. Almost the whole story of Troy is eventually told, along with other tales of gods and humans. There are references to the abduction of Helen, forebodings of the death of Achilles, and premonitions of the coming fall of Troy.

All these are things that oral narrative poets can do easily. If they find that they have a satisfied audience and time on their hands, they expand the story by adding incidents, often retold by one character to another. In the *Iliad*, we hear at length of Nestor's cattle raid (irrelevant to the plot but helpful in developing the character of Nestor) because he tells the story to Patroklos.

This is what happened, then: A certain admirer of the oral epic singers and their songs, observing political upheavals and widespread migrations, probably aware of the interest in Greek epic narrative among neighboring cultures, saw that the tradition was no longer reaching its potential audiences. The model of Hesiod's *Theogony* showed that writing could help. The aim was not to preserve or freeze the living oral tradition of the singers and their repertoire—that tradition would either survive or die, and writing could do nothing for it. The aim was to record and transmit the stories that many poets were telling in the traditional way and that one poet, personally known to the backer, could tell better than any others.

The backer—the admirer of this traditional poetry—may have been one of the "old men" and aristocrats who used to govern Greek cities, although we have little evidence that the Greek epic tradition was interesting or relevant to aristocrats. More likely it was one of the monarchs (*tyrannoi*, or "tyrants") who were supplanting some of these aristocrats at this time, with popular support. It is quite probable that the writing of the *Iliad* took place on the island of Chios or in one of the Greek cities of the neighboring coast of Asia Minor, as persistent legends and strong linguistic evidence connect the *Iliad* and the *Odyssey* with this region. We do not know the names of tyrants or aristocrats from these cities at this early date, so we do not know, and possibly never will know, the backer's name. Nor do we know the poet's name. But there is more to be said about the identity of the poet.

5

From Iliad *to* Odyssey

W e have scarcely any evidence of how many people read the *Iliad* in the first generation after it was made; nor do we know the name of a single one of its readers until, around 600 B.C., the poet Alkaios makes an unmistakable reference to the anger of Achilles. But we know one thing: the *Odyssey*, composed (many scholars believe) roughly twenty to thirty years later, takes the *Iliad* for granted. The later poem is in some way a sequel, a response, a reaction to the earlier one.

Why, then, was the *Odyssey* created? In what ways does it react to the *Iliad*? Was this twelve-thousand-line poem really the work of the same person who composed the *Iliad*? It is by attempting to answer these questions that we can get closer to the hidden personality that lies behind the two epics.

TWO POETS OR ONE?

First let's explore whether the *Odyssey* is the creation of the same poet who made the *Iliad*. Both answers have been forcefully argued. Many scholars prefer to think of the two poems as having a single composer, yet it is hard to give persuasive reasons. The question has been approached in several ways.

Some have compared details of the language of the two poems: the evidence of dialect, the choice of words, the choice of formulas, and the ways in which particular words and formulas are understood. There *are* differences, some of which are very much of the same statistical kind as the differences that persuaded scholars of later literature that Shakespeare did not write *King John*. The problem with all such investigations is that the method was originally developed to compare the works of authors who did not belong to an oral epic tradition and who were habitual users of writing. We have no idea how they would apply to the work of a singer or singers who usually composed orally but on one occasion developed for written preservation a definitive version of a traditional cycle to which many poets, over hundreds of years, had contributed—the *Iliad*—and then, on one other occasion, created a poem from different sources with less faithfulness to a tradition and greater inventiveness—the *Odyssey*.

This is why linguistic and stylistic approaches are bound to be inconclusive. They certainly show some small differences in language and style between the *Iliad* and the *Odyssey*, but what do the differences mean? They might show that different poets made the two, or they might show that one poet went back to work twenty or thirty years after making the *Iliad*. More confident, more mature, with a different commission and a different personal agenda, continually influenced by other singers and related traditions, this singer's poetic language might well have changed in all those ways. How can we know?

One kind of variation has been thought especially telling. The two poems depict an imaginary society that is self-consistent in most details, so what if the *Odyssey* seems to show an error in a detail that the *Iliad* seems to get right? That is exactly the case with the duties of a *keryx*, a "herald." In the *Iliad*, heralds make official announcements and participate in sacrifices; on one occasion they wash the hands of those about to pour a libation of wine to the gods. In the *Odyssey*, the regular function of heralds is to wash the hands of diners at the beginning of a meal. The poet of the *Odyssey*, unwisely generalizing from that single scene in the *Iliad* and using the same formulaic line, has mistakenly turned heralds into waiters.

But this and similar examples provide no final proof that two authors are involved. Suppose that the poet relied on a traditional context in the *Iliad* and so got the usage "right," then extended the usage in the *Odyssey* by mistaken analogy and so got it "wrong." Or suppose that the poet actually knew the traditional functions of *kerykes* and so got them right in the *Iliad*, but unwisely adopted an additional context for them in the *Odyssey* because a predecessor in that tradition had done the same. Either of these hypotheses could explain the new use of *kerykes*.

A much better way to answer the big question about the authorship of the *Odyssey* is to take the poem as a whole and ask how it stands in relation to the *Iliad*. The first point to make is that the *Odyssey* works remarkably well as a sequel to the *Iliad*, because it avoids repetition. Not even one episode is told in both poems. This may seem a very obvious remark—the *Odyssey* is set ten years after the *Iliad*—but in fact it is not obvious at all, because there are numerous anticipations in the *Iliad* and many flashbacks in the *Odyssey*. Yet somehow they never overlap.

The *Iliad* is in a way a poetic biography of Achilles and makes it clear to every reader that he is doomed to die before Troy falls, yet since he is still alive at the end, the poem can hardly tell us of his funeral. So the *Odyssey* does this, in a moving passage in book 24 in which Agamemnon's soul tells how Achilles was mourned by the Greek army and the Greek gods, how his body was burned, and how his bones, mingled with those of his friend Patroklos, were consigned to a golden urn.

The *Odyssey* in turn serves as a poetic biography of Odysseus. It tells us of his involvement with the wooden horse that brought about the fall of Troy, and of the time when he quarreled with Achilles, an incident that surely deserved to be mentioned in the *Iliad* yet somehow is not. The *Odyssey* even gives the story of how Odysseus first went to Troy to join the Greek forces, nine years before the sequence of events told in the *Iliad*. Yet it does not say a word about Odysseus's spying expedition with Diomedes or his participation in the embassy to Achilles. Quite clearly, these incidents are passed over because they have already been narrated in the *Iliad*.

It is curious that although both the *Iliad* and the *Odyssey* contain internal contradictions and loose ends, there are practically no contradictions between the two. How can this be?

We have been uncertain whether the *Iliad* was written by the poet or dictated to a scribe, and we have been puzzled by the question of why the poet, whether writing or dictating, did not tidy up the small discrepancies in the poem. As we consider the nature of the relationship between the *Iliad* and the *Odyssey*, the answer becomes clearer. We have already suggested that the poet was literate but still thought as an oral performer. Therefore, although it would have been possible to tie up the loose ends in the *Iliad* by rereading and correcting the written text, this was not done because in the poet's experience, one simply did not do that. One performed the poem before an audience, or in this case one dictated the poem and presented it to its audience, and that was that. The poem was done with. But unlike true oral epics, the *Iliad* did not disappear. In the next twenty or thirty years, the opportunity arose for what must have been an utterly new and strange experience— rereading or relistening to a poem in the oral tradition. By the time a new poem was demanded, the poet had become completely familiar, from end to end, with the fixed text of the *Iliad*, in a way that no singer had been able to achieve with any epic poem before. So of course there are no contradictions between the two.

Moreover, the *Odyssey* makes not the slightest claim to compete with the *Iliad*. In the *Iliad* we have a slice from the imagined narrative of the whole Trojan War, a well-chosen episode skillfully expanded, on the basis of an encyclopedic knowledge of the epic tradition, in order to tell or suggest almost the whole ten-year story. We have the essence of the Trojan cycle, which is itself the essence of Greek mythology. Thematically, the *Odyssey* is no rival to the *Iliad*: it is not central to Greek mythology but achieves something wholly different. It tells the story of one man's adventures, expanded with folklore elements until they constitute the definitive story of the resourceful, wandering hero who eventually succeeds in returning home.

Instead of competing with the earlier poem, the *Odyssey* ties up the loose ends. It answers the precise questions that the reader of the *Iliad* wants to ask. Q: We know Troy fell (see *Iliad* 12.15–29), but how? A: Using the stratagem of the wooden horse (see *Odyssey*, book 8). Q: What became of Helen and Menelaos? A: They are living happily together back in Sparta (see book 4), because Menelaos recaptured Helen in Deiphobos's house (see book 8). Q: Did Agamemnon return safely? A: Yes, but he was immediately murdered by his wife's lover, Aigisthos (see book 11).

We can now answer the question of whether these epics are the work of one poet or two.

Singers "hate" one another, said Hesiod; they are "enemies" of one another, said the Bosnian singer; they steal and plagiarize, said the later Greek scholars who worked out the succession of early epic poets. Let's say that a different but equally skillful singer had the opportunity, twenty years after the *Iliad*, to make another great poem to stand beside the first. That singer could not have resisted the temptation to steal and improve episodes, to contradict a rival, to compete with that rival's proudest achievement. That singer would have had not the slightest interest in tying up the *Iliad*'s loose ends. But let's say that the original singer, more mature and as skillful as ever, had this opportunity. That singer had no interest in competing with the *Iliad* but was now able to demonstrate equal skill in a different kind of story, a different area of the tradition. Showing total familiarity with the earlier work, the singer would naturally take advantage of this new request to answer some outstanding questions and deal with a little unfinished business.

That is how it was. The same poet who composed the *Iliad* was asked, perhaps twenty years later, for another such poem, and the result was the *Odyssey*.

The new commission offered further opportunities. The singer had learned much in the interim about Greece and the world beyond. Above all, the ability to reread the *Iliad* allowed a reconsideration of the complex relationships between people and the society they share, between truth and falsehood, between poets and the stories they tell. These thoughts are reflected in the complex moralities and conflicting emotions at the heart of the *Odyssey*.

EXPANDING THE WORLD

First we need to define the extent of the *Iliad*'s knowledge. The poet of
the *Iliad* (or the tradition that led to the *Iliad*) knew plenty about the
western coast of Asia Minor. What's more, distinguishing the geography of the present from the geography of the past in this region presented little difficulty. Very few passages of the *Iliad* imply the existence
of Greek cities along the Asia Minor coast, which seems odd at first,
because there had been Greek cities there for hundreds of years when
the poem was composed. But there is a very good reason for it: everyone
knew that these cities had not yet been settled by Greeks at the period
when Troy fell, so any mention of them would be anachronistic. Among
the big neighboring islands, Lemnos and Lesbos are similarly counted
as non-Greek in the *Iliad;* for example, the Achaioi at Troy have sacked
the cities of Lesbos and enslaved some of the inhabitants. This again is
real historical geography. It agrees (for example) with Hittite records,
according to which Lazpa, or Lesbos, like Wilusa or Troy, is in the
Hittite sphere of influence and not that of Ahhiyawa. Correctly, it
marks a contrast with the state of things in the poet's own time, when
Lesbos had become a center of Greek culture (Sappho and Alkaios
would soon be composing poetry there). So far, so good. Given the evidence that the poems come from the Asia Minor coast or neighboring
Chios, naturally this area and its history would be familiar to the poet.

When we look further afield the situation is different. True, the
Trojan Battle Order and the Catalogue of Ships are well informed
about almost the whole of Greece and the lands surrounding the
Aegean, but we have to set these two catalogues aside, because they
both have special origins and must have been incorporated more or
less wholesale into the *Iliad*. They do not represent the poet's active
knowledge. True, the neighborhood of Troy is handled convincingly
throughout the poem, but that might result from a strong tradition
about Troy and the Trojan War rather than from personal knowledge.
For proof of this fact we can look to book 12 of the *Iliad*, where the
poet allows us to learn in advance that Troy will fall, the Greeks will
sail away, and the gods who favor Troy will finally wash the walls of
the Greek camp into the sea:

So then Poseidon and Apollo devised a plan
To overwhelm the wall, harnessing the force of rivers,
All those that flow out to the sea from the mountains of Ida,
Rhesos and Heptaporos and Karesos and Rhodios
And Grenikos and Aisepos and divine Skamandros
And Simoeis, where many shields and helmets
Fell into the sand, and many of the tribe of half-divine men.

(Iliad 12.17–23)

The eight rivers of northwestern Anatolia form an interesting catalogue. Four of the names (Grenikos, Aisepos, Skamandros, and
Simoeis) were well known in later times; the other four were completely
unknown, and curiously, three of these crop up again, as do the four
well-known ones, mixed into a much longer list of rivers of the world,
the children of Okeanos and Tethys, in Hesiod's *Theogony*. The list
surely existed in the epic tradition before any of the poems known to us
were composed. If you were suspicious, you might think the list was not
originally connected with the Greek siege of Troy at all, because only
two of the rivers, Skamandros and Simoeis, are close enough to Troy to
be relevant to the story. In other words, although the two poets built
this list into the *Theogony* and the *Iliad* respectively, they did not necessarily know where the rivers were.[1]

Beyond the Asia Minor coast, and beyond the two big lists, the *Iliad*
poet's geographical knowledge is notably vague. Not much is known
about Greece, and practically nothing is known beyond Greece. It is
quite impossible to explain logically why Agamemnon should have the
power to make a peace offering to Achilles of seven cities *on the
seashore, on the border of sandy Pylos*—cities that lie on the edge of
Nestor's domain but are separated by many miles of mountainous
country from the nearest frontier of Agamemnon's kingdom, Mykenai.[2]
Outside Greece, the poet knows that northward there are Thracians
and Mysians along the coast of the Hellespont; beyond them are only
the vaguely named nomadic *Hippemolgoi*, "horse-milkers." Southward
there is Egypt, and even the city of Karnak, capital of Upper Egypt, for
which the customary Greek name of *Thebai* is first recorded in the *Iliad*,
but beyond that only the *Aithiopes*, or "burned faces," who live by the

streams of Ocean. Eastward there is the Phoenician trading city of Sidon, where Paris and Helen called on their way to Troy (one suspects the poet had no idea how far away it was), and nothing else.

The poet of the *Odyssey* knows more than this. First, the geography of Greece is more firmly anchored in reality. Telemachos's voyage from Ithake to Pylos and his ride from Pylos to Sparta make perfect sense. Odysseus's description of Ithake and its neighbors is puzzling in some details, but that may arise from our ignorance rather than the poet's:

> *I live in clear-seen Ithake. There is a mountain on it,*
> *Neriton with swaying leaves, seen from afar. Around it islands,*
> *Many of them, live very close to one another,*
> *Doulichion and Same and wooded Zakynthos;*
> *But Ithake lies land-bound, highest of all in the salt sea,*
> *Toward the dark, the others further off toward the dawn and the sun;*
> *Rough, but a good mother of children.*
>
> (*Odyssey* 9.21–26)

Ithake is not the farthest north or west of the group, as this suggests, and Doulichion is a strange name for Leukas. Still, there really is a group of four islands in those western seas, and Ithake is the roughest of them. Few Greeks except their own inhabitants ever got to know them better than the composer of these lines.

Second, the *Odyssey* contains many more names to place in the nebulous world map beyond Greece. For example, it has many mentions of Egypt and two visits there, on one of which we learn of the island Pharos, where, long afterward, the Greeks of Egypt would build a lighthouse (admittedly, Pharos was not really a whole day's sail out from Egypt with a following wind, as Menelaos says, and it was far too small to accommodate the strange events that he narrates to Telemachos).[3]

It's true that when Odysseus has left the land of the Kikones behind (in Thrace, on the northern coast of the Aegean), he disappears from the real map of the world and does not return to it until, ten years later, the Phaiekes land him on the coast of Ithake. Yet things are not quite so simple. Some clues support the many readers of the *Odyssey* who like to think that the Lotus-eaters lived in north Africa, the monstrous Kyklops in Sicily, Aiolos in the Aeolian islands (whence their name), the cannibal Laistrygones in Sardinia, Kirke on the coast of Lazio in central Italy. These identifications were first made by classical and Hellenistic scholars who were convinced that the poems we know were composed by Homer and that Homer lived long before Greeks had begun to settle these coasts. They recognized the places anyway, and it merely confirmed their view that Homer knew practically everything. Our assumptions are different. We date the making of the *Odyssey* as late as 630 B.C.—at any rate, after the beginning of Greek colonization—and we know that a poet of that period ought to know all about Mediterranean trading voyages. To us it seems even more likely than before that the fantasy geography of Odysseus's narrative corresponds in some ways with the real geography of those newly familiar seaways.[4]

The most confident of all the identifications was that of the fictional Scherie, land of the Phaiekes, with the real island of Kerkyra, or Corfu. This is Odysseus's description of the approach to the house of Alkinoos, where he was to be made welcome:

> *Outside the yard is a big orchard on both sides of the gates,*
> *Of four acres, and a hedge runs along each side of it,*
> *And there tall trees have grown, lush with leaves,*
> *Pears and pomegranates and shiny-fruited apples*
> *And sweet figs and olives lush with leaves,*
> *Whose fruit never fails or falls short,*
> *Winter or summer, all the year, but forever*
> *The West Wind, blowing, engenders some and ripens others.*
> *Pear upon pear grows old and apple upon apple,*
> *Grapes upon grapes and fig upon fig.*
> *And there his fruitful vineyard is planted,*
> *Where a drying platform on an open ground*
> *Is baked by the sun, and where they are gathering more*
> *And treading more; there again are unripe bunches*
> *That have just cast their blossoms, and others turning color.*
> *Rows of vegetables live alongside the orchard,*
> *All kinds of them, plentifully flourishing.*
> *There are two springs. One irrigates*

> *Every part of the garden; the other runs under the yard*
> *To the tall house, and there the citizens get water.*
>
> (*Odyssey* 7.112–131)

Although not rejecting the identification with Corfu, modern scholars
have preferred to consider Scherie more than half imaginary—a fairy-
tale place where the West Wind pollinates the blossoms and fruit ripens
all through the year.

Scherie is a recently founded colony *far away from barley-eating
men*. The real Corfu was a recently founded colony (traditionally 733
B.C.), admittedly not so very far away, yet it had increased the distance
by fighting a war with its mother city, Korinthos (in 665 B.C.), a most
unusual thing for a new Greek colony to do. As for the magic of the
orchard, it is worth recalling that no ancient writer knew that flowers
are pollinated by bees, and then glancing at the description of Corfu in
an early Baedeker guidebook: "The island is covered with fine olive
groves. . . . The olive-trees, which are allowed to grow without pruning,
here attain a height, beauty, and development elsewhere unparalleled in
the Mediterranean, if indeed in the world. They blossom in April, and
the fruit ripens between December and March. . . . The vine culture of
Corfu . . . is not inconsiderable. . . . The oranges, lemons, and figs are of
excellent quality, and afford several harvests in the course of the year."
We certainly do not need to claim that Scherie *is* Corfu, but it is in some
ways a fictional mirror image of Corfu.[5]

SUBVERTING SOCIETY

The world of the *Odyssey*—even the fictional world of Odysseus's narrative—was created by a poet whose familiarity with the real
Mediterranean world had continued to grow during the twenty years
since the *Iliad* was written. Meanwhile, that poet had not ceased to
think about the society that Greek epic describes, which is itself a mirror image of the society in which its poets and audiences lived.

Even in the *Iliad* the poet occasionally subverts the society that is so
compellingly described. When the goddess Athene tells Odysseus to use
gentle words to persuade the Greeks to go on fighting (2.180), he carries

out her instruction by making a political argument, putting the case for obedience to monarchs. In addressing *kings and outstanding men,* Odysseus expresses this view mildly, but whenever he turns to a *man of the people* he is more direct:

> *He would hit him with the skeptron and correct him with this speech:*
> *"Friend, sit quiet and listen to the speech of others*
> *Who are better than you. You are cowardly and weak*
> *And count for nothing in war or council.*
> *We Achaioi here will never all be kings.*
> *Rule by many is not good. There should be one ruler,*
> *One king, to whom the son of devious Kronos has given*
> *The skeptron and the laws so that he may judge for others."*
>
> (*Iliad* 2.199–206)

We may well wonder whether Athene or Odysseus speaks for the poet here, and whether we are meant to approve or disapprove of Odysseus's monarchical views. He is certainly out of sympathy with the views of most Greeks.

Some have used this scene as the keystone of an argument that the poet was a monarchist, or that the *Iliad* is designed as pro-aristocratic propaganda, and it's true that in book 2 of the *Iliad* Odysseus is allowed to carry his point. In the debate that follows these political comments, Thersites, who is ugly, bandy-legged, lame, hunchbacked, bald, and recklessly insubordinate (no other character in either epic is described in such relentlessly negative terms), is the only one who speaks out against Agamemnon, and he is beaten with the *skeptron* to the applause of everybody else. The divine right of kings has a field day, in fact.

But it is unwise to suppose that any single character in an epic (or a novel, for that matter) simply speaks for the author. If that really were the case, so much the worse for the epic. It is for us to decide whom we agree with. We reflect that the Trojan War is caused by a dispute among aristocrats irrelevant to nearly all Greeks or Trojans—whether Helen is to live with Menelaos or Paris—and that much of the *Iliad* story concerns a dispute among aristocrats about an issue irrelevant to the war—whether Agamemnon or Achilles is to have Briseis. We reflect that the first dispute "launched a thousand ships / And burnt the topless towers of Ilium," resulting in thousands of deaths after a ten-year war, and that the second dispute threatens to cause the whole Greek war effort to be wasted and to end in defeat.[6] All in all, we are not likely to conclude that the *Iliad* works as pro-aristocratic propaganda.

The poet clearly continued to think about these issues until the *Odyssey* was composed. In book 1 of the *Odyssey*, we observe events in the city where Odysseus himself is ruler. We learn that life can go on and a political discussion can be held in due order even when the leader has not been seen for twenty years. All is not well in Ithake, however; his absence raises the problem of finding a substitute or successor, a problem that no assembly of citizens can deal with, because it is a family matter, and that the suitors, who are Ithake's young aristocrats, cannot solve either. If the *Iliad* is ambiguous about the value and efficacy of aristocrats, in the *Odyssey* the balance finally tips against them. Things happen, problems are resolved, necessary secrets are kept, and all ends peacefully, if not happily, thanks to the decisions of people much lower on the scale of recognized power—the girl Nausikaa, the swineherd Eumaios, the housekeeper Eurykleia, and the people of Ithake, who decide not to pursue their vendetta against their king.[7]

In the *Odyssey*, even aristocratic generosity is not what it seems. When the leaders of the Phaiekes agree to make gifts to Odysseus, they determine to reimburse themselves later:

> Come, let us give him a big tripod and caldron,
> Each man, and then recover it from the people
> With a tax.
>
> (*Odyssey* 13.13–15)

SUBVERTING EPIC

In the passage of the *Theogony* quoted on page 95, Hesiod recites these words once spoken to him by the Muses: "We can tell many lies that are as if true, and when we want, we can speak the truth." This is a dangerous admission, although elsewhere Hesiod claims firmly to have truth on his side; in the *Works and Days*, he promises "to speak true things" to his brother Perses.[8] The same claim is made in another wisdom text, the biblical book of Proverbs, in a poetic passage spoken by Wisdom in person:

Ignorant ones! Study discretion. Fools! Come to your senses.
Listen, I have serious things to tell you; from my lips come honest words.
My mouth proclaims the truth; wickedness is hateful to my lips.
All the words I say are right, nothing twisted in them, nothing false.

(Proverbs 8.5–8)

"Truth" applies to the past, the present, and the future equally. In the Greek view, humans, without help from the gods, cannot see any of it clearly. The gods can see all of it. Their chosen vehicles, poets and prophets, can tell as much of it as the gods decide to allow. Poets may see further than others, but their inspiration does not guarantee that they see the truth; if the Muses tell lies, then so do the singers whom the Muses inspire.

A century later, around 600 B.C., Solon, lawgiver and political poet, was simply putting the same thought another way when he said bluntly that "singers tell many lies." If these words were not already in the public domain, they became so after Solon used them. Aristotle and Plutarch both quote them as proverbial, without troubling to acknowledge Solon. "Singers" (*aoidoi*) sang many kinds of songs, and Solon himself was a singer, but it is likely that rather than criticizing himself, he was focusing on tales of the *deeds of men and gods made famous by singers*—he was criticizing traditional oral narrative poets.[9]

A similar view was expressed by Xenophanes, the philosopher-poet of Kolophon, who was writing at least sixty years after Solon. Xenophanes boasts of his own work when he says proudly that "my skill is better than the strength of men or of horses." He is clearly setting up an argument in favor of his own kind of poems and of praise poetry (such as Pindar would soon be singing), and at the same time sharply criticizing the old traditional epics, when he ends his picture of an ideal banquet with these not-so-bland lines:

Song and dance and festival fill the halls.
First the gods must be hymned by cheerful men
In proper tales and pure compositions . . .
It is not wrong to drink as much as one can and still arrive
Safe at home without an assistant (all but the very old);
And to honor the man who has drunk yet seems noble,

> *Who has the mind and the muscle for virtue;*
> *And not to draw up battles of Titans or Giants*
> *Or Centaurs, fictions of earlier men,*
> *Or violent disputes (there is no good in these),*
> *But always to have true respect for the gods.*[10]

Why praise the warriors of today? Because praise poetry and exhortations to bravery are what Xenophanes himself writes. Why not tell the old stories of the battle of the Gods and Titans, the fight with the Centaurs, or the ancient quarrels between Greeks and Trojans? Because those are the lying tales that the epic poets told, in popular, artless, interminable, old-fashioned hexameter verse. Oral narrative poetry is falling from fashion, though Xenophanes may well have begun his career as a performer of it; traditional religion and myth are coming into question. The fashion now is for rethinking the world from first principles, for praising our own friends and contemporaries, and for composing our verse logically and with the help of writing. It is no coincidence that Xenophanes is the very first Greek poet who shows awareness that by writing he is creating "fame that will reach all of Greece, and never die while the Greek kind of songs survives."[11] He is conscious that by using writing, in the new Greek kind of song, he can address future generations in his own words, a thing that the old oral poets never thought of doing.

Once people had begun to doubt the truth in epic poetry, they continued to do so. Moreoever, Greek educationalists tended to equate truth with utility in literature. If it wasn't true, it wasn't good and was dangerous to students. Plato, Aristotle, and the Christian writer Clement of Alexandria are among many thinkers who question epic poetry on these lines. Aristotle, for example, argues that the divine power is not necessarily jealous and thus that poets are wrong to say that gods are jealous. Yet even the most severe of philosophic critics could not ban the *Iliad* and the *Odyssey*, however wrong they might be. The conflict continued, and could be resolved only when it began to be recognized that there is more than one truth and that there is truth in fiction.

If we trace this fruitful and long-running debate in philosophy and education back to its beginning, we find that it began with the words the Muses spoke to the young Hesiod when he was tending his sheep. It was briefly taken up in a single passage of the *Iliad*, partly quoted on page 120, in which Odysseus obeys the instructions of Athene in two quite different ways, depending on the status of those he is addressing. This is a shocking scene in its *Iliad* context. Elsewhere in the *Iliad*, as in epics from some other traditions, whenever a message is given and passed on and whenever an instruction is given and obeyed, the significant text is repeated verbatim; this is part of the structure of oral narrative, as are the formulas and the repeated scenes, and it has a profound and soothing effect on audiences and readers of epic, reassuring us that there is only one way to do it (whatever it is) and that that is the right and true way. Odysseus, by doing it two ways, throws us briefly into confusion.

The *Odyssey* is the work of a poet who has been consciously thinking about the relationship between words and truth. In the *Iliad*, speeches tell the truth. We may question the motives of speakers such as Agamemnon and Achilles and even Nestor, but we do not doubt their statements. In the *Odyssey*, our task as audience is much more complex. Do we believe Menelaos? Do we altogether trust Helen, or Kirke, or Kalypso? When is Odysseus telling the truth?

Part of this reconsideration has to do with the relationship between poets and the stories they tell. In the *Iliad*, the only poems that are retold within the body of the work are the women's laments. This tradition of laments was no doubt as rich in its own way as that of epic, but it was surely separate. In the *Iliad*, perhaps, the poet was not yet bold enough to depict a narrative singer at work. In the *Odyssey*, things have moved on. This time we have narrative poems (and this time the singers are men), and they pose a new question. Are the Trojan narratives sung by Phemios and Demodokos as true as the *Odyssey* narrative itself, or less true, or more true? And what about the love affair of Ares and Aphrodite? There is no other early evidence for this myth—later retellings depend purely on the *Odyssey*. Perhaps we are to take it that Demodokos, or rather the poet of the *Odyssey*, has invented the story, but we cannot be sure.

It is Odysseus himself—the very man whose alternative political speeches in the *Iliad* put us momentarily into doubt—who poses the most insistent questions. We disbelieve his two or three shorter narratives; the poet never says he is lying, but we think he is. He admits that he sometimes lies, in any case: he claims to have given a false name,

Metis, or Nobody, to the Kyklops when they were drinking together. Well, then, why should we accept anything in his long narrative, told to Alkinoos and the Phaiekes, with its magical events, fantastic animals, and not-quite-human peoples?[12]

SUBVERTING GENDER

The first of the narrative performances described in the *Odyssey*— Phemios's song of the return of the Achaioi from Troy—is the cause of a woman-man dispute, between Penelope and Telemachos, about what topic the singer should choose. Telemachos concludes sharply:

> Go back to your room and attend to your tasks,
> The loom and distaff, and instruct your maids
> To set to work. Public speech shall be the business of men,
> Any men, but especially myself, since I rule this house.
>
> (Odyssey 1.356–359)

This claim is empty, whether we look at it in relation to the suitors, to the maids, or to Penelope herself. He rules none of them, but of course Penelope does not tell him so, or question his assumed authority in any way.

In the *Iliad*, the poet was prepared to be frank about sexual relationships. We noted that Helen describes herself as a "bitch" in her conversation with Hektor, using the term because of her shamelessness in living publicly with Paris while married to Menelaos. Earlier she has had an encounter with Aphrodite, the goddess who drove her into the arms of Paris and now intends to do so again. Helen is just as brutal to Aphrodite as to herself, and the goddess is no less brutal in reply.

> When Helen recognized the beautiful neck of the goddess
> And her desirable breasts and flashing eyes
> She was stunned; but then she spoke out to her in reply:
> "Madam, why are you so keen to be a procuress?
> Will you now drag me to some other fine city
> Further off, in Phrygia or lovely Lydia,
> Because there too you have some male friend? . . .

Go to Paris yourself, then! Stray from the high road of the gods,
Never again turn your feet toward Olympos;
Whine around him and watch him all the time
Till he makes you his wife, or rather his slave girl!
No, I will not go—it would be shameful—
To make his bed. If I do, all the women of Troy
Will blame me. I have endless miseries in my heart."
But divine Aphrodite answered her angrily:
"Don't rouse me, wretch, or I shall be angry, and abandon you,
And hate you as wildly as until now I have loved you,
And expose you to the hatred of both armies,
Trojans and Greeks. You would die a vile death."

                                        (*Iliad* 3.396–417)

Doule, "slave woman," was a common word in later Greek, but in the epics the word *dmoe* is used in that everyday sense. *Doule* is used only here and at one point in the *Odyssey*, when Menelaos is said to have fathered a son by an unnamed *doule*. Its apparent meaning, therefore, is "slave used for sex." Helen is insulting the goddess, and the goddess responds fiercely, threatening to hand her over to the soldiers who have fought the war that she caused.

If there is any one issue on which the poet is bold enough to subvert everyday assumptions, it is that of the relative position of men and women. As readers of the *Odyssey*, we have to work hard on gender relationships, and our task is made no easier by the strange case of the goddess Athene, who spends a good deal of time accompanying Telemachos *en travesti*—a point the poet will not allow us to forget for a moment, because her real (feminine) name is used in introducing each one of her speeches, yet naturally her interlocutors address her as a man. In advising Odysseus, she is not above using her feminine power; in advising Telemachos, she takes the role of a young man, a first, fictional foreshadowing of a fact demonstrated many times in ancient and medieval literature: that by boldly risking a male role and male dress, women can gain power, or at least freedom, in a patriarchal society.

Setting Athene aside, we as readers have to keep the peace through much of the poem between Penelope and Telemachos, and our judgments had better be less one-sided than those of earlier commentators (see pages 88 and 98). We have to decide whether we are with Odysseus against twelve of his maids:

> *[Odysseus] called Telemachos and the cowherd and the swineherd*
> *To him and spoke winged words: . . .*
> *"When you have cleansed everything in the house,*
> *Take out the slave girls from the well-built hall*
> *Between the roundhouse and the high garden fence*
> *And stab them with sharp swords until you have taken*
> *The lives of all, and they quite forget the sexual pleasure they felt*
> *When under the suitors, coupling with them secretly."*
>
> (*Odyssey* 22.435–445)

The Greek words are blunt but not obscene. "Sexual pleasure" is *aphrodite*, which is also the name of the goddess who provides sexual pleasure; "couple" is *meignymi*, literally "mix," which is what bodies do in the sexual act.

This episode too makes us work hard. In the following verses the women are actually hanged and not stabbed to death, and as readers we have to understand why. The answer is that Telemachos decides to countermand his father's orders because he *will not take cleanly the lives of women who poured insult on my head and my mother's;* the insult, as Telemachos goes on to explain, is that they *slept with the suitors,* and their punishment will be to die uncleanly, which is how hanging was regarded in early Greece. More basically, we have to decide why it seemed right for Odysseus, his son, and his farmhands to kill their slaves at all and whether we agree that it would be right. The question forces us to look into the heart of a slave-owning society, one in which the women of a household were the sexual property of its head. Squeamish commentators try to find evidence in the text that Telemachos and Odysseus did not personally carry out the killing ("Odysseus, and probably Telemachus too, being excluded from such a degrading task," according to the new standard commentary on the *Odyssey*; "the swineherd, the cowherd, and perhaps—one hopes not—Telemachus," according to Stanford). We could willingly bypass that issue; we know that ordering a killing is no less degrading than performing it. In any case, the commentators are misguided. Telemachos, as the poet imagines him, though too weak to "rule [his father's] house," was not too weak to kill unruly slaves after his father had come home.[13]

We still have to decide whether we want Odysseus to go home to Penelope or stay with Kalypso or marry Nausikaa, and all this on the assumption that it is Odysseus's decision—but perhaps it isn't. Athene, as his divine patron, makes practically every decision and facilitates every choice. Kirke, after his stay with her, guides him to the next and most terrifying episode of his wanderings; Kalypso allows him to build a raft, shows him where the tall trees grow (he really ought to have noticed that for himself), and gives him the tools he needs. Commentators have shed tears over the parting of Odysseus and Nausikaa (E. V. Rieu, translator of the *Odyssey* for Penguin Classics, admits that "some of us, steeped in the traditions of later fiction, may regret Homer's failure to pursue Nausicaa's romance to a more exciting conclusion"),[14] but the girl herself dismisses him with a few friendly words, reminding us, irreverently, of the closing lines of an English folksong:

> *"I can't marry you, my pretty maid."*
> *"Nobody asked you, sir," she said.*

If these arguments are accepted, the *Odyssey* is no rival or supplementary *Iliad*, put together in the same way by a different singer and the same scribe. It is a new, original, different work by the same poet. The *Iliad* distills the oral tradition; the *Odyssey* builds on it. After twenty years of reconsideration, with greater maturity and confidence, this poet is readier than before to strike out individually. Relations between men and women in human society are already a major theme of the *Iliad*, in spite of its military setting; in the *Odyssey*, these gender relations are at the very center of the story.

6

Identifying the Poet

Now we reap our reward for refusing to identify the legendary oral poet Homer with the creation of the *Iliad* and the *Odyssey*. We have taken nothing for granted about the making of these poems. We know that it must have taken time, leather, ink, a rich and powerful backer, and a singer skilled in the making of epics, but we need to know more about the singer. Where did this singer live and work? When were the poems made and written? Who was the creator of the two great epics?

LANGUAGES IN THE *ILIAD* AND THE *ODYSSEY*

We already have some clues that connect the making of the poems with the Aegean islands or the Aegean coast of Asia Minor. The poet's historical and geographical knowledge of this coastline is particularly confident, and the linguistic environment of the epics strongly encourages us to focus our search on this region, from Euboia to the eastern Aegean, with Chios at the center.

Let's begin with a bird's-eye view of the language patchwork in the seventh century B.C., when the *Iliad* and the *Odyssey* were composed. In most of the lands lying directly north of the Mediterranean, people spoke languages of the Indo-European family (to which English, modern Greek, and many other modern languages belong), including Thracian in the southern Balkans, Greek (in its various dialects) in Greece and the Aegean, and the Anatolian group, including Lydian, Carian, Lycian, and others, in western and central Anatolia. To the south and east, languages of the Afroasiatic or Hamito-Semitic family were spoken: Libyan in most of north Africa, Egyptian in Egypt, and Semitic languages such as Phoenician and Akkadian along the eastern edge of the Mediterranean and in Mesopotamia. A few unrelated languages were scattered among the members of these two major families, including more than one language in Crete, at least one (Pelasgian) in Greece, and at least one in Cyprus.

Therefore, Greeks lived in a multilingual world. Some inhabitants of Greece and its borderlands were of necessity bilingual: there were bilingual speakers of Greek and Pelasgian, whatever that may be; there were bilingual speakers of Greek and the old local languages in Crete; there was much bilingualism in Cyprus; there were bilingual speakers of Greek and at least three Anatolian languages along the western edge of Asia Minor. One of the Greek-Lydian bilinguals was the Greek iambic poet Hipponax, later in date and even more unbridled in his humor than Archilochos.

The *Iliad* shows some awareness of language variation, though not where it might be expected. Curiously, although Greeks and Trojans are at war and are not imagined to belong to the same ethnic group, they are not shown to speak in different ways. When the leaders on opposing sides meet under truce, they have not a moment's difficulty in understanding one another. It is important to notice this, because it is a feature that later authors of fictional narratives across Europe have been happy to adopt. It certainly makes things easier in plotting fiction if you can forget about language problems, but it is not the kind of convention that would occur to everyone, and in this case we have to consider whether the poet is being more realistic than we first thought. Helen will no doubt have become fluent in "Trojan" in her ten years in Troy (foreign languages are sometimes said to be best learned in bed); perhaps we are also to think of Paris, Hektor, and Priam, though members of a royal family with Anatolian allegiances, as bilingual in Greek.

I put "Trojan" in quotes because we do not know what language was really spoken in the city and neighborhood of Troy. It was thought by later Greeks that Trojan was a different language from that of some surrounding peoples, which is why in an early myth, Aphrodite, disguised as a Phrygian princess when she goes to Mount Ida to seduce the Trojan Anchises, explains to him that she is bilingual and knows his language because she was brought up by a Trojan nurse. In other words, Trojan was different from the neighboring Phrygian (*Homeric Hymn to Aphrodite*, 112–116). Even the find of a late Hittite official seal in Luwian in 1995 does not tell us what everyday language was spoken in the city; it only tells us that official contacts were maintained in Luwian with some other Hittite authority after the fall of the kingdom at Hattuša.[1]

With the Trojan Battle Order in book 2, the *Iliad* shows undoubted linguistic realism. The list of Trojan allies is preceded by a divine instruction to Hektor by the goddess Iris:

> *Many are the allies of Priam, gathered under the great citadel,*
> *And each different people has a different language:*
> *You must have each man give orders to those he rules,*
> *Draw up his countrymen, and lead them to battle.*

> (*Iliad* 2.803–806)

Assuming, just as we must with the Catalogue of Ships, that the real setting for this passage is the beginning of hostilities, not the tenth year of the war, this instruction is wise and necessary. The allies about to be listed would have spoken several different languages, mostly of the Anatolian group. The leaders themselves, just as in any military alliance, would need some shared language. Five hundred years later, the poet would probably not have been able to put a name to that language, but *we* know that it would have been Luwian. The troops would not all speak it, so the orders must be translated to each contingent by its leader. The poet returns to the language issue in book 4, where the Trojan allies, expressing their concerns at once in different languages, are compared to sheep bleating to their lambs.[2]

In the Battle Order, the Kares of southwestern Anatolia are characterized as *barbarophonoi*, or *of foreign speech*.[3] Since many speakers of strange languages are named in the *Iliad*, including some far stranger to a Greek ear than Carian would have been, why is this formulaic adjective applied only to Carian? It may be that nothing is meant; many formulaic adjectives say nothing distinctive about the noun to which they refer. It may be, however, that Carian was in some way special to the epic tradition or to the poet, perhaps as the most commonly encountered foreign language (to those of Miletos and its region, including neighboring islands, or because Greeks and Kares often fought side by side as mercenaries). It may even be that Carian is recognized as a special case because in late Hittite times, Miletos, unlike its neighbors, was a buffer state independent of the Hittites. Its Carian language, though a member of the Anatolian family like Luwian, was not a Luwian dialect.

Like the *Iliad*, the *Odyssey* gives an impression of linguistic sophistication. Readers of the *Odyssey* are reminded that the part of the world inhabited by Greeks has room for many languages. In lovers' talk between Ares and Aphrodite, the Sinties, inhabitants of the northern Aegean island of Lemnos, are called *agriophonoi*, "wild-spoken." In fact there was an Etruscan base on Lemnos, and the language was utterly different from Greek. Again, at the southern limit of the Aegean

> *There is a land called Crete in the middle of the wine-dark sea,*
> *Fair and rich, well watered, and there are people in it,*
> *Numerous, uncountable, and ninety cities.*
> *Each tongue is mixed with others: there are Achaioi,*
> *There are brave Eteokretes, there are Kydones,*
> *Doriees in three tribes, and divine Pelasgoi.*
>
> (*Odyssey* 19.172–177)

It is a nice list, showing real awareness of ethnic and linguistic complexity, even if the presence of the Dorians is anachronistic. It's hard for us to see how to fit as many as five peoples into the known prehistory of Crete, but that is best ascribed to our ignorance rather than to the poet's mistake.

We can be reasonably confident from this evidence that the poems come from an environment in which encounters between languages were an everyday occurrence.

THE LANGUAGE OF THE GODS

Apart from these hints at a multilingual world, even in their own milieu "the poems give some slight indication of two tongues existing side by side," as Maurice Bowra wrote in 1930.[4] What Bowra meant was that the poet regularly makes a distinction between the *language of men* and the *language of gods*. Incidentally, there is never even a hint that this distinction causes communication difficulties, so we must assume that either men or gods or both were bilingual. Here are the details supplied in the *Iliad*. A mythical monster is called *Briareos* by the gods, *Aigaion* by men. A landmark near Troy is *Myrine* to immortals, *Batieia* to men, and the river of Troy is *Xanthos* to gods, *Skamandros* to men. A bird (possibly the roller, *Coracias glaucus*) is *chalkis* to gods, *kymindis* to men.[5]

A reader familiar with Greek is likely to notice that these word pairs all have something in common. As Bowra puts it, "The language of the gods is Greek": the words in the gods' language, as listed by the poet, make immediate sense in Greek.[6] The words in men's language do not make sense in Greek, and at least three of them—the place-names *Batieia* and *Skamandros* and the bird name *kymindis*—are definitely of non-Greek origin. Those two place-names are real local names in north-western Asia Minor, from the period (after the burning of Troy VIIa) when the language of the Troy region was more closely related to Thracian than to any other. The bird name is Lydian (which is historically one of the Luwian dialects), and it is next used by the bilingual poet Hipponax, who sang of a "*kymindis* croaking on a shithouse roof."[7]

In the *Odyssey* too there is occasional mention of a "language of the gods." A medicinal plant is called *moly* by gods and is given by Hermes to Odysseus to protect him from Kirke's magic potion. The rocks that the *Argo* passed on its famous voyage but that Odysseus managed to avoid on his wanderings were called *Planktai* by the blessed gods, according to Kirke's instructions to him.[8]

Of course, the idea that there is a distinct "language of the gods" was not invented by the poet of the *Iliad* and the *Odyssey*. It goes back thousands of years in the poetic tradition, to the long-lost poetry that was spoken in proto-Indo-European. We can be sure of this because the same idea is found in various other poetic traditions in Indo-European languages.[9]

But we are interested in the use of this idea by one particular poet and in the information we can extract from that use. First of all, it is important to emphasize that the *other* language is described not as "language of humans" but as *language of men*, a phrase that translates accurately the name chosen by the poet, who in this context always uses the sex-specific Greek word *andres*, "men," and not *anthropoi*, "humans." This makes us look for an explanation outside that Indo-European commonplace of a "language of the gods." We have to look instead at the rare historical cases in which there has been a separation between the "language of men" and its obvious corollary, the "language of women," within a single community. The best-recorded example was on the Caribbean island of Dominica, where, in the seventeenth century, men's and women's languages were entirely different in vocabulary though identical in structure. This had happened because men from the South American mainland (who spoke an Arawakan language) had invaded the island one hundred years earlier. They had driven off the Dominican men and settled with the women and children (who spoke Island-Carib). Then followed a period of several generations during which each sex had its own language and both sexes were bilingual. Eventually it was the men's language that disappeared.[10]

Although the poet never suggests this, we have to ask whether, in the case of the *Iliad* and the *Odyssey*, a real bilingual community with an eventful history provided the idea of the two differentiated languages. This brings us back to certain cities of the Aegean coast of Anatolia, notably Miletos, where there had indeed been a mixture of language communities. In Miletos, Greek and Carian had existed side by side, and there were some unusual rules separating male and female society. Women in Miletos, Herodotos tells us, "are not to share food with their husbands nor to call their own husbands by name." In other cities of this coast there was surely linguistic mixture involving Greek and Anatolian languages, though we have fewer details.[11]

In the *Iliad*, then, the language of the gods turns out to be Greek; the language of men turns out to be Anatolian (sometimes Lydian, sometimes not). In the *Odyssey*, the language of the gods is again Greek, but this time we are not told anything about the other language, not even that it is the "language of men." Perhaps that designation now seemed a giveaway, offering as it does a hint that language may be gendered. At all events, the multilingual world of the two epics and in particular the opposition between *language of the gods* and *language of men* are probably linked with the poet's own experience.

THE LANGUAGE OF EPIC POETS

Aside from their knowledge of distinct languages, Greeks were also sharply aware of the dialect divisions within their own language, which were important and of long standing. We can be certain of this because the Mycenaean dialect of Greek, as written in Linear B tablets around 1300 B.C., is ancestral to later dialects of Arkadia and Cyprus but not to other Greek dialects, so these others already existed in parallel with Mycenaean as early as 1300 B.C.

The most notable among the dialects of archaic and classical times are Ionic, Doric, and Aeolic. Ionic was the dialect of most of the new Greek cities of western Asia Minor; a variant, Attic, was spoken in Athens. Doric was spoken in much of the Peloponnese—where it apparently replaced Mycenaean—and also in Crete, Rhodes, and the southwestern corner of Asia Minor; it is first recorded in Alkman's poems. Aeolic is best known as the dialect of Lesbos, soon to be employed by Alkaios and Sappho.

Classical Greeks had this strong awareness of language and dialect for several reasons. There was plenty of seaborne trade across the Aegean and around the coasts, which brought relatively distant Greek-speakers into regular contact with one another. There was travel on pilgrimage, and the major Greek and Anatolian shrines attracted speakers of all the dialects and of several languages. New Greek cities on far-off coasts were often settled by an amalgam of different dialect-speakers; at the outset they must have been multidialectal as well as multilingual.

In addition, from the earliest periods of written literature, Greek writers adopted conventions that tended to link each genre with a dialect. Because Alkman, first and best, wrote choral poetry, the Doric of Sparta always seemed right for choral poetry. That's why Pindar, a Boiotian who flourished 150 years after Alkman, wrote his poems in a watered-down Doric, a dialect quite different from his mother tongue. Because the texts attributed to the legendary Hippokrates are in Ionic, later medical writings are also in Ionic. Some of these conventions must already have been in existence when literature was still purely oral, because Hesiod uses the same dialect as the poet of the *Iliad* and the *Odyssey*, although as the autobiographical narrator of the *Works and Days*, he makes it quite clear that he lived in rural Boiotia (where the everyday dialect was a form of Aeolic) and never crossed any sea but the narrow straits that divided Boiotia from Euboia.

However, when we compare this "epic dialect" with all that is known of early Greek dialects from other sources, it becomes clear that, in contrast to Alkman's and Sappho's, it cannot be pinned down to any single geographical locality. The dominant and most recent layer in it is close to the western subdialects of Ionic Greek, which were spoken in Euboia and some of the Aegean islands; therefore, it is also close to the dialect written by Archilochos, who was born in Paros, in the central Aegean. The most prominent among the earlier layers are the various features that match Aeolic.[12]

These facts strongly suggest that the language of epic had developed separately from any and all local dialects over a long period. All epic singers who composed in Greek, in hexameters, used a similar poetic language; all epic audiences must have been able to understand it, though not necessarily to speak or sing it. The language of Hesiod's poetry differs very little from that of the *Iliad* and the *Odyssey*. There are differences—certain features belonging to various dialects not found in the *Iliad* or the *Odyssey*—but they are occasional and they do not point to any one town or district, certainly not to the town of Askra, where Hesiod actually lived. Just as with Hesiod, so with the Homeric poems. Even if we can pin down the dialect of the texts geographically, it does not tell us where they were composed.[13]

It can tell us something about these poets, however. They belonged to the same tradition but learned from different exponents. Hesiod learned from the Muses—he insists on that—but he also learned from humans, from older singers. We can deduce that at least one of these came from the east Ionic dialect area, one was an Aeolic speaker (from Lesbos or the facing coast of Asia Minor), and one from a West Greek dialect area; scattered examples suggest an even wider range of influences. Fewer teachers, or at least teachers from a smaller geographical range, influenced the maker of the *Iliad* and the *Odyssey*. The language of these poems incorporates elements from several local dialects, but with the exception of west Ionic and perhaps Aeolic, they are historical rather than recent traits. The poet of the *Iliad* and the *Odyssey* was not an inveterate traveler.

LANGUAGE, HISTORY, AND THE DATE OF THE POEMS

We have assumed that the *Iliad* was composed around 650 B.C., and the *Odyssey* at least twenty years later. Let's look directly at this issue. Since the poems tell of events in the distant past and make practically no reference to current events, the question of their date is a very difficult one, made more difficult by an apparent conflict between linguistic and textual evidence.

The linguistic evidence cannot be fully explored without study of the Greek texts. Those familiar with the language of early Greek hexameter poetry tend to agree about the order in which surviving poems were written. The evidence does not provide absolute dates, and it is impossible to gauge the writing of these hexameter poems against the dates of other genres of Greek literature because the epic dialect stands apart from all the others, but the usual conclusion is that the *Iliad* came first, then the *Odyssey*, then the *Theogony* and *Works and Days*, and then the Homeric hymns, which were written at various different periods. The evidence is carefully set out by Richard Janko in *Homer, Hesiod, and the Hymns*. However, the conclusion has a shaky basis, because it tacitly assumes that these poems come from the same linguistic community and that this community's language was developing gradually and smoothly. If we make that assumption, we look to the poems for evidence of this gradual development. But if the poets lived far apart (as seems likely), in different social circumstances (as seems possible), and were not even influenced by the same members of the tradition (as is indicated by the dialect evidence), our initial assumption is false.[14]

Other evidence suggests a quite different answer to the question. Clues to the dating of Hesiod and his poems, as conveniently set out in Martin West's edition of the *Theogony*, suggest that he was at work between 730 and 690 B.C. Certain apparent anachronisms in the *Iliad* and the *Odyssey* hint at the date of these epics. Most startling is the passage in book 9, in Achilles' hot-tempered speech rejecting the peace offerings of Agamemnon, referring specifically—almost as an afterthought—to Egyptian Thebes (Karnak, capital of Upper Egypt):

Not even as much wealth as arrives at Orchomenos or Thebes
Of Egypt where so much property lies in the buildings,
The hundred-gated city, where at each gate two hundred
Men ride out with their horses and chariots . . .

(*Iliad* 9.381–384)

Lying far inland, politically detached from Lower Egypt and the Delta under its Nubian rulers, Egyptian Thebes was surely highly obscure to Greeks in the archaic period, until around 663 B.C., when it fell to the Assyrian king Assurbanipal. Even then it was a place of legend, for in reality it had no city walls and no gates. It is added in here, it seems, specifically because it was in the news.[15]

To set beside this evidence, books 13 and 16 of the *Iliad* contain descriptions of what looks very much like hoplite fighting, by massed warriors with their shields locked together, a style of warfare gradually adopted by Greeks in the course of the seventh century. These two passages have worried many commentators, because it is widely assumed that the *Iliad* was composed before hoplite tactics were invented. Some argued that the passages were interpolated (added to the text by a later editor), though no convincing reason was proposed; others explained them as depicting a little-known forerunner of the seventh-century system.[16]

A similar clue to the date of the *Odyssey* is given by the mention of the town of Ismaros on the north coast of the Aegean, as Odysseus's first port of call on his wanderings. It belonged to the Kikones, a Thracian tribe listed in the Trojan Battle Order, and is otherwise unheard of except by way of the poems of Archilochos, because the warriors of the new Greek city of Thasos, with Archilochos among them, fought at Ismaros at some date close to 650 B.C. Ismaros, like Egyptian Thebes, is likely to have been included in the *Odyssey* because it was in the news. A prophet or quack Kikon, presumably a member of the tribe, is named by the poet Hipponax in the sixth century, after which the Kikones disappear from history.[17]

Taking the evidence as a whole, then, we have two poets composing in very similar dialect, though not quite similar enough for us to place them in the same linguistic community. Neither refers directly to the other (or to any other named poet). Historical evidence suggests that Hesiod is the older of the two; linguistic evidence suggests that the poet of the *Iliad* and the *Odyssey* is the older. The dating of Hesiod and his work is relatively uncontroversial; many scholars would agree with a date around 700 B.C. The problem is in the dating of the *Iliad* and the *Odyssey*, because some scholars, relying on the linguistic details and on a long-standing assumption that these poems are older than the lyric poetry of the mid-seventh century, place them a whole century earlier than the historical evidence suggests, around 750 rather than 650 B.C.

APPROACHING THE POET

We seem to know plenty about Hesiod, even if only a proportion of what he says about himself and his family is literally true. In the same way, and with exactly the same caveat, we seem to know plenty about Archilochos, Alkaios, and other early lyric poets. Even Alkman, mysterious as he and his work may be, is prepared to get personal and to dream of a cooking pot "full of bean soup, such as hungry Alkman lusts for, hot, when the nights are long: he eats no fancy dishes, but looks for common fare, like the people."[18]

There is one other early Greek author of whose life, unlike these others, we are almost wholly ignorant, though plenty of guesses have been made: Sappho. She is a very personal poet, a singer of feelings and emotions, but her poems are as if addressed to a closed circle. They were written down, yet when we read them we almost feel we are eavesdropping. If we dare to do this, we can learn a great deal about what Sappho thought and felt, but we are still shut out from a knowledge of how she lived. This is partly to be explained by her individuality as a poet and partly by the great difference between male and female ways of life in early Greece. To generalize, men lived in a public sphere; they talked for everyone to hear, and everyone knew what they did. Women lived in a private sphere; they seldom spoke for men in general to hear, and men knew little of what they did. Even their names were seldom mentioned in male society.

Having noted this difference between known male poets and the one early female poet, we have to wonder whether it can tell us anything about the poet who composed the *Iliad* and the *Odyssey*, someone about whom we have no information, not even a name. Do we dare to speculate whether this poet was a woman? The idea offers an obvious answer to some of the questions we have faced. First, there is this extreme personal reticence, commonly explained by the poems' subject matter. It is an explanation that does not work perfectly. After all, Hesiod can boldly put himself in the foreground, not only in the *Works and Days* but also in the *Theogony*, and yet the theme of the latter poem is no more closely related to its poet than are the themes of the *Iliad* and the *Odyssey*.

Then there is the conflict over the dating of the epics. In many traditional societies we see a noticeable difference between the sexes in the adoption of linguistic changes: if a certain sound change is noted in the speech of the majority of men in a traditional community, the same change may be noted in the speech of the majority of women a generation later. One of the earliest observations of this sociolinguistic effect was made by the Roman orator and politician Cicero about six hundred years after the *Iliad* and the *Odyssey* were written down:

> Of course women more easily keep the old fashions unaltered, because however many people's speech they may encounter they always retain what they first learned: so, when I listen to [my mother-in-law] Laelia, I seem to be listening to Plautus or Naevius [classic authors of the previous century]. Her speaking voice is so correct, so plain, that no artificiality and no imitation could possibly be present, and I feel sure that her father and her ancestors spoke just so.[19]

Cicero's observation is accurate, though his reasoning differs from that of modern researchers. In modern times such differences have been noted among the Aromunians of Albania, the Yiddish-speakers of eastern Europe, and many others. This is not in any way a genetic or inborn effect, and the actual time difference varies because of variations in the extent of the contrast between women's and men's lives. In general, however, in traditional societies it is typically men, and not women, who engage in travel and trade and meet speakers of strange dialects and foreign languages. Women meet fewer people; there are fewer external influences on their language, and external influences prompt linguistic change.

Incidentally, the impression that dialect influences on Hesiod are more disparate than those on the poet of the *Iliad* and the *Odyssey* fits very well with this observation. A boy or young man learning the singer's art would be much freer to learn from a variety of older poets than would a girl or young woman, who might have no poetic models beyond her own family and immediate circle.

Since we begin with no facts at all about the poet who saw the *Iliad* and the *Odyssey* written down, no one can deny that she might have been a woman. But is it likely? Before going further, let's set this possibility on a firmer footing. To do this we have to look first at the whole world of oral poetry. The risky assumption that oral epic poetry is made by men has been very widespread, and we have to range widely if we are to combat it.

WOMEN AND MEN AS ORAL POETS

Early researchers on oral epic poetry were often outsiders to the society they were investigating. In many traditional societies, it was far easier for outside observers (nearly all of whom were men) to move in male society, and it was easy for them to accept the widespread assumption that the chief exponents of oral poetry were men. They wanted oral performances. So long as performances by men were available for recording, they had no need to look further. Somehow the great number of women performers who contributed folk songs to researchers in Britain, Ireland, and the United States in the nineteenth and early twentieth centuries did nothing to change these general attitudes. It's true that one of the very earliest folklore researchers, the eighteenth-century collector Thomas Percy, demonstrated from written evidence that medieval singers included women as well as men, yet it is only quite recently that attention has begun to be focused once more on the real place of women in the creation of oral literature.[20]

Poetry is often a family business, and it is sometimes the case that men and women perform together. So John Smith has found in Rajasthan: "The *par*-epic is typically performed by a man and his wife of the Nāyak caste." Elsewhere Smith observes that some men sing with their aunts or brothers or sisters-in-law: "As well as fiddler and dancer, the male performer has the rôle of lead singer: the musical and verbal material of each stanza is divided between him and his wife according to clearly fixed patterns." We can imagine something similar for epic performances by *jongleurs* in medieval France, to judge by the following aside from performer to audience in *Huon de Bordeaux*:

> *Now be quiet, please, and listen:*
> *I'll tell you the song if you want.*
> *I'll tell you—by the love of God—*
> *That I composed this song that I've recited,*
> *And you have given me hardly any money.*
> *Be sure of this: if God gives me health,*
> *I'll stop this song that you are hearing*
> *And all shall be deprived, I promise you,*
> *Of Auberon's power and honor,*
> *Who do not go to their purses to give something to my wife!*[21]

(For the last line, admittedly, one manuscript has a different text: "who do not go to their purses to give some money to me!") In West Africa, in oral epics that tell the story of Sunjata, the narrative is performed by men while the lyric sections require a chorus of women. In these examples, however, the general pattern seems to be that men are the "lead singers," in Smith's terminology; it is they who create the narrative.

Aside from team performances, women have become known in many parts of the world as makers of oral literature, but they are most often assumed to be specialists in love songs, laments, and tales told to children. The *Iliad* mentions women as singers of laments. The anonymous poet of the greatest Anglo-Saxon epic, *Beowulf*, gives additional support to the generalization that laments, as a genre of oral literature, are often composed and performed by women:

> *And a Geatish girl,*
> *Her hair bound up, sorrowfully sang*
> *A poem of lament, ever repeating*
> *Her dread foreboding of invasion,*
> *Mass deaths, the army fleeing,*
> *Capture, rape, slavery . . .*[22]

Because of these classic precedents, researchers into oral tradition were from the beginning ready to regard women as appropriate performers of laments. They duly found them in Russia in the early twentieth century: "In the backward and more conservative districts," as Henry and Nora Chadwick explain, "every woman can give expression to her grief in poetical form, either by composing a new *zaplachka* ('lament'), or by adapting one already in existence to the new circumstances." They go on to cite an earlier researcher, Rybnikov, who had recorded four laments recited by a young woman who was not a skilled poet; although judged by Rybnikov to be cruder than compositions by professional singers, these four personal and private laments were in classic form. Many other examples could be cited.[23]

In Ethiopia in the early twentieth century, women were makers of poetry in several genres. Laments were among their specialties, but another women's specialty, less commonly encountered elsewhere, was the song of satire or abuse, the same genre that in early Greece Archilochos had made his own. For this kind of performance in Ethiopia, groups of men or women (but usually women) gathered to abuse a king or nobleman, especially one who was not generous enough in rewarding the praise poetry that they had made earlier. The only way to stop the flood of poetic insult, some subjects found, was with gifts— a cow was a suitable payment. Women were also the composers of poems of abuse in the Nigerian language Igbo.

Rulers of the Galla, in southeastern Ethiopia, employed women poets—court poets—who made war songs and praise poetry for rulers and their guests. Women were praise poets also among the Tuareg of southern Algeria, and it is reliably said that young Tuareg men who were imprisoned by the French colonial government feared more than anything else that they might become the subject of women's songs of abuse. Women were present on the field of battle (admittedly, less often than men) and were makers of war songs among the pre-Islamic Arabs.

With examples such as these we are getting closer to the epic genre, the making of long narrative poetry, but we have not yet reached it. Women are not so often recorded as performers of epic narrative, so the cases in which they can be identified in this role are all the more interesting.

Returning to prerevolutionary Russia for a moment, there were as many women as men among the strange companies of *kaleki*, wandering Christian singers, who even in the early years of communism drifted from place to place in Russia and Siberia performing *stikhi*, religious stories in verse, including miracles and saints' lives; often they performed short epics too. The *kaleki* were beggars and sang for money, and it is possible that their special position as religious vagrants neutralized assumptions about the social roles of women, allowing them to perform publicly when other women would not.[24]

Medieval Icelandic sagas (a prose genre, but with many similarities to epic elsewhere) are narratives of what appears to be a very masculine world. The importance of women in that world can easily be overlooked, and yet their role in the stories is crucial, beginning with Aud the Deep-Minded, once queen of Dublin, ancestor of many famous Icelanders. The sagas in their written form are nearly all anonymous, but there is every reason to suppose that women played just as important a part as men in their transmission. The Chadwicks develop the argument that both of the early sources for the Norse discovery of America—the saga known as *Thorfinns Saga Karlsefnis*, or Saga of Eric the Red, and the version of the same events in *Flateyjarbók* known as Groenlendinga Saga—originate in the story told by Gudrid, Thorfinn's wife, of her own part in the adventure, and that this story developed in different ways in oral tradition until the two versions now known were set down in writing. They also note the part played by Thurid, daughter of Snorri the Priest, as one of the major oral sources for Ari the Learned (a descendant of Aud) in his compilation of *Íslendingabók*, the Book of the Icelanders, a sagalike catalogue of founders, their families, and their settlements. Snorri appears as a character in many sagas, and perhaps these traditions too are to be linked to his daughter. Finally, Ari is some-times thought to be the writer of the anonymous *Laxdaela Saga*, one of the greatest of all the sagas, a story that centers on the four marriages of Gudrun, Ari's great-grandmother: these traditions too must have come to him through the storytelling of women.[25]

With this glance at Iceland we begin to grasp the circumstances in which, in many traditional societies, women come into their own as performers of oral narrative and epic. In their family roles they may be originators, performers, and transmitters of classic texts, some of which are among the greatest in the world. Outside their families, their contribution to world literature may often be unknown or overlooked, since whoever contributed to the creation and transmission of such texts, men are much more likely than women to perform them to a wider audience. Most of the very meager historical evidence about ancient Roman oral narrative traditions relates to male performers, and yet the poet Ovid, whose works *Fasti* and *Metamorphoses* take the form of frame narratives incorporating stories told by others, makes use repeatedly of female storytellers, depicting them performing in pri-vate and family settings. The *Metamorphoses* even includes a fictional competition in narrative singing between two groups of goddesses, the Muses and the Pierides, the whole scene afterward narrated by the Muses to Minerva.[26]

Women have been numerous among the informants used by collec-tors of British and American folk songs, but they performed more often at home than in bars or public houses. Pádraigín Ní Uallacháin, who has collected the Irish oral poetry of Ulster, provides information on the women who have been among the greatest creators of this poetry. Often they were members of families in which both men and women were per-formers (her own father, Pádraig Ó hUallacháin, was a collector and performer like herself); often they were well known to be skilled singers with a large repertoire, but it was sometimes difficult for strangers to persuade them to perform. The Sokolov brothers, who collected Russian short epics in the neighborhood of Lake Onega in the late 1920s, likewise found that women were in the majority among their sources. They believed that this represented a new development, but in reality it was surely because of the unusually adventurous way they did their research. In a society that was consciously rejecting old patriarchal attitudes, they went to people's houses and asked about old songs, whereas earlier scholars had set up a public office and asked singers to come to them. In prerevolutionary Russian society, it would have been far more difficult for women than for men to respond to such a call. Women knew and were able to perform the epics—in fact, by the Sokolovs' time, women such as Marya Krivopolenova from Archangel were much better able to do so than most of the men—yet it had usually been men who performed the epics in public. This is paralleled by an observation by Nigel Phillips in his study of *tukang sijobang*, the epic performers of Sumatra. There had been few women, he was told, among the performers because the late hours and the traveling could not easily be combined with a woman's domestic work.[27]

Phillips does not discuss to what extent women knew and took part in the transmission of *sijobang* within their families; perhaps he was unable to find out. Of a previously unknown oral tradition shared by women among the Gond of central India, Gregory Nagy (a specialist in Homeric epic with a wide knowledge of oral traditions) rightly observes: "It may well be worth asking whether this discovery about women's traditions in India would have been possible if the researcher in this case, Joyce Flueckiger, did not happen to be a woman." It is an important point: some oral poetic traditions—certain genres or subgenres, in certain societies—are performed only by women to audiences that consist only of women.[28]

It is now becoming clear why women seldom figure among performers of epic reported by the less innovative folklore collectors. Some collectors do not look for them. Some focus on public performers and therefore overlook women, who in many traditional cultures are likely to perform at home or in private. Some are not allowed access to women's performances. And the problems do not stop there.

DIFFERENCES BETWEEN MEN'S AND WOMEN'S TRADITIONS

Some investigators have been sufficiently incomplete in their reporting as to gloss over the fact that they used women as informants. Shocking as it may seem, some even revise women's performances and attempt to transcribe them as if they are men's. This was notably done by a research team working with the Kabyle storytellers of northern Algeria. Kabyle, a Berber language, is one in which there are clear distinctions between men's and women's speech. Daniela Merolla, who recently examined this material from a new viewpoint, observes that the original researchers dealt differently with women's narratives, "standardizing" them into men's language where that could easily be done, although "it is still possible to find a few elements that indicate women's language." We can add that they were clearly adopting "the androcentric frame of reference, in which the male represents the 'unmarked,' or normative, category while the female is 'marked,' that is, treated as the exception to the norm." I'm quoting here from Lillian Doherty, who is not discussing modern anthropology but has observed the same attitudes in Homeric criticism.[29]

These last, dubious attitudes derive partly from simple male chauvinism but partly from a more complicated desire, still surviving from nineteenth- and early twentieth-century folklore research, to find an illusory "original text," compared with which all other versions are corrupt or interpolated. Researchers must have assumed, first, that the "original" stories or poems, lying somewhere in the background of the texts they were recording, had been created by men, and second, that the "best" or most faithful copies of these would be performed by women; they concluded (without ever making their reasoning explicit) that to transcribe a woman's performance while concealing all textual signs that it came from a woman would give the best possible approach to the male "original." Why else should Dallet, the Sokolov brothers, and many other folklore collectors give special attention to women informants and afterward downplay or even conceal the fact that they did so?

Gregory Nagy has been quoted for his comments on a specific oral tradition in India that is performed only among women. He raises the issue because it demonstrates that such traditions exist, and because he has dared to ask whether the *Iliad* was made by a man or a woman. He is one of the very few modern scholars who have considered this issue at all. Having looked at Joyce Flueckiger's research on the modern Indian epic tradition of *Candainī*—she was told that women do not perform *Candainī*, and when she observed a woman singing the Candainī story, it was in a distinct, "exclusively female" poetic form—Nagy concludes that if women performed *Iliad* stories, they would do so in a different genre, as Sappho did in her poem on the wedding of Hector and Andromache. "Epic, as a public performance genre in India, is performed almost exclusively by male singers."[30]

The comparison is interesting, and it is certainly true that in her narrative poems Sappho gives the impression of being very close to an oral tradition. But the implicit conclusion, that women singers did not share in the Greek epic tradition, is not compelling. There exist distinct genres practiced exclusively by men and exclusively by women, yet there are also genres that men and women share. In the particular case adduced by Nagy, men such as Stesichoros, as well as women such as Sappho, told stories belonging to the Trojan War cycle in nonepic genres. We have found other epic and narrative traditions in which men and women share. Thus we cannot safely extrapolate from the Indian information to show that the Greek epic tradition was restricted to male performers.[31]

One shared tradition is particularly interesting in this context. Both women and men were among the informants used by J.-M. Dallet and his team in their research among the Kabyle. Merolla notes that six *timucuha*, "fictional prose narratives," were told to the research group by a woman singer named Yamina at-Saedi, a large enough collection to make it possible to look for differences between women's and men's narration. In contrast with the Gond traditions investigated by Flueckiger, in Kabyle there was no formal difference of style, meter, or genre between men's and women's performances. Merolla found that Yamina at-Saedi's narratives, like those of male narrators, never question the fundamental male and patrilineal authority structure of Kabyle society. The plots are the same and the outcomes are the same. Yet there are differences. In cases where the male ethic leads to an unreasonable overreaction (as when, in one story, a misunderstanding over relationships can be solved only by killing the woman involved), a male narrator glosses over the incident, while Yamina at-Saedi highlights it and makes the unreasonableness explicit. Where men's narratives may reinforce unfavorable views of women and their actions, women's narratives will tend to bring out the good sense and individuality of women.[32]

The last piece in the jigsaw of evidence is contributed by Donald Philippi's study of Ainu epic poetry, from the now vanished culture of Hokkaido (northern Japan). In earlier centuries, it appears, there were both men and women poets among the Ainu, but during their final decline, in the nineteenth and early twentieth centuries, it was the women who remained in the villages and kept the traditional culture alive. During this period, when their epic poetry was for the first time being recorded in writing, most of the outstanding performers were women. While reporting these facts, even Philippi is a little coy about admitting that women performed *all* of the thirty-five long and short Ainu epics that he selects and translates. The simple fact is that these women were the very last recipients of the tradition. They were possibly its most skillful performers, and assuredly its final ones, for the Ainu language is no longer spoken; no one is now able to perform or to listen to its oral epics. The greatest performer of all, Imekanu (1875–1961), after retiring from her work as a Christian missionary, wrote 20,000 pages of epic poetry from the tradition that she had learned orally as a child.[33]

Strangely enough, the facts concerning this particular epic tradition run parallel with the observation made by Cicero and by modern linguists: that in traditional societies, the language spoken by women is typically slower to change than that spoken by men. Women are in practice often the last competent speakers of a disappearing language; in Ainu society, at least, they were the last skilled performers in a now lost epic tradition.

We have other examples to set beside Ainu. In eighteenth-century Britain, the ballad collector Thomas Percy based his work on existing manuscript records; in just three cases he or his informants found it possible to gather oral material parallel to the manuscript texts, and for each of the three the informant is said to be "a lady." None of the ladies is named; they, or their families, would probably have thought it improper for them to be named in public print. In southeast Ulster in the late twentieth century, Pádraigín Ní Uallacháin collected oral poetry from both men and women, but in one district after another she found that women were the most knowledgeable singers. What's more, they were the last survivors, because in this region, the tradition of spoken Irish has now come to an end, just as the Ainu language tradition has come to an end and just as the oral tradition of British ballads has come to an end.[34]

In oral literature every performance is a creation; the last creator may show at least as much originality as the first (if there ever was a

first). It's enough to have shown that women have been the last and perhaps greatest creators in various traditions. From these facts we can
argue that this may have been the case in the archaic Greek epic tradition also. Still, it's not without interest that women are also among the
earliest recorded performers in many traditions. Sappho is not alone.
The first named poet in the world was a woman, if we dare to take literally the Sumerian tablet in which a certain Enheduanna is named; she is,
we are told, the daughter of Sargon of Akkad, high priestess of the love
goddess Inanna, and composer of a poetic hymn supplicating the
dreaded goddess, though the written text of this hymn comes to us by
way of another poet.

A FEMALE POET OF THE *ILIAD*

In many societies, women who have become skilled oral narrative performers have learned their skills through their families and have used
them in family contexts—and also to researchers, when researchers
happen to have discovered their abilities, and in writing, as did the great
Ainu poetess Imekanu, who learned to create epics and afterward
learned to write.

It was in a private context that the *Iliad* was created. It must have
been, because as we already know, it cannot possibly have been copied
down from any normal performance.

Of course, any singer who had the skill might theoretically have
been encouraged to devote time to making this enormous poem. Yet it
might well have been difficult in practice to persuade the singer to give
up all normal work, the kind of work that must usually provide food
and shelter. Oral epic singers in traditional societies are often described
glibly by Homeric scholars as "professional." In terms of skill they are
professional indeed, but in scarcely any known society have they been
full-time professionals. In some places women have been less likely than
men to perform publicly as singers because the long journeys and the
overnight stays cannot easily be combined with their traditional household roles. For this reason, women who have the necessary skills are in
some societies more likely than men to be able to undertake the task of
gradually creating a really long epic, since the work can—indeed, it
must—be done at home.

Remember too that the *Iliad* had to be made privately, with an extended effort of voice and concentration, without the reward in audience appreciation that a singer normally enjoyed. Some people nowadays think that nothing is more desirable than the gift of a sabbatical year in which one doesn't need to do anything except write, but others regard this as hell on earth. How would a popular ancient oral singer, accustomed to vocal praise and varied rewards from live audiences, have regarded such an offer? Recent researchers have found that it can be easier to persuade women singers than men to undertake the work of dictating, simply because they are more accustomed to performing privately, to *please themselves* or for a few friends or family members; the appreciation of a small and select audience is familiar to them.

There was a corresponding reward, however, a reward that would have been infinitely more meaningful to a woman skilled in the epic tradition than it would have been to a man. Male singers reached very large audiences; writers in other genres described them, half enviously, as singing "to the peoples." These audiences were not strictly segregated by gender; both men and women attended festivals, for example, and in book 1 of the *Odyssey* Penelope and her maids, along with Telemachos and the suitors, can listen to Phemios's song. Yet women lived a relatively secluded life in early Greece. At informal gatherings, when singers might perform, many men and very few women would be there to hear. The suitors, just like the men who went to *symposia* in classical Athens, left their womenfolk at home. Male singers might see little likelihood of reaching larger audiences by creating a written epic. By contrast, a woman skilled in the tradition would have performed to please herself or to family and intimate friends. Such a woman, if she were as perceptive as the poet of the *Iliad* and the *Odyssey* must have been, might have realized that a new potential audience undreamed of by male singers—an audience of women—existed and could be reached with the help of writing.

The hypothesis that we are building here is a new one, yet nothing in Homeric criticism is wholly new, and it is foreshadowed (for different reasons) by some earlier authors, most obviously by Samuel Butler in *The Authoress of the Odyssey*. The atmosphere of the *Iliad*, the poem of war, is certainly different from that of the *Odyssey*, a story rooted in a largely peaceful society. Butler believed that this could best be explained by hypothesizing a woman poet for the *Odyssey*.

We have discussed the differences between the two poems already, and we have shown that the hypothesis of two different poets does not work well; the best explanation is that the *Odyssey* is a new departure by the same poet who composed the *Iliad*, twenty years older, more independent, more adventurous. Butler dared only to suggest a woman poet of the *Odyssey*—he left the *Iliad* alone—but his suggestion makes good sense on this basis. A woman singer, the most skillful of her generation, had already produced the *Iliad*, the quintessence of the old oral tradition. With added confidence and greater maturity, she was now able to create something newer and freer, a poem that would quietly and subversively build a woman's viewpoint into the traditional framework.

There will be objections to the hypothesis that a woman singer created the two poems. The first is that no early author says it. This objection fails completely, however, because no early author describes or names the singer who saw these two poems written down. We are given no sex and no name—certainly not Homer, who is seen as a singer of the distant past. The idea that Homer was the person whose performance of the *Iliad* and the *Odyssey* was written down is first proposed in one ill-informed postclassical text, the anonymous *Life of Homer*, fraudulently ascribed to Herodotos, and has been re-invented by modern scholars.

The second objection is that early Greek singers and poets, including the so-called children of Homer who kept up the oral tradition, were nearly always men. This objection fails for two reasons. First, we know that some early Greek poets, including one of the very greatest, were women. Second, although superficial inquirers into many oral traditions find only male singers, later and more sensitive inquirers often find that women are the best singers of all. The fact that women did not usually perform for a public audience that included men explains why no ancient source exists to tell us how Sappho's poems were performed—and it also explains why no one tells us that women were among the children of Homer.

The third objection is that the *Iliad* feels like the work of a man. This is serious: the *Iliad* is largely about male heroics in war, and the great majority of its characters are men whose aim is to kill one another. But this objection also fails for two reasons. First, although there are women's genres and maybe also men's genres, the sexes share the major poetic forms. Women and men belong to the same tradition and tell the same stories; this was observed even in the case of Berber oral narrative, in a society that is more rigorously secluded than that of early Greece. Second, the same research demonstrates that women, though telling the same stories, are capable of telling them from a different angle and with an added depth, dealing sympathetically with the feelings and motives of women characters. No one will deny that the poet of the *Iliad* does this; no one will deny that in the *Odyssey* it is done even better.

CONCLUSION: THE POET

In spite of the long poetic history that precedes the poems, we are focusing on two events that took place at precise dates. In each case the act of composition was the act of writing, and in those acts the *Iliad* and then the *Odyssey* came into existence. We have placed these events around 650 and 630 B.C. These datings are speculative. They intentionally place more weight on historical than on linguistic evidence, because the linguistic evidence rests partly on invalid assumptions and assumes that the poet was a man. But a survey of the ancient sources combined with modern understanding of oral tradition leads us to separate the legendary Homer from the composition and writing of the two epics, and having done so, we have found sufficient reason to suggest that the poet was a woman.

It's probable that this will not be proved. It's enough at this stage to have shown that there is no direct evidence of the poet's identity and therefore no justification for the customary assumption that the two epics were composed by a man.

PART THREE

THE RESPONSE

7

From Oral Epic to Written Classic

On this new basis we can now explore what happened next: how the *Iliad* and the *Odyssey* became classics, and how they catalyzed a new understanding of oral literature.

We begin to find evidence of a readership of these epics around 600 B.C., a long generation after the poems were created. We should not be surprised at this apparent lapse of time. It took many weeks to copy out a manuscript of either poem. Leather remained a costly commodity; so were scribal man-hours. Therefore, although we cannot guess how many copies were made in that first half-century, it cannot have been a large number. We do not know how many people in Greece could read, but it cannot have been many. And we have no idea whether the typical reader of one of these early copies read alone, read to others, or memorized in order to recite to others.

We do of course know that epic poetry was heard at public gatherings, such as the funeral games at which Hesiod won his prize. By the fourth century B.C., extracts from the epics attributed to Homer were sometimes recited from fixed texts, word for word, on such occasions, but whether this was a late development, occurring only after oral transmission had disappeared completely from Greek epic tradition, or whether the written texts began to usurp this authority as soon as they existed is completely unknown.

Perhaps it took longer for private reading to catch on. In the long run, however, the *Iliad* and the *Odyssey* would never have reached their astonishing level of popularity without private reading. Once written, they were able to circulate (like the poems of Archilochos) among audiences of a completely new kind: people who would never otherwise have heard them but could now read and reread them to one another. People could listen whenever they wished and wherever they were, in small circles of friends or larger gatherings, as long as someone in the group could read. They could even read, meditatively, on their own, pleasing themselves as Achilles pleased himself. Literacy was by no means universal, but it was far more widespread than the ability to create an oral epic. Whether or not the poet guessed that this would happen, it was certainly true that the written epics, unlike their oral counterparts, reached an audience of women as well as men. Richard Bentley, the best textual critic of the eighteenth century, was aware of this dual audience. He supposed that Homer "wrote a sequel of songs and rhapsodies, to be sung by himself for small earnings and good cheer, at festivals and other days of merriment. The *Ilias* he made for the men and the *Odysseis* for the other sex." In Bentley's view, the gender of the intended audience explained certain differences between the *Iliad* and the *Odyssey*.[1] Though preferring to attribute these differences to the poet's increased confidence and maturity, I would agree that in creating the *Odyssey* she may have been addressing a potential audience of women more directly than before.

THE EARLIEST READERS OF THE *ILIAD*
AND THE *ODYSSEY*

Down to the fifth century B.C., no one, in sources known to us, admits directly to having read or heard the *Iliad* or the *Odyssey*. The only information about readership comes from writers and artists who in some way responded to the poems, leading us to conclude that they read them or heard them read.

One of the oldest individual scraps of evidence is a vase that illustrates a famous episode in the adventures of Odysseus: the blinding of the Kyklops. Only one early version of this popular scene shows the Kyklops being blinded with a tree stem, a strange choice of weapons, but the same choice that is made by the poet of the *Odyssey*. It is on a large storage jar whose exact date and provenance are unknown, but it was certainly made before 600 B.C., not in Greece but in the Etrurian lands in central Italy. Curiously, the wine with which the Kyklops was previously supplied by Odysseus is represented in this scene by an amphora, not a goatskin, as in the text. But this is easy to explain. The wine has to be on show, because the story says that the Kyklops was rendered drunk and helpless before the sailors attempted to blind him. An empty goatskin is difficult to draw; an amphora is easy and immediately recognizable, which is why the painter chose it. It seems clear that the painter of this vase, or a patron, must have known the Kyklops story in a version practically identical with that of the *Odyssey*. Most likely he or she knew the *Odyssey* itself.[2]

A Corinthian vase made around 590 B.C. depicts Achilles returning to battle in new armor. But in this scene Achilles is being encouraged by Thetis, while Phoinix and Odysseus look on. That disagrees with the *Iliad*, in which Thetis delivers Achilles' new armor and then goes away; Phoinix and Odysseus find him still inconsolable at the death of Patroklos, and only the goddess Athene can finally persuade him to fight. Here are the crucial lines:

> *So saying he sent away the other basileis,*
> *But the two sons of Atreus stayed, and godlike Odysseus,*
> *Nestor and Idomeneus and the old horseman Phoinix*

To please him in his bitter sorrow, but his heart was not
Pleased . . .
[Athene] in the form of a wide-winged, shrill-voiced falcon
Plunged through the air from heaven, while the Achaioi
Were arming themselves afresh in the camp. She instilled
Nectar and lovely ambrosia into the breast of Achilles
So that hateful hunger should not weaken his knees . . .
And then godlike Achilles armed himself among the rest.

(Iliad 19.309–364)

This painter and patron apparently did not know the *Iliad;* at any rate, they settled on a quite different version of Achilles' return to battle, probably based on some other recently heard epic.[3]

As to artists, so to early poets the Trojan War story was familiar. Eventually we see signs that poets know the *Iliad* and the *Odyssey,* but it can be hard to recognize them. It's possible that Sappho (c. 600 B.C.) had read the *Iliad* or heard it recited before she composed her poem of the wedding of Hektor and Andromache, but there is no proof of it. Hektor and Andromache were surely known before the *Iliad* was composed.

When Sappho's contemporary Alkaios tells of Achilles' appeal to his mother, Thetis, and his prayer to Zeus and attributes the story to the anger (*mânin*) of Thetis's offspring, it's evident that in his time the Achilles story, focusing on Achilles' anger and his quarrel with Agamemnon, was popular. Alkaios is making a direct allusion to it, and in this case there is a strong possibility that he is alluding to the *Iliad,* in the very first line of which the anger of Achilles (*mênin . . . Achilêos*) is announced as the theme.[4]

At about this same time the Athenian poet Solon refers to the lies told by the singers—the earliest specific reference from any outside source to the *performance* of Greek oral narrative poetry. Solon is not alluding to any particular poem here (unless he is thinking of the Muses' address to Hesiod in *Works and Days*); instead, he is glancing at the theme of truth and lies in poetry and whether we can tell them apart— the theme originally broached by Hesiod and explored at length and in depth by the poet of the *Odyssey.*

None of these references or allusions can be precisely dated, but all five are to be placed between about 620 and 580 B.C. If we accept them at face value, we know of five early members of the audience or readership of Greek epic. Solon of Athens, a widely traveled man, alludes to epic singers and apparently knew an example of their work that raised the question of truth and lies. Sappho knew the Hektor and Andromache story, and an unnamed Corinthian knew of Achilles' return to battle in new armor; both of these surely knew epics of the Trojan cycle. More unexpectedly, a painter or patron in far-off central Italy knew the *Odyssey*, or at the very least knew the Kyklops story in precisely the way in which the *Odyssey* tells it. Finally, and most tellingly, Alkaios of Lesbos knew the *Iliad* by its theme and alludes to it in a way that he must expect his own audience to recognize. However small his audience, this is the first, crucial indication that the *Iliad* was in general circulation.

THE EMERGENCE OF HOMER

One of those earliest readers, Alkaios, was close enough to the event to have heard the name of the singer who saw the *Iliad* and the *Odyssey* written down. He did not make a note of it, because the singer was not of special interest to him.

The reasons for anonymity in oral narrative traditions are easy to see. When these traditions are purely oral, the singer's own name and personal history do not need to be included in the song. The audience knows who the singer is. In any case, everyone knows that the tradition is greater than any individual singer. The singer, while aware of those who have gone before, is also aware that the necessary skill and inspiration are not a matter for boasting but a divine gift. As a sign of this, in Greek epic, divine inspiration is invoked at the outset, and we can see from the opening words of the *Iliad* and the *Odyssey* that their tradition has not yet crossed over to the author-centered approach typical of other kinds of writing. Admittedly, divine invocations are copied in later poetry as a literary conceit; even Dante and Milton, in their Christian epics, claim the help of the Muses, and the Portuguese epic poet Camões acknowledges the aid of the Tágides, imaginary river nymphs of the Tagus. In early Greek oral poetry, by contrast, we must take these invocations literally. If the Muses withdrew their gift, as they did from Thamyris (see page 96), the poet lost the power to sing.

But the tradition of anonymity was coming under threat. While acknowledging divine inspiration, even Hesiod expressed his personality bluntly in *Works and Days* and included his own name in the text of *Theogony*. Other, shorter poems were newly circulating in writing and were similarly linked with their authors' names, from Archilochos and Alkman onward. What's more, these shorter poems provide exciting and even titillating biographical information. And so it became natural to ask parallel questions, and to require similar answers, about the *Iliad* and the *Odyssey*.

In the course of the sixth century, as if in answer to such questions, the name of Homer began to emerge in written texts. Nobody yet names the *Iliad* or the *Odyssey*, and nobody yet links Homer with these two poems in particular. To all the earliest writers who mention him, he is a name without a biography. He lived in the distant past and was a *rhapsodos*, a singer of hexameters; the symbol of his profession was a *rhabdos*, or "wand" (actually, in the *Iliad* and the *Odyssey* it would have been called a *skeptron*). He had composed all the epics that singers sang, or all the good ones, or all except those that seemed to belong to Hesiod. He was definitely not a writer; all the early sources describe him as singing or speaking his poems, and there is never a hint that he saw them written down. In the first century A.D., the Jewish historian Iosephos (Josephus), in a quick survey of the antiquity of various historical records, states this tradition explicitly: "They say that even Homer did not leave his poetry in writing, but that it was transmitted in memory and afterwards collected from the songs, which is why there are so many inconsistencies in it."[5]

Homer stood for the whole Greek epic tradition. In the sixth century B.C. this was still universally regarded as an oral tradition, in spite of the existence of written texts of the *Iliad* and the *Odyssey*. Thus the first thing to be said about Homer is that he was "sweet-singing"; because of that (according to poets who worked in writing), he was all the more likely to mislead, deceive, and corrupt. He was uniquely skilled but irresponsible and not to be trusted. "To begin with Homer, since all people have learned . . . ," said the philosopher-poet Xenophanes (c. 510 B.C.), opening his case for the prosecution. The rest of that sentence is lost, but it seems likely that "all people" have learned something about the world or the gods from Homer, and therefore Xenophanes must begin by reacting to Homer. The stinging reaction came in a following passage:

> *Homer and Hesiod have ascribed to the Gods*
> *All the faults and misdeeds that exist among humans,*
> *Thieving and whoring and deceiving one another.*[6]

Yes, we are certainly talking about the *Iliad* and the *Odyssey* here. It's easy enough, skimming through these poems, to find a few episodes of whoring and deception that Xenophanes might have in mind. Zeus's memory of his early lovemaking with his sister Hera without their parents' knowledge, Hera's later seduction of Zeus, the illicit love affair of Ares and Aphrodite: all of these will fit the bill. According to this argument, Homer is corrupting and sacrilegious because these songs show the gods as immoral.

At about the same date, the poet Simonides made a much more specific reference to Homer, in an aside concerning the hero Meleagros,

> *Who by his spear*
> *Overcame all the young men, driving them*
> *Beyond the swirling Anauros out of Iolkos rich in grapes:*
> *Thus Homer and Stesichoros sang to the peoples.*[7]

But in this case Homer is being credited with some epic now unknown. Neither the *Iliad* nor the *Odyssey* says a word about Meleagros's triumph at the funeral games for Pelias at Iolkos; nor does any other early text, and that serves to demonstrate how little we know of the range of Greek oral epic around 500 B.C. However, Simonides also knew a line that does occur, word for word, in the *Iliad*.

> *The man of Chios spoke a very beautiful line:*
> *"As are the generations of leaves, so also are those of men."*[8]

Glaukos, the speaker in the *Iliad* at this point, explains that the autumn leaves are succeeded by a new generation next spring and that humankind passes and is renewed in the same way. Although the line could well be proverbial and might have been used by many singers, it seems likely that Simonides is really thinking of the *Iliad* as known to us. The phrase "the man of Chios," which means Homer, demonstrates that Homer's identity was as familiar to Simonides' audience as the theme of the *Iliad* had been to Alkaios's audience: both would be recognized from an allusive phrase.

This is, as it happens, the first solid detail in what would eventually be a full-scale biographical tradition about Homer. Whoever he was, whatever he sang, he came from Chios, the big island in the eastern Aegean.

Let's turn to a contemporary of Simonides'. Herakleitos was a thinker—a philosopher, in fact—in the tradition of Xenophanes but with a radicalism of his own. His work too is placed around 500 B.C., making him one of the very earliest Greek writers of prose. "What mind or sense have they? They follow the peoples' singers; the gathered crowd is their teacher," says Herakleitos, criticizing those who fail to question common assumptions, as he himself continually did. He means that "the peoples' singers [and] the gathered crowd," traditional singers and their audiences, are bad guides for those who intend to think for themselves. Yet Herakleitos is ready to acknowledge the special abilities of Homer, writing elsewhere that the legendary hexameter poet was "more skilled than all the other Hellenes."[9]

The full text of Herakleitos's book is lost, but another trenchant opinion concerning traditional poetry is reported from it: "Herakleitos claimed that Homer deserved to have been thrown out of the contests and beaten, and Archilochos just the same." To understand what Herakleitos means by this, we need to know first that in ancient athletic contests, those who caused a false start, by crossing the starting line before the signal, were penalized with a beating. Beating was the penalty not for weak competitors but for those who broke the rules. Evidently, therefore, Herakleitos is agreeing with Xenophanes. He is lampooning Homer and Archilochos not for any lack of poetic skill but for the bad moral example set by their narratives.[10]

Now to the praise poet Pindar, a generation later than Herakleitos and his contemporaries. Pindar makes three specific references to Homer in his poems on athletic victories. The first of these, in an ode of 476 B.C., sets the tone: Homer is a powerful and deceiving voice.

> *You know the might of Aias,*
> *Stained with blood at dead of night*
> *With his own sword, spilling disgrace*
> *On all the sons of the Hellenes who went to Troy:*

> *Yet Homer made him honored among humankind,*
> *Raised his fame and spoke it to the* rhabdos
> *In magical words, an amusement to later people.*[11]

In a later poem Pindar follows the same pattern of thought. Odysseus, like Aias, does not deserve the fame that Homer gives him.

> *The tale of Odysseus, I take it,*
> *Has become a greater thing than his suffering*
> *Because of sweet-spoken Homer.*
> *Over the hero's lies and subterfuges*
> *Something majestic extends: thus*
> *Skill in storytelling, by distracting, tricks us.*[12]

Sophia, which means "skill" in this quotation and in the one by Herakleitos above, acquires in later texts the familiar sense of "wisdom," but Pindar and Herakleitos do not mean to say that Homer is wise.

Pindar's third mention of Homer appears to be a direct quotation:

> *When sharing in the words of Homer,*
> *Attend to this: a good messenger, he said,*
> *In whatever affair, brings highest honor—*
> *Why, from a well-told tale the Muse herself gains stature!*[13]

But it isn't quite a direct quotation after all. The more optimistic readers think that this is a reminiscence of *Iliad* 15.207, in which, in a conversation on Mount Olympos, Poseidon says politely to the messenger goddess, Iris, *"When the* messenger *is in accord with destiny, this, also, leads to a* good *outcome,"* though only the two words in roman type are shared between the texts. Pindar's lines could just as well be a reference to a lost epic or a hexameter proverb with an epic ring to it. In the first two quotations, however, Pindar certainly thinks of Homer as the composer of the *Iliad* and the *Odyssey*. The suicide of Aias does not feature in the *Iliad*; Homer has been irresponsible in that poem, Pindar is telling us, by showing Aias as a hero while failing to mention his disgraceful death. He has been equally irresponsible in the *Odyssey*, in which the lies and subterfuges of Odysseus are a recurrent theme.

Notice that the innovative poets and philosophers of the late sixth and fifth centuries liked to criticize the *Iliad*, the *Odyssey*, and the early singer Homer. They did so with some assurance that their own relatively restricted audience would understand these references. We can be quite certain that the two great epics, now beginning to be associated with Homer, were in circulation in sixth-century Greece, but it is evident too that a tradition of oral epic persisted alongside them, at least up to the time of Herakleitos and Pindar.

While criticizing the epics, these newer writers made frequent use of the stories that were found in them. They treat these stories as current information, in the public domain, as we might say, rather than as the work of any single author or the subject of any particular poems. It is said that Pindar's younger contemporary Aischylos, the earliest Athenian dramatist whose works survive, acknowledged that his tragedies were "steaks from the great dinners of Homer." If Aischylos really said this, he is the first author known to us who acknowledged Homer as a principal source. He is probably crediting not just the *Iliad* and the *Odyssey* but all the early epics, for indeed Aristotle later argued, with some justification, that—unlike the others—the *Iliad* and the *Odyssey*, with their well-constructed and unified plots, could provide material for only one or two tragedies each.[14]

Herodotos, the "father of history," a generation later than Aischylos, takes a somewhat different attitude toward the epics. He questions various points of detail in them, such as the river Ocean that surrounds the world. The *Iliad* makes several mentions of *the streams of the river Okeanos, which is the beginning of all things*, but Herodotos has his doubts: "I do not know that any river Okeanos exists; I believe that Homer or one of the poets who preceded him devised the name and put it into poetry."[15]

Herodotos naturally attempts to discover the facts about Homer, since he uses the epics as sources.

I think that Hesiod and Homer lived four hundred years before our own time, and no more than that. These two were the makers of divine genealogy as far as the Greeks are concerned; they gave the gods their names and titles, allocated their various honors and powers, and described their appearance. The poets who are said to have preceded these two men actually came later, I believe.[16]

Herodotos also attempts to verify the canon of Homer's works (page 173). In short, he doubts some of Homer's facts but treats him with respect, as a fairly reliable predecessor in a slightly different genre.

From this point on, poets, playwrights, and philosophers continue, through the later centuries of Greek literature, to debate the moral qualities of the work of Homer. As we read further in these debates, we realize at last that writers such as Plato are indulging in a literary game. The general moral standpoint of the *Iliad* and the *Odyssey* is so unshakable, and their position as classics has become so secure, that no criticism over details will really threaten them.

Strangely enough, the immediate legacy of the maker of the *Iliad* and the *Odyssey* is not to be found in written verse. Instead, traditional oral narrative leads on gently to written narrative—to history, in fact. Historians wrote in prose, not hexameter verse. Their inspiration came from their own inquiries, not from any goddess. But their knowledge is comparable to that of an epic poet: they know what people did and said in the past. Their skill is comparable too: they are telling stories of the past, and at first their stories are read aloud to a gathered audience in public. They sometimes disagree with earlier historians, including the maker of the two epics, but they also often use earlier histories, including the epics, as sources.

THE *HOMERIDAI*, THE *RHAPSODOI*, AND THE HOMERIC CANON

In the poem quoted above (page 165), Pindar speaks of "sharing in the words of Homer." At least, that is my attempt at a rendering of his word *syntithemai* (it is a lifetime's task to grasp the implications of the unexpected words that Pindar likes to use in unexpected senses). Here, he is certainly reminding us that "Homer," or epic poetry, is something in which one participates in a different way from his own choral lyrics. Pindar schooled his choruses to keep to a text that was planned in every detail; the audience enjoyed it precisely as he had written it down. It had been very different with epic. Evidently it still felt somewhat different, even in Pindar's day. Each member of the audience was a potential contributor to a performance in an oral tradition, in just the same way that the *Odyssey* shows Odysseus, Telemachos, and Penelope contributing with interruptions that might well determine the singer's theme. Each member of the audience would appreciate the resulting performance individually, and each might have something different to bring away from it.

Both Herakleitos and Simonides say explicitly that oral singers address "the peoples." In their time, the singers were truly popular. Epics from the oral tradition commanded far larger audiences than any newly written text, and what is more, their audiences were international, as we know from the Etruscan painting of the blinding of the Kyklops. Thus, for at least a hundred years after the *Iliad* and the *Odyssey* were first written down, whatever changes might meanwhile have been going on in the new world of written literature, hexameter narratives continued to be sung to attentive audiences in very much the same way they must have been before.

By the early fifth century B.C., when Pindar was at work, some of the traditional performers belonged to a professional guild called *Homeridai*:

> In the same way as the Homeridai,
> Singers of woven words, usually
> Begin—with an address to Zeus—so this man
> Has taken his first installment of victory in festival games
> From the widely sung grove of Zeus of Nemea.[17]

This, in about 485 B.C., is the very first mention of the *Homeridai*. The name looks as though it means "children of Homeros." We can compare it with a similar name. The *Asklepiadai*, or "children of Asklepios," were not truly descendants of the legendary healer, a man of the distant past who was said to have become a god; they were a guild of physicians whose skills were passed from teacher to apprentice. Likewise, the "children of Homer" were not necessarily descendants of a legendary poet; they too were in reality a professional guild. Their reputation was questionable—Plato would certainly question it—but they were a part of everyday life.

Following that first reference by Pindar, in the early fourth century the name of the *Homeridai* crops up several times in Plato's writings—once, naturally enough, in the dialogue *Ion*, which is a fictionalized encounter between Sokrates and a professional performer of the works of Homer. This performer, Ion, is proud enough of his skills to assert that he deserves "to be crowned with a golden wreath by the *Homeridai*," though he does not claim to be one of them. A second time, in Plato's *Republic*, in a context in which Homer's contribution to Greek civilization is being played down, a character admits that "even the *Homeridai* themselves don't make the claim" that any Greek city owes its constitution to Homer.[18]

Plato's third mention of the children of Homer (in his dialogue *Phaidros*) is the most informative. Sokrates is speaking:

> "I believe that some of the *Homeridai* recite two hymns to Eros from among the esoteric poems. One of them is quite disrespectful to the god, and what's more, the meter is incorrect! This is what they sing:
>
> *Now this winged god is called by mortals Eros,*
> *But immortals say 'Pteros' because love must grow wings."*[19]

Pteros is an invented portmanteau word in which *pteron*, "wing," is added to *eros*, "sexual love." The error in meter to which Sokrates refers is in the second line of the original Greek: the consonant group *pt* is treated as if it were a single consonant.

These lines are not otherwise known. They are certainly not by the poet of the *Iliad* and the *Odyssey*, but there is no reason to think that Plato has made them up. Playing with gods' names is quite typical of later Greek divine hymns, some of which were indeed esoteric, semi-secret, and intended for initiates only. This is probably a real fragment from a hymn to the god Eros sung by "some of the *Homeridai*." There were other hymns in their repertoire, as we shall see.

One more scrap of information about the *Homeridai* comes from the essayist Isokrates, who wrote around 350 B.C. He asserts in his *Praise of Helen* that "some of the *Homeridai* tell the story that Helen appeared to Homer in a dream and told him to make a poem about the Trojan expedition." It is likely that Isokrates is telling the truth. In many poetic traditions, especially those in which authors are named and credited, it comes to be seen as part of the task of a reciter to introduce poems by explaining how they came to be composed. The legendary biography of Homer, some of whose details had already been devised, is part of this impulse. Eventually there were fictional biographies of other early poets, notably Archilochos, made up out of cleverly interpreted scraps of their poetry.[20]

For no good reason, it is traditional among Plato specialists to explain the word *Homeridai* as "admirers of Homer." What Plato actually says or implies about the *Homeridai* is quite different from this, makes perfect sense, and is supported on one side by Pindar and on the other by Isokrates. The *Homeridai* were a guild who performed hexameter poems, including the *Iliad* and the *Odyssey* and hymns to the gods, all of them piously linked with the name of Homer. They also told stories about Homer, especially the kind of stories that "explained" the poems. Possibly (if Ion is not fantasizing), they even awarded honors to performers who raised Homer's reputation.

Now Ion himself is not a member of the *Homeridai*; Plato's dialogue makes this point quite clear. Ion is a *rhapsodos*, and we know exactly what *rhapsodoi* did because Pindar, not always the most explicit of writers, is explicit about this, addressing the *Homeridai* as "singers of woven words." It is immediately certain that these woven words, *rhapta epea*, are what *rhapsodoi* must perform; the phrase *rhapta epea* is there so that Pindar's audience will make the easy link to the word *rhapsodoi*, "weavers of songs" (*epea* are words; *odoi* are odes or songs).

If Pindar were a mathematician and not a poet, he would have said that *Homeridai* were a subset of *rhapsodoi*, and these in turn were a subset of *aoidoi*, or "singers." To take *aoidoi* first, any singers or poets who performed orally deserved this name. Pindar himself was an *aoidos;* so are the fictional Demodokos and Phemios and the other unnamed performers who lead the singing and dancing in various incidental scenes in the *Iliad* and the *Odyssey*; so was the legendary Homer. *Rhapsodoi*, a more closely defined grouping, were performers of "woven words," or hexameter poems (including those attached to the name of Homer but not excluding others). Some were narratives, like the *Iliad* and the *Odyssey*, while others were lists, genealogies, and repertories of wisdom, like the Catalogue of Ships and like the *Theogony* and *Works and Days* by Hesiod. The special thing about the *Homeridai* was evidently their repertoire, which they linked with Homer, and their membership in a lineage that made them (metaphorically, if not literally) the children of Homer.

What we do not know fully, however, is where and on what occasions *rhapsodoi* (including *Homeridai*) performed. Hesiod says that he performed at the funeral games for Amphidamas at Chalkis and won a prize; Amphidamas was, one supposes, an aristocrat who had an expensive funeral. Such occasions surely did not arise often. We may be prepared to guess, on the basis of more recent texts, that Hesiod and his colleagues also competed at religious festivals. On such occasions hymns were addressed to the gods, and these hymns were often in hexameter verse like the epics. On the sacred island of Delos, it was Apollo who was addressed in this way:

> *There the Ionians in their trailing robes gather*
> *With their own children and their chaste wives.*
> *With boxing and dancing and song*
> *They recall you and give you pleasure whenever they set up the*
>   *contest.*[21]

But that too was scarcely an everyday event, and singers have to live. Many poets have found a second profession, a "day job," helpful (Hesiod makes it very clear that he was a farmer, as several modern oral poets have been). Most performances were likely to have been rewarded not with a rich prize but with food and a place near the fire, such as Odysseus earned for the tale he told to Eumaios.[22]

To judge by the careful phrase "some of the *Homeridai*," adopted by Plato as well as Isokrates, the *Homeridai* were far from monolithic in their attitude to their canon. In the fifth century a range of poems alongside the *Iliad* and the *Odyssey* was attributed to Homer; many authors disagreed over these attributions, and Plato seems to assure us that the *Homeridai*, like other people, were divided over which poems belonged to their eponymous ancestor and which did not.

A later source happens to name one of the early *Homeridai* and in so doing helps us to identify some of the additional poems. Here's the text, which comes from a Greek commentary on the lines by Pindar quoted above.

Originally people gave the name *Homeridai* to the descendants of Homer, who were his successors in the performance of his poetry. Afterward reciters who did not trace their parentage to Homer were given the same name. Particularly prominent were the followers of Kynaithos, who are said to have made many poems and inserted them among Homer's works. Kynaithos was from Chios, and is said personally to have written the *Hymn to Apollo*, which is one of those ascribed to Homer. This Kynaithos was the first to recite the works of Homer at Syracuse, in the sixty-ninth Olympiad [504 to 501 B.C.].[23]

Well, this makes us feel more at home. Greek scholars know all about the *Hymn to Apollo*. Some lines have already been quoted from it, and more will be quoted soon. Since its two parts commemorate Apollo in two aspects (the god of Delos and the god of Delphoi), some have argued that it was first performed in 522 B.C. at the unusual double festival held under the patronage of Polykrates, ruler of Samos, to honor Apollo in these aspects. This suggestion would tie in with its attribution to Kynaithos, a *rhapsodos* who was active at the right period.

The *Hymn to Apollo* is among several relatively short hexameter poems whose main purpose is to tell mythological tales in honor of various Greek gods. These hymns are now familiar to us under the label *Homeric Hymns*. No one believes that they are by the same author as the *Iliad* and the *Odyssey*, but the name has stuck. Unfortunately, the *Hymns* do not contain any hymn to Eros; if they did, it would support Plato's statement about the *Homeridai*. A hymn to Zeus would support Pindar's early reference to the *Homeridai*, but the short and scrappy hymn to Zeus that does exist in the collection can hardly have struck Pindar as typical or worth mentioning at all. However, there are also other, less venerable collections of Greek hymns. The so-called *Orphic Hymns* include another to Zeus and one to Eros; like the lines quoted by Plato, the *Orphic Hymns* are continually concerned with secret names and hidden meanings.

All in all, the additional poems ascribed to their progenitor by the *Homeridai* seem to overlap with texts known to us today, but they do not coincide entirely. Many believed that Homer had composed the *Kypria* and other epics of the Cycle (see pages 27–30), which no longer survive except in brief fragments, but Herodotos, writing about 440 B.C., already opposed that view. He had noted that there was a conflict between the *Kypria* and the *Iliad* about the route that Paris and Helen took on their way to Troy. Taking it that the *Iliad* was by Homer, Herodotos concluded from his evidence that the *Kypria* must be by a different author.[24]

What is really interesting is the initial assumption. Only 60 years after the name of Homer is first mentioned in ancient texts and 160 years after the first external allusion to the *Iliad*, beliefs concerning the two have come together to the point at which Herodotos assumes that the *Iliad* is the one self-evident work of Homer and that all other attributions to him must be tested against it. Some scholars today make the same assumption.

At the same time, Herodotos was aware of a wider grouping of hexameter poetry which he was prepared to call more vaguely *ta Homereia epea*, "the Homeric epics." He had heard that 150 years before his own time, Kleisthenes, ruler of Sikyon, after a war with Argos, had forbidden the competitions of *rhapsodoi* at Sikyon because their Homeric epics glorified the rival state of Argos. Whether or not the story is accurate, Herodotos must have some specific poem in mind. Possibly he is thinking of the *Iliad* (because *Argeioi*, "the Argives," is one of the regular names for the Greeks at Troy in this poem); more likely he is thinking of the *Thebais*, a lost poem of the Cycle, whose first line began "Sing, goddess, of thirsty Argos . . ." In the Greek text, *Argos* is actually the first word of the poem. For Herodotos, it seems, "the Homeric epics" encompassed the *Iliad* along with other poems, including the *Odyssey*, *Kypria*, and *Thebais*.[25]

He might well have included some of the *Homeric Hymns* in the same group. Later scholars attributed them doubtfully to "Homer or one of the *Homeridai*" (such as Kynaithos), but in the fifth century B.C. many did not question that they were by Homer. As it happens, the *Hymn to Apollo* is cited in evidence by Thoukydides, the Greek historian of the Peloponnesian War in the late fifth century. "Homer himself shows that this is how things were," says Thoukydides, "in the following lines, which come from the Address to Apollo." With that, he quotes the lines of the *Hymn* (already cited on page 171) that deal with festival performances at Delos. Incidentally, the version known to him is different in many small details from the *Hymn* as we read it, yet it is the same poem.[26]

You may be wondering why it matters so much who composed the *Hymn to Apollo*. It matters because it is a very personal piece of writing. That is why Thoukydides cannot resist the temptation to go on and make a second quotation from it, even though the point being made here is irrelevant to his history.

In the following lines from the same poem Homer makes it clear that there was a poetic competition, and that people used to go to Delos to compete. Addressing the Delian chorus of women, he ends his praises with these words, in which he actually speaks of himself:

> *Come now: may Apollo favor you, along with Artemis;*
> *Good health to you all; and afterward*
> *You will remember me, when any man of this earth,*
> *Any other weary stranger, comes here asking:*
> *"Girls, who is the sweetest of singers*
> *That comes here? Who has given you most pleasure?"*
> *You shall all reply in chorus:*
> *"A man who is blind, and lives in rocky Chios . . ."*[27]

The next line, which Thoukydides does not quote, is one of those predictions of greatness that poets cannot always forbear from making—

> *". . . All his songs are victorious afterward."*[28]

Every reader of this hymn is surely charmed by the poet's artless pride— "the sweetest of singers," "all his songs are victorious"—and by his neat self-description as "a man who is blind, and lives in rocky Chios." These lines are actually the oldest surviving evidence of the popular legend that Homer was blind.

To set beside the *Hymn to Apollo*, there still exist three lines from a lost poem in which (so it seems) Hesiod categorizes Homer and himself as *aoidoi*, "singers," of the special group called *rhapsodoi*, "singers of woven words":

> *Then the two singers, Homer and myself, first performed*
> *In Delos, weaving our verses into new hymns*
> *To golden-haired Phoibos Apollo, child of Leto.*[29]

It would be pleasing if this little fragment had really been composed by Hesiod, but it surely was not. It comes in much too neatly and ties off too many loose ends. It makes Hesiod (the real maker of the *Theogony* and *Works and Days*) a precise contemporary and colleague of the mysterious Homer, and it almost proves that Homer is the blind man from rocky Chios who speaks of his own successes in the *Hymn to Apollo*.

That is impossible for us to believe, although Thoukydides evidently did believe it. The person who composed the *Hymn to Apollo* was a fine poet, was working in the same tradition as the maker of the *Iliad* and the *Odyssey*, and was a forger. Study of the language of these poems strongly suggests that the *Hymn* was composed later than the two epics; moreover, it was composed in a tradition in which the use of writing played a growing part.[30] Even among ancient investigators, although there was a strong tradition that Homer was blind and an almost equally strong tradition that he came from Chios, little weight was placed on this line from the *Hymn to Apollo* in justifying such views. It was always clear to critical observers that the *Hymns* and the epics of the Cycle were simply not as good as the *Iliad* and the *Odyssey*. The passage already quoted from the ancient commentary on Pindar, naming Kynaithos as one of the *Homeridai* and the real author of the *Hymn*, adds that the "followers" of Kynaithos—a subset of the *Homeridai*—were particularly active in expanding the canon of poems ascribed to Homer.

This is how modern scholars have reached the conclusion that the author of the *Hymn*, whether or not it was Kynaithos, was not speaking of himself at all. He intended the poem to be taken as a genuine Homeric composition. He meant us to say: "Why, this is Homer!"[31]

HOMER BECOMES A CLASSIC

If we look at the matter geographically, knowledge of the *Iliad* and the *Odyssey* appears to have spread inexorably across Greek-speaking lands in the course of the sixth century B.C. Two hundred years later, an Athenian author believed that Hipparchos, the dictator of Athens around 520 B.C., had been "the first to bring the epics of Homer to this country of ours." Curiously, Herodotos had already recorded a tradition that the prophetic verses of Mousaios, another legendary early poet, were put into writing at about the same date by a compiler who worked with Hipparchos at Athens. But Herodotos said nothing about Homer in this context.[32]

The claim about Hipparchos has no strong backing, but the evidence for it is much earlier than that for the other "discoverers" of Homer mentioned on page 29, and we should perhaps tentatively accept it. Athens is only one city, but if the *Iliad* and the *Odyssey* really did begin to be better known in that city around 520, perhaps they were also spreading to other places at the same time, and this helps to verify one other reported dating. Kynaithos, "one of the *Homeridai*" and the supposed author of the *Homeric Hymn to Apollo*, is said to have been the first to perform the works of Homer at the Greek colony of Syracuse in Sicily, an event dated to "the sixty-ninth Olympiad," or, in our terms, 504 to 501 B.C. There can be no doubt that in the fifth and fourth centuries, written texts of the *Iliad* and the *Odyssey* spread far and wide; when Alexandrian scholars attempted to produce reliable editions of the epics, they were able to draw on numerous "city editions" from as far afield as the Greek colony of Marseille.

Somehow, by that time "Homer" had become a classic—the oldest and most venerable member of the canon. When and how did this happen?

The Athenians were telling one another in the fourth century B.C. that their ancestors had determined (that is how the political writer Isokrates puts it) that the Homeric epics should figure "in poetic contests and in the education of the young." Or (this is what the orator Lykourgos says) their fathers had made a law that singled out the poems of Homer among those of all other poets: "they should be performed by *rhapsodoi* at every quadrennial festival of the Panathenaia." There is supporting evidence too. By about 400 B.C. boys were studying the *Iliad* and the *Odyssey* at school, and some adults even claimed to know them by heart. On the Athenian comic stage in 405, a list of four great ancient hexameter poets is given: Orpheus the mystic, Mousaios the prophet, Hesiod the poet of farming, and "the divine Homer." It's a very odd list from our perspective—two mythical figures to whom third-rate forged verses were ascribed, one proudly individual poet, and one legendary singer of anonymous epics—but it helps to prove that Homer was accepted as a classic in Athens by the early fourth century.[33]

Schoolchildren and other readers enjoyed the *Iliad* and the *Odyssey*. They found the story line tragic and compelling, the details of warfare and practical matters instructive, the style hypnotic.

By 400 B.C. the actual maker of the poems, woman or man, was already long forgotten. By now the legendary singer Homer was in undisputed possession. To satisfy the hundreds of thousands who now studied the two epics, Homer was gradually given a detailed biography (or rather, several biographies). He was a descendant of the prophet Mousaios and the divine Orpheus. He was born at Smyrna (Izmir), his real name was Melesigenes, and he composed his epics in a cave that was afterward sacred, overlooking the springs of the river Meles near Smyrna. No, he was born in Chios and taught there, seated on a rock, which was afterward shown to tourists (indeed, it still is); he was blind; he was a lover of Odysseus's wife, Penelope; he was buried on the island of Ios, where his mother was born. He took part in a poetic duel with Hesiod, and Hesiod was judged victorious.[34]

In the revival of epic as a written genre, a revival led by Kallimachos and Apollonios in the third century B.C., Homeric verse (of a new, stylish, very literary kind) became fashionable once more. Apollonios wrote *Argonautika*, or "The Voyage of the Argonauts," a new epic on a traditional theme. Kallimachos, poet, scholar, and librarian at Alexandria, wrote *Hymns* in literary imitation of the *Homeric Hymns*. He also wrote a now lost antiquarian epic, *Aitia*, or "Explanations," a collection of myths that explained current rituals and beliefs. This is certainly not what the *Iliad* and the *Odyssey* were about, but it demonstrates that this is how the two epics were looked at by readers and scholars of Kallimachos's time. They were indeed mined for historical and linguistic information; they became the subject of commentaries and glossaries. Libraries at Alexandria and Pergamon mounted searches for variant manuscripts across the Greek world, and editors based in these libraries used the variants—and their own assumptions about Homer— to create new, authoritative edited texts.

There's room to mention only the most famous of the many later epics that belong to the lineage of the *Iliad* and the *Odyssey*. The time of Augustus, the first of the emperors, was the heyday of Latin literary epics. Virgil's *Aeneid* (he also wrote *Georgics*, a poem on farming, as a nod to Hesiod) was written at the emperor's request; as a parallel to the *Odyssey*, it tells the story of the fall of Troy and of a party of Trojan refugees, led by Aeneas, whose descendants founded Rome. The *Metamorphoses* of Ovid, a retelling of Greek myths of transformation, has a more desultory structure, like Kallimachos's *Aitia*. Both of these Roman authors glorify Augustus and his adoptive father, Julius Caesar (who claimed direct descent from Aeneas). In this they differ totally from the poet of the *Iliad* and the *Odyssey*, who shows no interest in any contemporary person or any noble family. Among several later classical epics I will name only the Latin *Civil War*, often called "Pharsalia," by Lucan; the unfinished *Achilleis*, or "Story of Achilles," by Statius; and a Greek epic by Quintus of Smyrna that narrates the last months of the Trojan War, thus forming a sequel to the *Iliad* and perhaps a replacement for the almost-forgotten early epics *Aithiopis* and *Sack of Troy*.

Medieval narrative epics are not in this family line: their makers knew little of classical precedents. First among later descendants of classical epic is Dante's *Divine Comedy*, written in Italian around 1300, in the first part of which the spirit of Virgil serves as the narrator's guide to Hell. The whole idea of a visit to the underworld is borrowed from the *Odyssey* via the *Aeneid*. Although the theme and structure of Ariosto's romantic Italian epic *Orlando Furioso* ("The Madness of Roland") have a medieval feel, there is still much that is classical in its style. It is the direct ancestor of Spenser's *Faerie Queene*, while Milton's *Paradise Lost* draws most heavily on Virgil. More heroic in feeling than any of these are Torquato Tasso's *Gerusalemme Liberata* ("Jerusalem Freed"), a crusading epic, and Luís de Camões' *Lusiads*, the national epic of Portugal, a stirring narrative of the explorations of Vasco da Gama.

Almost everything about the *Iliad* and the *Odyssey* was imitated by later writers of epic, first in Greek, afterward in Latin and in modern languages. The synonyms for proper names, such as *Achaioi = Argeioi = Danaoi, Dardanoi = Troes, Agamemnon = Atreides* ("son of Atreus"), *Paris = Alexandros*, were of course confusing for casual readers, but literary poets found them a good idea and continued to use similar sets of alternatives. Thus Virgil in the *Aeneid* has two names for the son of Aeneas, *Ascanius = Iulus;* Milton in *Paradise Lost* has at least four names for the villain of his Christian epic, *Satan = the Arch-Fiend = the Arch-Enemy = the lost Archangel;* and Camões has at least three names for his hero's homeland, *Portugal = Lusitânia = a ocidental praia lusitana* ("the westerly Lusitanian shore").

The later narrators, like the narrator of the *Iliad* and the *Odyssey,* are always omniscient: they know everything that happened on earth and everything that was discussed in heaven. These poems display their literary ancestry from their very first lines. The *Odyssey* begins, *Muse, tell me of the man;* therefore the *Aeneid* begins, "I sing of arms and the man" and *Gerusalemme Liberata* begins "I sing the pious arms and the soldier" and the *Lusiads* begins, "The arms and the famous warriors." Even *Paradise Lost* begins, "Of man's first disobedience . . ." Only Ariosto (like Stesichoros) is detached enough to mock this translinguistic formula, which must set out with a man because the first line of the *Odyssey* does, and must include arms, meaning battles, because the first line of the *Aeneid* does. Perhaps after all Ariosto was the only one perceptive enough to see that the inherited formula omits half of humanity. His opening line is *Le donne, i cavalier, l' arme, gli amori,* "The ladies, the knights, the arms, the love affairs . . ." Only the poet of the *Divine Comedy* is bold enough to break the pattern entirely. He decides that his story needs no introduction; he begins, *Nel mezzo del cammin di nostra vita,* "Midway on the road of our life . . ."

Some details of the "Homeric" style seemed so strange to later readers that they were imitated rather less closely than this. The formulas, especially the standard combinations of a common noun or personal name with an adjective, one of which would be used in the *Iliad* and the *Odyssey* almost every time a certain object or character was mentioned, were found memorable by readers even though no one understood the original logic behind their use; but poets who composed in writing decided that they could do better. Since they worked slowly, with glossaries or dictionaries at hand, they were able to multiply the adjectives for variety and appropriateness to the context, not merely according to their position in the line. Yet with all his variation, Virgil often returns to his favorite, *pius Aeneas* and *pater Aeneas.*

As for the repeated scenes (such as shared meals and sacrifices) in similar or identical words, they turned out to be convenient to manuscript copyists of the *Iliad* and the *Odyssey*, who were tempted to write these passages from memory without checking the text. In fact, it is believed that because of this understandable but lazy practice, the repeated scenes have become more numerous, and more repetitive, in the surviving manuscripts of Homer than they would have been in the earliest ones. Later poets, however, took the view that this level of repetition was boring and were careful to vary the vocabulary when they wished to describe similar scenes more than once in a narrative.

8

The Rediscovery of Orality

EARLY WORK ON ORAL POETRY

Through the many centuries that followed, down to the nineteenth century A.D., it was generally remembered by all those who thought about the matter seriously that the maker of the *Iliad* and the *Odyssey* was an oral poet. Some believed that Homer worked in writing, but few doubted that the poems were composed for oral delivery. It is easy to demonstrate this, whether from the writings of Greek and Roman commentators on the two epics or from those of later classical scholars such as Richard Bentley, whose view was that Homer wrote "a sequel of songs and rhapsodies, to be sung by himself for small earnings and good cheer, at festivals and other days of merriment."

Current everyday oral poetry existed all through that period of two thousand years. It has formed a vital part of practically every historical culture. Unfortunately, until the eighteenth century, such poetry was not generally considered to be literature. It did not interest those who studied literature, still less those who studied the classical literature of Greece. It did not occur to most classicists that they might be able to learn something about the difference between oral and written composition, something that would help them to understand the special nature of Homeric epic, by comparing oral and written composition in their own language. This prolonged failure to make a short imaginative leap may seem incredible, but it was part of a wider failure. Classical studies were the highest peak of the humanities; therefore, although Greek and Latin classics were allowed to illuminate modern literature (Bentley even tried to produce a text of Milton's *Paradise Lost* using the methods of textual criticism that he had perfected in his classical work, and failed ridiculously), it was hard for scholars to imagine that modern literature could illuminate the classics.

One of the first clear attempts to compare the early Greek epics with later oral poetry was made by a now half-forgotten figure, James Macpherson. In 1773 he published the final version of his "translations" of a sequence of Gaelic tales that he attributed to a legendary oral poet, Ossian. Macpherson also issued translations of the *Iliad* and the *Odyssey* in the same florid and incoherent English prose. He chose to treat "Homer" like "Ossian" because he believed, correctly, that the Greek epics had emerged from an oral tradition, just like the Gaelic tales.

Ossian and Macpherson were eventually discredited, but Ossian's supposed works, highly popular and widely translated, encouraged the recording of oral poetry in many European languages. Attitudes to modern literature broadened. Teachers of modern languages were to be found in more and more universities. This development went hand in hand with the growth of political nationalism, because national awareness included the awareness of a literature in the national language. The groundwork was beginning to be laid for a new approach to Homer.

Across Europe, in the course of the nineteenth century, popular oral literature in prose and verse was gathered, published, and eagerly studied. In Britain and the United States, narrative ballads, folk songs, and fairy tales were collected from oral performers, largely by amateur scholars working in a discipline known as "folk-lore." More and more analogies were noted between modern ballads on the one side and ancient and medieval epics on the other; it was noted too that English ballads belonged to a tradition that could be traced at least as far back as the fourteenth century, and that some fine ballads recorded at early stages in the tradition, such as *Chevy Chase*, were of near epic length. Lord Macaulay wrote his balladlike *Lays of Ancient Rome* (1842) as a way of working out in practice the theory that the legendary history of early Rome, surviving only in Latin prose narratives, had originally been transmitted in the form of oral poetry very much like that of early Greece. The *Iliad* and the *Odyssey* were now often said to have been woven together out of earlier, much shorter ballads and lays by Homer, and ancient statements that supported this were now taken more seriously than before. To be honest, one reason that this view found favor was that there happened to be no current tradition of oral epics in the countries where classical studies were strong (Britain, the United States, France, Germany, and Italy); in those countries, ballads and folk songs were the only modern analogy to the Homeric epics. There is even an English translation of the whole *Iliad* from the late nineteenth century, in a pastiche of early modern English, with a balladlike meter.[1]

To be equipped to compare the *Iliad* and the *Odyssey* with modern oral epics, a nineteenth-century scholar needed rare linguistic skills. Oral epics comparable in length and tone to the *Iliad* and the *Odyssey* were actually being collected, but not in North America or in western Europe. In Europe the richest sources were the countries that were later to be temporarily united as Yugoslavia. In the Christian mountain fastness of Montenegro and among the Muslim people of Bosnia, people performed epics telling of the fighting between Christians and Muslims five hundred years earlier; they were in the same language, then usually called Serbian. Across central Asia, adventurous Russian ethnographers collected a great quantity of oral poetry, including many narrative epics, in Yakut, Tatar, Kyrgyz (these three are Turkic languages), Mongolian, and Tibetan. Among the Russians themselves the *byliny*, "ballads" or short epics, told stories of fighting between Russians and Tatars hundreds of years before. In Finland and among the Finno-Ugric peoples of

northern Russia, epics of varying length were collected; the Finnish traditions became famous because they were gathered by Elias Lönnrot
into a long and fairly coherent epic, *Kalevala* (of which the first version
was published in Finnish in 1835), just as the "lays of Homer" were
believed to have been gathered by Lykourgos, Hipparchos, or some
other. In Africa and Oceania, missionaries and colonial administrators
made abstracts of historical traditions that were enshrined in oral verse
and prose narratives.

The collectors of these oral epics naturally saw analogies between
the modern material that they were collecting and the ancient epics.
They were also encouraged by the knowledge that there had been popular epics in several languages of western Europe in medieval times.
These texts now came into their own: the major Icelandic sagas, the
Anglo-Saxon *Beowulf*, the *Song of Roland* and many other French
epics, the German *Nibelungenlied*, and the medieval Greek *Digenis
Akritas*. Some modern ballads even turned out to be retellings of the
same stories. To nationalists, the newly discovered oral poetry in their
own languages helped to prove for the first time that these languages
could claim to be on an equal cultural level with classical Greek,
French, German, English, Italian, and Spanish.

Yet scholars who studied the *Iliad* and the *Odyssey*, and the
medieval epics too, treated these texts as if they had belonged to a tradition of written literature from the beginning. What else could they do?
There was as yet no theoretical underpinning for the study of oral literature. If you collected variants in manuscripts of the *Iliad*, the *Odyssey*,
and the *Chanson de Roland*, it was because you aimed to reconstruct an
original text. If different manuscripts offered alternatives, the "correct"
alternative must be chosen. If passages were present in some manuscripts and not in others, or seemed to be inconsistent with the rest of
the text, you employed literary logic to decide whether the doubtful lines
were "genuine" or "interpolated." The variant versions could have been
seen as signs of a complex oral/written tradition. Instead, all variants
except the chosen one were stigmatized as corrupt or contaminated,
and the evidence for them was swept into footnotes or appendices and
omitted entirely from translations.

The structure of the *Iliad* and the *Odyssey* was subjected to searching investigation. Ancient commentators had excused many minor

inconsistencies, either with marvelously ingenious explanations or with the remark that "even Homer nods." However, modern classical scholars generally assume that the texts on which they work were once perfect and consistent; if they are not, someone must have altered them. Noting continual inconsistencies of language, style, and plot in the Homeric epics, many nineteenth-century scholars (the separatists) concluded that the epics were a pasteup of the work of several authors; others (the unitarians) argued either for a single author named Homer or for one author per epic, whose work had later been tampered with. Was Homer one person or many people? Could the "original" epics be excavated out of the surviving texts?

SERBIAN-BOSNIAN EPIC TRADITIONS AND MILMAN PARRY

Traditional poetry in Serbian (now also called Bosnian and Croatian) was to play a crucial role in the development of oral studies—and in exploring the origins of the *Iliad* and the *Odyssey*.

At the birth of central European nationalism in the mid-eighteenth century, when the Serbians were subjects of the Ottoman empire, Andrija Kačić-Miošić compiled a national history of the Serbians and southern Slavs, published in 1756. Ottoman archives were few and secretive, so Kačić, having drawn what he could from medieval chronicles, had no choice but to look for additional source material among oral epics and ballads, still favored as popular entertainment in his homeland. Some of the most stirring of these epics dealt with incidents in the Christian-Muslim warfare of four hundred years earlier that had ended in Ottoman conquest. Reluctantly at first, then with growing enthusiasm, Kačić employed source material that practically any other historian of his time would have condemned or ignored.

He reworked this material in very much the same way that James Macpherson and Elias Lönnrot would do, in Gaelic and Finnish respectively. Kačić got in ahead of them; his work also precedes by nine years the publication of the first serious collection of English ballads, Thomas Percy's *Reliques of Ancient English Poetry*. Thus modern oral poetry in Serbian came under the scholarly spotlight before that of any other people or region. In the mid-nineteenth century, Serbian national pride was fostered by a big collection of oral literature, highlighting the famous battle of Kosovo in 1389, gathered by the writer and political activist Vuk Stefanović Karadžić, known as Vuk. At the beginning of the twentieth century, Matija Murko, a Slovene academic, carried out pioneering research into the origins, transmission, and social context of modern oral epics that he collected in Bosnia and Herzegovina. Kačić, famous in his time, was by now almost forgotten, Vuk's work known only to those who read Serbian. Murko, however, wrote in German and French, the major languages of literature and philology, so his work was accessible to the wider world of scholarship, and it was studied with great interest by Milman Parry, an American classicist who was working for a doctorate at the Sorbonne in the late 1920s. Antoine Meillet, Parry's teacher and one of the great comparative linguists of the twentieth century, guided him toward Murko's researches, offering the opinion that the peculiar style of the Homeric epics, on which Parry was working, might be explained by reference to their traditional origin as oral poetry.[2]

Such explanations, as Parry began to work them out, made good sense, but no proof could be given within the discipline of classical philology, because scholars had no adequate samples of any other oral narrative poetic tradition in classical literature. By now engaged in teaching classics at Harvard College but still conscious of unanswered questions on oral epic poetry, Parry looked toward Soviet central Asia and Yugoslavia as possible areas for fieldwork. Partly because of the long history of scholarly interest in Serbian oral poetry, partly because Murko had begun to ask the questions that Parry also needed to ask, partly because the tradition of oral narrative verse in Yugoslavia was still active and widespread, and partly because he could not get a visa for central Asia, Parry determined to go to Yugoslavia.

But why Bosnia and its Muslim singers? Vuk and Kačić had focused on the Christian history of the Serbs; their publications had become classics and school texts in Serbia. Therefore, the Christian Serbian singers of Parry's day, if they had ever attended school, had learned their repertoires not just from older singers, in the traditional way, but also from school texts. This was no longer a simple, uncomplicated oral tradition; writing was involved. Therefore, it did not meet Parry's research needs. But the repertoires of Bosnian Muslim singers had not been published at all till Murko came along, and Murko's work was almost unknown in his native Yugoslavia. Bosnian singers had had little or no education, were mostly illiterate, and still learned to sing in the traditional way.

It was true that Murko had been there before Parry. He had even made phonograph recordings, one of the methods that Parry was to adopt. But this scarcely reduced the originality of the work that Parry now undertook. Bosnian oral traditions were extremely rich, and a great number of poems, a mass of potential research material, was still uncollected. In 1934–1935, using high-quality recording equipment and sometimes working from dictation, Parry and his research team recorded well over twelve thousand performances, and this collection, now at Harvard, formed the basis for work by Parry himself (before his accidental death in 1937), his assistant Albert B. Lord (afterward professor of comparative literature at Harvard), and many others who have wanted to know at first hand how narrative poetry in an oral tradition comes into existence and what it sounds like. Lord's well-known work *The Singer of Tales* (1960) is both a study of the Bosnian-Serbian tradition and a survey of what it can contribute to our understanding of other oral traditions past and present, beginning with the *Iliad* and the *Odyssey*.

ORALITY AND THE NATURE OF GREEK EPIC

It took nearly three decades for Parry's researches concerning oral composition to become widely known among classical and medieval scholars. The insights of Parry, Lord, and others are referred to in shorthand as the "oral theory." Their application to the study of the *Iliad* and the *Odyssey* has also been called the oral theory, which can be confusing. As regards the two Greek epics, ancient sources tell us that they were performed orally and at first transmitted orally; no modern theory is involved. As for the discoveries of how oral poets in Yugoslavia do their work, these amount to confirmed fact. However, when generally applied to the understanding of oral traditions elsewhere, these discoveries and insights become a theory, and that is why Lord entitles Part One of *The Singer of Tales* (which largely sets out these confirmed facts) "The Theory."

The oral theory made plain for the first time the origins of the *Iliad* and the *Odyssey*, though leading to some misunderstandings along the way. The problem that Parry originally undertook to tackle had been set out by his teacher, Antoine Meillet, in a groundbreaking book tracing the prehistory of poetic meters in Indo-European languages:

> Homeric epic is entirely composed of formulas handed down from poet to poet. An examination of any passage will soon reveal that it is made up of lines and fragments of lines which are reproduced word for word in one or several other passages. Even those lines of which the parts happen not to recur in any other passage have the same formulaic character, and it is doubtless pure chance that they are not attested elsewhere. It's true, for example, that *Iliad* 1.554 does not appear again in the *Iliad*, nor anywhere in the *Odyssey*, but that's because there was no other occasion to use it in those poems.[3]

This is a slight exaggeration: the *Iliad* contains some passages that are not formulaic, and the *Odyssey* contains more of them. But it is largely true, and the reason for this formulaic structure had always been a mystery to later readers. Already in his dissertation Parry had demonstrated for the first time the economy of the formulaic system. For each name or noun that is likely to occur in the poem, there will be different formulas that permit it to fill any required position in the line. With rare exceptions, there is no redundancy; for each noun or name the poet uses only one formula in each position. This is why the formulaic phrases *pius Aeneas* and *pater Aeneas*, used by Virgil for the hero of the *Aeneid*, could not simultaneously be true formulas in a Homeric system: they are synonymous (they mean Aeneas) and they fill the same gap in a metrical line.

But why are the two epics structured in this way? If Meillet was correct, why were such formulas "handed down from poet to poet"? Parry's answer to this crucial question was stated in two articles published in the early 1930s. The formulas, along with the repeated scenes, are an indispensable part of the singer's equipment in building a long narrative poem. They come automatically to the lips, allowing more time for forward planning. An oral epic must be structured in this way;

otherwise, it could not be composed at all. This theory was abundantly confirmed when Parry explored the Bosnian oral epic tradition, which has a similar system of formulas.

Parry's insight offered, for the first time, an answer from the *poet's* point of view to the problem discussed from the reader's point of view on page 69—the problem of why some adjectives in the Homeric poems are inappropriate to their immediate context, as in *the noisy dogs were silent*. Folklore scholars already knew that would-be oral poets learn from existing practitioners. Parry and Lord showed what they learn: not only themes and stories but, crucially, the poetic or narrative language, and in particular the system of formulas.

In general we are talking of peoples who do not use writing and do not have formal schools. Among such peoples, those who learn several languages do so by listening, practicing, and observing audience response. They know nothing consciously of grammar, but those who become bilingual or multilingual unconsciously develop a perfect command of grammar and an ability to switch between grammars. That is exactly how it works with poetic language; a singer learns the vocabulary (the existing poetic language and formulaic system) and controls the grammar, as shown by the ability to adjust and create formulas, to misuse the system creatively, and on occasion to bypass it.

Controlling the language and the repertoire of stories, the singer develops the skill of producing, on demand, a poem that will satisfy the audience. Some imagine that an oral narrative poem will necessarily be unstructured or poorly structured, but that is to misunderstand the relation between literature and its audience. Structure aids understanding and pleases an audience. Any singer needs to please the audience, to ensure an adequate reward and a return engagement.

The fact that singers learn formulas, repeated scenes, themes, and whole story lines does not mean that any singer is compelled to repeat them without changing them or adding new stories to the list. As classical scholars slowly came to terms with the oral theory in the 1950s and 1960s, some lost sight of this point; they could not see how a poet who composes in formulas can show originality. They failed to realize that the oral poetic language is a real language, one in which formulas act as words. *Any* poet shows originality by choosing which word to use next, and which theme to introduce, and what attitude to take, and how each conflict is to be resolved. The oral narrative poet does this too, but works on a larger scale, choosing (at times) two-word formulas, whole-line formulas, and many-line standard scenes. From these, he or she builds an epic which may show at least as much originality as any written poem.[4]

Scholars who forget that written composition has imperatives just as oral composition does, and that poets are nonetheless free, may assert that an oral poet was "forced" to follow a certain path and was unable to change a formula or to reimagine a scene. Don't believe it. A poet who works in writing seldom needs to invent a word and if wise uses few newly invented words, because too many strange words make a text difficult to read. In the same way, in formulaic poetry, a poet will seldom need to invent a formula and has many more effective ways of showing originality. Still, each existing formula was devised by an oral poet; any oral poet in a living tradition is similarly free to invent a new one and to use it once or many times, and others are free to adopt it or not. Richard Martin, following an insight by Adam Parry, observes that the poet of the *Iliad* shows more than usual independence of tradition when speaking through the lips of Achilles; in Achilles' words, he argues, we find the real voice of Homer, and one form that this originality takes is the wealth of apparently new formulas to be found in Achilles' speeches.[5]

Some describe the composition in performance of oral narratives as improvisation, but that is not quite the appropriate word. The story, the possibilities for its elaboration or adjustment, and the words and formulas with which it will be expressed are in the performer's repertoire in advance. And there is no rule against premeditation. Sometimes, says Albert Lord in *The Singer of Tales*, "Singers prefer to have a day or two to think the song over, to put it in order, and to practice it to themselves. Such singers are either less confident of their ability, or they may be greater perfectionists."[6] Ahead of an important engagement, the singer will spend time thinking out the choice of theme, the nature of turning points in the plot, the aspects of character that need to be emphasized, the hints of later victories or disasters that will keep the audience balanced between suspense, shock, and satisfaction. Of course the singer who created the *Iliad* considered its general structure before beginning and continued to plan in advance of each session. With the *Odyssey*, with its two plot lines running in parallel, there's even more evidence that an experienced singer was working with a premeditated plan.

Parry and his followers showed, then, that singers learn from their predecessors the poetic language, the system of formulas, the traditional stories and characters. What they do *not* learn from each other is the precise wording of a story or poem. Whole poems are *not* transmitted from one poet to another.

It was long believed that this *was* the way in which oral narrative poems are transmitted, by being memorized and recited by each new poet in the tradition. Parry and Lord demonstrated a most important fact: this mistaken belief about memorization and accurate transmission is encouraged by oral singers themselves, because if asked, they often claim to have repeated a text word for word, just as they had heard it or just as they performed it on a previous occasion. Parry already knew that this issue would be a central one, and he planned his fieldwork carefully, collecting multiple performances by single poets and performances of the same story by different poets to answer it. It was crucial because of the ancient tradition that poems composed by Homer had been transmitted orally, over what might have been a long period, before being written down as the *Iliad* and the *Odyssey*. Parry's researches, supported by those of others who have investigated oral traditions elsewhere, show that we must reinterpret this ancient tradition, because the "same" poem is in fact never transmitted accurately in an oral narrative tradition. That is, an oral epic is never performed in the same words twice.

The Bosnian singer Đemo Zogić's report of the learning and transmission of a song makes clear how singers themselves view the matter. This quotation is followed by Albert Lord's reaction to Zogić's report:

> I engaged this Suljo Makić [said Zogić]. I sat down beside [him] and in one night I picked up that song. I went home, and the next night I sang it myself. . . . The same song, word for word, and line for line. . . . If I were to live for twenty years, I would sing the song which I sang for you here today just the same twenty years from now, word for word. . . .

> Was Zogić lying to us? No, because he was singing the story as he conceived it as being "like" Makić's story, and to him "word

for word and line for line" was simply an emphatic way of saying "like." As I have said, singers do not know what words and lines are.[7]

Lord's last assertion may seem surprising, but there is independent evidence that the concept "word" is not necessarily familiar where writing does not demand it. Chinese script, for example, portions out the language strictly into syllables, and according to a famous formulation by Benjamin Whorf, "there is no word for 'word' in Chinese."[8]

The fact that long oral narratives are not repeated or transmitted accurately (in the sense in which we would understand the term) has been so fully and convincingly demonstrated that classicists who ignore it are burying their heads in the sand. This is why the act of performing an oral epic cannot be distinguished from the act of composition. Every skilled singer is a poet. Parry was not alone in seeing this; Henry and Nora Chadwick, in their world survey of traditional literature, published while Parry was at work in Bosnia, say of Russian and Yugoslav oral poetry that "each recitation is, in some measure, a creative work. . . . Among the peasants of Lake Onega a singer never sang a *bylina* twice alike"; "Every minstrel is a more or less creative poet. . . . A poem is never repeated in exactly the same words even by the same man."[9]

ORALITY AND THE WRITTEN *ILIAD* AND *ODYSSEY*

Epic poems in Bosnia were performed in various settings, Parry discovered. The most formal was during the Muslim holy month of Ramadan. Constrained to daytime fasting, men gathered in the cafés in the evening and stayed there all night. Café owners engaged singers in advance, and sometimes a single poem lasted through a whole night. Performances at other times of year were not always planned; the audiences came and went, and there were various unpredictable interruptions. But Parry hoped to verify that a singer could produce a poem as long as the *Iliad*, and for this he had to create the setting himself, as no normal Bosnian audience would listen to such a marathon performance. On Parry's request, the singer Avdo Međedović, plied with sufficient cups of coffee, was able to dictate over three days in 1935 a respectable poem about as long as the *Iliad* on a traditional theme. Long afterward, Harvard

University Press published it under the title *The Wedding of Smailagić Meho.* Parry and a local assistant had played the part of the backer and the scribe in the production of this experimental modern *Iliad.*[10]

But the *Wedding*, unlike the *Iliad*, never became a bestseller. It's not really very good. It feels fattened, ornamented, stuffed. It can be compared with the later reworkings of the French *Song of Roland* (which in its oldest known form is short, poignant, and very good indeed); to quote Maurice Bowra in 1930, "they add nothing significant or fundamental. They merely say more elaborately what has already been said simply. And this is the point where the *Iliad* differs from them."[11] Parry tried to prove that a singer could produce something as long as the *Iliad*, but he seemed instead to have proved Bowra's point that a long oral poem would be less than half as good as the *Iliad*. Some recalcitrant scholars have continued to argue that for this reason the *Iliad* and the *Odyssey* must have been composed by a poet who worked in writing, but they haven't proved the point. That would entail showing that a writer who was *not* an oral poet, struggling to adapt an unfamiliar medium (writing) and an untried method of work (written composition) to a genre that had till now been purely oral, could do better. Meanwhile, Parry's demonstration stands, and the difference in quality between the *Wedding* and the *Iliad* does not invalidate it. If Avdo had not known, as he did, that hundreds of other epics of his tradition, sung by him and others, had already been put in writing; if he had been performing not for a foreign professor's files but to be read by people he respected; if he had been asked to perform a poem that would encapsulate the whole story of Christian-Muslim warfare in one sequence of episodes and had taken the time to plan it; and if he had wanted to; and if Parry had been very lucky, then he might have produced something that more closely equaled the *Iliad*.

In spite of his precautions, Parry sometimes found that he was observing the performance of poems that had been learned from printed texts. In fact, the marathon performance by Avdo Međedović had originated in a much shorter printed song that the singer's next-door neighbor, who knew how to read, had long ago spelled out to him. Parry did not exclude such performances from his research (many of them are present in the Parry Collection at Harvard) but he did avoid working with singers who could read. He knew beforehand that this might happen, and he chose Bosnia precisely because fewer people were literate there. He wanted to find an oral tradition that was as far as possible entirely uncontaminated by the influence of writing.

It was a good aim. With the spread of literacy in the twentieth century, it became more difficult every year to find a large and complex oral tradition that was similarly pure, and it is fortunate that Parry did his collecting when he did.

Parry and Lord concluded that an oral poet cannot continue to practice the profession with the same skill after learning to read and write and that an oral tradition dies as literacy spreads. The oral theory went wrong here, because the conclusion was not properly compared with what was known of the effect of literacy on other oral traditions. The evidence of ancient and medieval sources, and of information from beyond Europe, would have led to a more nuanced view. Literacy can have very different effects in different societies. A great deal depends on the balance of power between orality and literacy, which differs in each case. If, as in medieval western Europe, the usual language of literacy is that of an elite, and literacy does not become widespread among the participants in oral literature and is not in evidence in any popular forms of entertainment, there may be no immediate reason for oral literature to disappear.

This is an important issue for scholars of the *Iliad* and the *Odyssey*, because of the variants in early manuscripts of the two epics. Their transmission was evidently complex, and we cannot assume that the different versions developed out of one another entirely through written interpolations and copying errors by scribes. As with some of the medieval European epics, the possibility of a mixed textual tradition, in which oral transmission coexists with limited literacy, cannot be ruled out.

It is important too for all those interested in the growth of Greek culture. We have already seen that the tradition of *rhapsodoi*, and of the special group called children of Homer, continued to exist for about three hundred years, to the time of Plato and Isokrates, while the genres of Greek poetry were gradually spreading into writing. No doubt the later *Homeridai* made far more use of writing than their seventh-century predecessors had. Yet oral tradition ran on even as literacy spread; in fact, it has never died. There were still storytellers in Greece under the Roman empire. In Byzantine times a new epic tradition grew up (known to us, as with the *Iliad* and the *Odyssey*, mainly because some texts were written down), centering on Digenis Akritas, the hero of the Christian-Muslim borderland; some of these Byzantine tales are still told in oral ballad form in modern Greece and Cyprus.

Finally, then, Parry's work forces us to reinterpret the ancient tradition about the origin of the *Iliad* and the *Odyssey*. The tradition still tells us most of what we need to know—only omitting the name of the poet who saw the epics written down—but it grew up among people who thought that epics can be and are transmitted accurately in oral tradition over a long period. Everyone thought so then, and most people continued to think so until the mid-twentieth century. Thanks to Parry and others, we now know that this does not and cannot happen.

The usual reinterpretation, adopted by Albert Lord and by many others, is that Homer was not (as the sources tell us) an early poet who sang the *Iliad* and the *Odyssey* and transmitted them orally to his successors but the poet who saw the *Iliad* and the *Odyssey* written down. This flatly contradicts the ancient consensus. No ancient authority (except the unconvincing author of the pseudo-Herodotean *Life of Homer*) thought that Homer came into contact with writing.[12]

Our reinterpretation is simpler. As the tradition says, Homer was a famous singer who worked long before the use of writing. We are therefore reading not his work but that of a later singer in the same tradition, the one who composed the *Iliad* and the *Odyssey* and saw them written down. She (or he) was a seventh-century contemporary of Archilochos and was among the greatest creators of literature that the world has known, but is not named in the poems.

Oral poets do not need to name themselves: their audiences know them already. To us, the name does not matter. Like a live audience, we are beginning to know this poet.

9

Reading the Iliad *and the* Odyssey *Afresh*

A true oral epic is as ephemeral as a jazz performance or a story told to children. It disappears at the moment of performance; it can be recalled only in the audience's memory.

It is different with the *Iliad* and the *Odyssey*. We know that they are not oral texts, because we have them before us in writing. We seem to know it anyway, because they speak to us directly, more than 2,600 years after their creation. They make us a part of their audience.

The special style and structure of oral texts, fully shared by the *Iliad* and the *Odyssey*, are essential to their existence. They are the keys that enable singers and storytellers to create texts on each successive occasion, to satisfy audiences each time, and to learn new themes from others. Although real oral poems are so ephemeral, we have already seen how formulas and repeated scenes make the epic world and its characters quicker to grasp and easier to get to know; in this way the oral style makes it possible to transmit ideas not just to contemporaries but to later audiences and readers down to the present day. The same style and structure enable oral epics to channel ideas and information not just from the poet but from the distant beginnings of what may amount to hundreds of years of earlier oral tradition.

This is no random assertion—its truth can be demonstrated. First, although the poet of the *Iliad* and the *Odyssey* was no historian, and although there was no written record of these things, various small details surrounding the events of the poems, including the central fact that there was a fall of Troy, have been shown to belong to a period up to *five hundred years* before the poems were composed. Second, scholars explain some of the roughness in the rhythms of these poems by showing that in the forms that those same words had in Greek *seven hundred years* earlier, they would have fit together correctly without any roughness; later singers, all the way down to the time when these two poems were written, must have retained the phrases (because they sounded right) although they no longer gave the correct rhythm. Third, some of the formulaic phrases that are the building blocks of the poetic narrative style have been shown to have exact equivalents in the verse of other Indo-European languages. The most famous example is the phrase *kleos aphthiton*, "undying fame," clearly a formula; it occurs only once in the *Iliad* but again in Sappho's poem of the marriage of Hektor and Andromache. One single ancestral phrase with this meaning surely underlies both the Greek phrase and the Vedic Sanskrit words *śravah . . . akṣitam*, used in the lyric poetry of the *Rigveda*. The parent formula must have been used by poets in the unrecorded proto-Indo-European culture of around *three thousand years* before the poet's time.[1]

Thus, in reading the *Iliad* and the *Odyssey*, we are in touch with the poet (as when we read any text), but we are also in touch with the long and unwritten tradition that lies behind her. We are exploring not only this poet's original ideas but also those of tens or hundreds of generations of earlier singers. A text from an oral tradition opens a window on many centuries of human experience. As we read, we can ask questions that no other text can be expected to answer quite so well—

questions about the beginnings of all literature and music, about how texts become classics, about why we read and why we listen.

We can set out in several directions when beginning to read the epics. They have been regarded as authorities on carpentry and boatbuilding (true, we are told how Odysseus builds his raft), and on the ground plan of royal palaces (commentators on the *Odyssey* will give you plenty of information on Penelope's chamber, yet the poet was not too clear where Ithake was, let alone where Penelope's bedroom was), and as textbooks of kingship and warfare (and we do see a great deal of how poets imagine that kings and warriors go about their business). They have been taken as aristocratic propaganda and as an anthropological survey of an ancient society. The tradition was greater than any such special focus, and that is why the *Iliad* and the *Odyssey* carry such conviction. We can believe in such details as the Kyklops's cheesemaking, and the boat, and Odysseus's house, and the drugs mixed by Kirke and Helen, and even the single combats before the walls of Troy because the tradition, to which innumerable poets and audiences had contributed, embodied good solid depictions of these things.[2]

We can believe in the hospitality offered to Telemachos and in every other tiny detail of Homeric society—as we can believe in every detail of medieval Icelandic society in the Icelandic sagas—because these details too were shaped by many performers and audiences. We are not learning exactly how people lived in the poet's time (certainly not kings or aristocrats, because the audiences were not mainly kings and aristocrats), nor how they lived in the past, because there was no way of remembering exactly. We are learning how audiences thought in the poet's time—rich and poor, men and women, slave and free, in Greece and even beyond— because poems of the epic tradition were sung "to the peoples" in large numbers; the formulas, the plots, the morality of such poems were known to many. They were the popular culture of their day. They helped to shape how people thought and what people said.

A singer's conscious aim was to give pleasure. While doing so, and almost unconsciously, singers achieved far more than this. Epic poems were examples from which listeners learned how to deal with the big issues of life. The epics—the *Iliad* and the *Odyssey* in particular—made their audiences think about life and death, humans and gods, men and women, right and wrong. We know they did, because philosophers from

Xenophanes to Plato and beyond, whenever they raise these issues, appeal to Homer as an expert witness. As modern readers, we too form part of the audience for the epics. We too are made to think afresh.

Who makes the rules for human society? Characters in the epics tell one another that the gods impose rules and punish transgressions. When Antinoos, the most vocal of Penelope's suitors, refuses to give food to the mysterious beggar (Odysseus in disguise) and instead throws a stool at his head, his companions react sharply:

> *Antinous, you did badly to throw [the stool] at the unlucky vagrant;*
> *Fatally, if he happens to be one of the heavenly gods.*
> *For indeed the gods, in the semblance of strangers from abroad,*
> *All take existence and wander through cities,*
> *Observing the wickedness and the lawfulness of humans.*
>
> *(Odyssey* 17.483–487)

This view is reinforced by a clichéd scene in later Greek and Roman poetry in which poor peasants, faced by unexpected visitors who are actually gods in disguise, have only the most rustic of food to offer them but manage nonetheless to provide a nourishing meal. However poor the fare, the anonymous visitors always relish the hospitality and always reward their hosts.

Very cleverly, the *Iliad* and the *Odyssey* tell us about our relation with the gods in a way that makes sense to us whatever our religion. Advice and instructions come to individuals in the form of nocturnal visits by gods and goddesses, but the plot does not suffer if we take them to be dreams. We can decide that Telemachus's companion on his visit to Nestor is really his friend Mentor and not Athene in Mentor's shape. We can assume that the shipwrecked Odysseus drifted for several days at sea without Athene's help, and that he was not endowed by her with more-than-human strength and radiance but merely (as Sir Arthur Conan Doyle might have said) "threw off his rags and drew himself up to his full height." If we wish, we can believe that when Helen goes to bed with Paris again, after watching his cowardice on the battlefield and expressing her disgust for their relationship, it is not because a goddess named Aphrodite forces her to do so but because she remains obsessed by him.

Some have concluded that the poet did not believe in the traditional gods but used them as a poetic convention, but this would make nonsense of the invocations with which each poem begins and of nearly every twist and turn in their plots. The suitors tell one another that the gods are watching us, and most people in ancient Greece agreed. Dreams were sent by the gods. People (such as Sokrates) heard voices advising on a certain course of action. Belief in divine influence was all-pervading, and the poet shared it.[3]

And yet we must make our own decisions. If our actions are immoral, we and not the gods take the blame. Consider the destruction of Troy. We never quite see this event: the city still stands when the *Iliad* closes, and it is merely a memory when the *Odyssey* opens. The fall of Troy is still the defining event for both poems. It was inevitable, because of the unjust cause for which its people were fighting. Helen was taken away by Paris from the husband to whom her family gave her and continued to be kept from him, with the support of King Priam (Paris's father) and the Trojans. The fact that she went with Paris willingly does not affect the morality of this; she is in the wrong, Paris is in the wrong, and those who help them are also in the wrong.

What the gods do, when they amuse themselves by getting involved in human affairs, has no effect on the morality of human acts such as this. Morally, it is irrelevant that Aphrodite, all-powerful goddess of sexual desire, has promised (in order to win a beauty competition) to bring about the love of Paris and Helen, and keeps her promise, allowing them no personal choice. When they do what Aphrodite compels them to do, Helen and Paris are to be pitied, because they are under compulsion, but nonetheless they are in the wrong. Priam and the people of Troy are to be pitied too; they are right to fight loyally for Paris, but the cause in which they are supporting him is still wrong. It is irrelevant, finally, that the gods are joining in on either side of the Trojan conflict, fighting in person and also helping and hindering individual humans. They can, if it interests them, change the tide of battle or the outcome of a war. Morally, it is irrelevant: the balance between right and wrong for us humans remains as it was.

Each significant event in the epics tends to have two distinct causes. One is human—the desires, wishes, purposes of women and men. The other is supernatural—the persuasion, instruction, interference of gods and goddesses. Dual causation is as relevant as ever. We still have a framework of law and morality that we maintain and fight for and place above individual human wishes and compulsions. Details of course differ: currently we are less likely than ancient Greeks to fight over an act such as the elopement of Paris and the already married Helen, while comparable acts (imagine the elopement of the underage Nausikaa to marry Odysseus) would seem less serious to ancient Greeks yet would anger us more. One point remains the same. Paris and Helen were under a compulsion: what they did remained punishable. The imagined modern Odysseus and Nausikaa are under a compulsion; what they do remains punishable. The *source* of the compulsion is seen quite differently by the ancient poet and by modern observers. The poet attributes it to a particular goddess. Many people between classical times and our own would blame the Devil, or "something inside my head," or would believe that God imposes such tests on his worshippers.

What we realize as we read the *Iliad* or the *Odyssey*, since they come to us from a time when human wishes and compulsions were understood differently, is that it does not matter so very much how they are understood. It does not matter whether it is the gods' fault or our parents' fault or even our own fault. We humans must still work out for ourselves how to make our actions agree with law and morality, and we must still decide what to do when law and morality have been breached.

Many commentators on the *Odyssey* say that the suitors are in the wrong. We have already seen that it isn't as easy as that. True, when we place ourselves beside Odysseus and Eumaios, we don't like the suitors. But when we place ourselves beside the citizens of Ithake, we find that we must decide whom we would choose for our leading citizen: we can stick with Odysseus, who never comes home, or we can go for a young and vigorous member of another family (perhaps our own family). And that's when we remember (and the poet reminds us) that by the end of the poem, Odysseus has wiped out two generations of Ithake's young men; that's when we wonder, briefly, whether his return has been the best outcome for the city.

Many commentators say that in the central quarrel of the *Iliad*—the one between Agamemnon and Achilles—Agamemnon is in the wrong. As before, it's not so simple. Agamemnon is hasty, petulant, and in many ways a bad leader. Achilles is proud, sulky, and a bad subordinate. Many human beings are just like them. The poet is not telling us this story so that we can criticize Agamemnon and Achilles for being human. To be angry with the characters because we wish they would act differently is a child's response to a fairy tale, not an adult's response to epic.

The gods, or the Fates, have decided that the Trojans are in the wrong. They will lose the war, and Troy will fall. But nothing in the *Iliad* allows us to say that the Trojans are less estimable, less good, less noble than the Greeks. Priam is a fine and tragic figure; Hektor is a hero; Andromache is as brave and faithful in the *Iliad* as Penelope is in the *Odyssey*. The fall of Troy is a tragedy in the making.[4]

Twenty years ago the Icelandic specialist Jesse Byock showed that the real purpose of saga was to make its audience explore the intractable problems of Icelandic law and society. Thirteen years ago the Homeric scholar Oliver Taplin concluded that the usefulness of Greek epic is that it sets up for its audience difficult questions in politics, social life, and traditional law, the kind of questions that in real life might well cause violent conflict.[5] Singers might never realize this consciously; they might be aware of no other aim than to give pleasure. Oral epic serves its purpose whether poets and audiences realize it or not. That's why, brave and resourceful though Odysseus is, noble though Achilles may be, we will scarcely get the smallest hint as to which of the contenders, in any such judgment, ought to emerge the winner. If, like the commentators, we finally decide in favor of Achilles or against the suitors, we're doing exactly what epic audiences are supposed to do—so long as we don't let the commentators persuade us one way or the other. There is more than one choice, and we have to explore the choices for ourselves.

There are many oral epics. In early Greece a whole epic cycle was eventually put into writing, with the fall of Troy as its high spot and the death of Odysseus as its dramatic close; many other epics were sung, and some of them were written down. As far back as we can discover, the *Iliad* and the *Odyssey* were more popular than any of the rest. Their popularity has ensured that they still survive when all the rest are lost.

A good epic singer takes a detached perspective, because that singer must set up the moral questions and give the audience the pleasure of finding answers. Somehow the poet of the *Iliad* and the *Odyssey* raised the right questions, and raised them in such a way that from

Xenophanes and Herakleitos onward, we have never ceased to argue over the answers. This poet achieved an even greater level of detachment, so that we are able to ask not only whether Achilles was right but whether the quarrel was worthwhile; not only whether Menelaos or Paris deserved to win Helen but whether such a fight deserved a resolution; not only whether Odysseus should go home but whether the people of Ithake should take him back.

The making of the *Iliad* and the *Odyssey* was an astonishing achievement—an achievement whose greatness is difficult to estimate, for these are the first written texts of such significance in any European language, and the oral texts that preceded them are lost to us. It is reasonable to wonder whether an oral epic singer whose life work was the entertainment of successive, unpredictable live audiences could easily have found the time, leisure, and detachment for this achievement. The need was for a singer familiar with the tradition, less tied to the demands of live audiences, free in thought, and potentially free to spend time on a wholly unfamiliar and apparently unrewarding activity. As we have seen, it is possible, and even probable, that this poet was a woman.

If so, her work demonstrates the rightness of the choice. She had reflected that the fighting and the public business in her society was the work of men. That fighting and that public business are the themes of the *Iliad* (and of most other early Greek epics whose subjects are known to us). Epic singers are reluctant to tell their audiences what to think, and in this poet's hands the *Iliad* tells its wholly traditional story. It is left to us as audience whether we notice that the initial dispute between men is over the fate of a woman, Chryseis; the real quarrel, which follows, is over the fate of another woman, Briseis; and the whole war is over the fate of a woman, Helen.

She knew that it is for women to mourn over men, as the *Iliad* often shows us. Even if men forbid the proper form of mourning, as happens on one occasion, the women will still mourn silently.

> *Great Priam did not permit lamenting; in silence they*
> *Heaped the bodies for burning, grieving at heart,*
> *And after burning them in fire they went away to holy Ilion.*
> *Just so on the other side the well-greaved Achaioi*

Heaped the bodies for burning, grieving at heart,
And afer burning them in fire they went away to the hollow ships.
                                        (*Iliad* 7.427–432)

She knew that it is for men to fight over women; she wanted us to know
(if we are interested) that it is the women who make the decisions that
cause this fighting. Helen's views are irrelevant to all male discussions in
the *Iliad*, yet it was Helen's decision, originally, to go with Paris. The
fall of Troy would result from her decision. Hundreds of years of epic
tradition, culminating in the *Iliad* and the *Odyssey*, resulted from the
fall of Troy. As Helen said of herself and Paris,

> *On us two Zeus has set a sorry fate, so that afterward*
> *We shall be themes of song for men of the future.*
> (*Iliad* 7.427–432)

Helen foresaw a poetic tradition concerning the warfare and suffering
that she had caused, a tradition extending far into the future. This text
may, after all, carry a hidden message. The poet, as well as Helen, could
look into the future; epic poets, unlike other mortals, can see the past
and the future as well as the present. The *Iliad* and the *Odyssey*, like all
oral epics, were created at the demand of a single audience. Perhaps the
poet foresaw that, uniquely, they were fated to be heard by generations
yet unborn.

Like all epic singers of the Greek tradition, the poet of the *Iliad* and
the *Odyssey* taught no lessons. She left it to us, her future audiences, to
draw our own conclusions.

NOTES

PREFACE

1. Shipley and Foxhall, *Cambridge Guide*; Kirk, *The Iliad*.

INTRODUCTION

1. The fall of Troy is narrated by the Roman poet Virgil in the *Aeneid*, book 2.
2. This story is told by the Greek playwright Aischylos in a series of three famous tragedies, the Oresteian trilogy, the first of which is titled *Agamemnon*.

1: ORAL POETRY IN EARLY GREECE

1. *Iliad* 18.468–615.
2. The *Catalogue of Women* was traditionally said to be by Hesiod; it forms a continuation to his poem *Theogony*. These lines are from Hesiod fragment 305, Merkelbach and West, *Fragmenta Hesiodea.*
3. Archilochos fragment 120, West, *Iambi* [Athenaios 628b].
4. Aristotle, *Problems* 19.15 [918b13–29].
5. Why are the tunics glossy with oil? See Shelmerdine, "Shining and Fragrant Cloth."
6. *Odyssey* 8.250–385.
7. *Odyssey* 6.99–140.
8. *Odyssey* 4.17–19.
9. Sappho fragment 111, Lobel and Page, *Poetarum Lesbiorum Fragmenta.*
10. Sappho fragment 44, ibid. See the full translation and commentary in Burnett, *Three Archaic Poets*, pp. 219–223.
11. Alkman fragment 98, Page, *Poetae Melici Graeci.*
12. *Homeric Hymn to Apollo* 514–519.
13. Athenaios 630e–f.
14. Ibid. 606a–607b. Pindar's *paieanes* survive only in fragments on papyri; his *epinikia* can still be read complete.
15. *Iliad* 24.720–761. On Greek laments, see Alexiou, *Ritual Lament*, and Holst-Warhaft, *Dangerous Voices.*
16. *Iliad* 18.316; 19.301; 19.338.
17. *Odyssey* 24.58–62.
18. Tyrtaios fragment 7, West, *Iambi* [Pausanias, *Guide to Greece* 4.14.5]; Hippias of Erythrai [Athenaios 259e].
19. Plutarch, *Life of Solon* 21.4. See Alexiou, *Ritual Lament*, pp. 4–23.
20. Hainsworth, *The Iliad*, pp. 37, 88; Segal, "Bard and Audience," p. 5; Nagy, *Poetry as Performance*, pp. 71–73. For the festivals at Athens, see page 176.
21. *Iliad* 9.524–525.
22. Alkaios 283, Lobel and Page, *Poetarum Lesbiorum Fragmenta.*

For full translation and commentary, see Burnett, *Three Archaic Poets,* pp. 185–189.

23. Antipatros, "On Stesichoros" [*Palatine Anthology* 7.75].

24. Stesichoros fragment 33, Page, *Poetae Melici Graeci.* The fragment is reconstructed on the basis of a parody by the comic poet Aristophanes.

25. *Odyssey* 1.336–355, 8.62–82, 8.471–531.

26. *Iliad* 11.670–762 (the quotation in the text is of the last line of this passage); *Odyssey* 4.235–264.

27. *Odyssey* 11.368.

28. Plato, *Symposion* 172a–173b.

29. The classical encyclopedia is Ziegler and Sontheimer, eds., *Der kleine Pauly* (vol. 2, p. 94). The quotation is Plato, *Symposion* 201d.

30. Plato, *Symposion* 215a–222b. The quotation in the text appears near the beginning of this passage.

31. Ibid., 203b.

32. *Iliad* 6.357–358.

33. Thoukydides, *Histories* 1.9, quoting *Iliad* 2.109.

34. For the Lykourgos story, see *Epitome of Herakleides of Pontos, Constitutions* 2.3; Plutarch, *Lykourgos* 4; Aelian, *Miscellany* 13.14; Dion of Prousa 2.45. For the Peisistratos story, see Cicero, *On the Orator* 3.137; an unnamed historian cited by Pausanias, *Guide to Greece* 7.26.13; cf. Aelian, *Miscellany* 13.14; Dieuchidas, cited by Diogenes Laertios 1.57. For the Solon story, see Diogenes Laertios 1.57. For the Thestorides story, see *Life of Homer* 15–17 in Lefkowitz, *Lives,* pp. 144–145.

2. THE *Iliad* AND HISTORY

1. See *Iliad* 20.285–287, 12.381–383, and 12.447–449.

2. For calculations based on African and Polynesian historical traditions, see Henige, *Chronology;* in general, see Vansina, *Oral Tradition.*

3. Pausanias, *Guide to Greece* 2.15–17. See also Strabo, *Geography* 8.6.19 [377].

4. Strabo, *Geography* 13.1.24–42 [592-602].

5. See Boedeker, *The World of Troy*.

6. Giovannini, *Étude historique*.

7. Page, *History and the Homeric Iliad*, pp. 124–132 and especially p. 161, note 28.

8. See Latacz, *Troy and Homer*, pp. 243–244, citing recent work by Frank Starke.

9. Kirk, *The Iliad*, vol. 1, p. 194.

10. Lorimer, *Homer and the Monuments*, p. 252; Page, *History*, pp. 245, 251–252, and 283, note 78.

11. Blegen et al., *Troy*; see also the journal *Studia Troica* vol. 1 (1990) to date. Some archaeologists use the form *Troia* as an international standard and call the successive layers Troia I to Troia VIII. On the issue of dating, see Hood, "Bronze Age," and Korfmann, "Troia."

12. Latacz, *Troy and Homer*, pp. 49–72.

13. Easton et al., "Troy in Recent Perspective." For the guess about horses, see Page, *History*, pp. 67, 70.

14. Based on a French translation by Christiane Desroches-Noblecourt, membres.lycos.fr/slave1802/article.php3?id_article=319#nb28. She and others identify Arwad with Arzawa. Compare the translation in Breasted, vol. 3, p. 136.

15. After Christiane Desroches-Noblecourt (above). Compare the translation in Lichtheim, *Ancient Egyptian Literature*, vol. 2, pp. 62–72.

16. Garstang and Gurney, *Geography*; Güterbock, "Troy in Hittite Texts?"; Latacz, *Troy and Homer*, with references to work by Hawkins and Starke.

17. After Garstang and Gurney, *Geography*, p. 101; cf. Latacz, *Troy and Homer*, p. 105.

18. After Garstang and Gurney, *Geography*, p. 101; cf. Latacz, *Troy and Homer*, pp. 108–110.

19. See Mellink, "Homer, Lycia, and Lukka."

20. Kirk, *The Iliad*, vol. 1, 252–253, 261–262.

21. *Iliad* 2.530; *Odyssey* 1.334 and elsewhere.

22. Examples include the French *Pèlerinage de Charlemagne*, the Anglo-Saxon *Waldere* and *Widsith*, the German *Nibelungenlied*, the Icelandic *Thidrekssaga*, and the Latin *Waltharius*. See page 222.

23. Herodotos, *Histories* 2.116–117. See page 173.
24. The Greek sources for the incident are Pindar, *Olympian Odes* 9.70; Euripides, *Telephos*; Strabo, *Geography* 1.1.17; and Proklos, *Chrestomathy*. The latter is a prose outline of the early Greek epics and is based at this point on the *Kypria*.
25. Garstang and Gurney, *Geography*, p. 97. For a completely different, folkloric interpretation of the Teuthranian episode, see Davies, "Euripides' *Telephus*."
26. Abridged translation based on Garstang and Gurney, *Geography*, pp. 121–122; cf. Latacz, *Troy and Homer*, p. 94.
27. Virgil, *Aeneid* 2.608–633; Quintus of Smyrna, *Fall of Troy* 14.632–655.
28. Based on the translation by John A. Wilson in Pritchard, *Ancient Near Eastern Texts*, p. 262.
29. Kirk, *The Iliad*, vol. 2, pp. 36–50.

3. THE *Odyssey* AND SOCIETY

1. For the lion's jaw at Troy, see Latacz, *Troy and Homer*, p. 28, citing *Studia Troica*, vol. 6 (1996).
2. See Edwards, "Homer and Oral Tradition."
3. Stanford, *The Odyssey*, vol. 1, p. 221 (abbreviations expanded), cf. vol. 2, p. 244.
4. Bowra, *Tradition and Design*; Ruskin, *Modern Painters*, p. 302; Arnold, *On Translating Homer*.
5. Compare the comments of Camps, *Introduction*, pp. 44–49.
6. Reece, *Stranger's Welcome*, p. 63.
7. Ibid., p. 67, note 9.
8. Eustathios, *Commentary on the Odyssey* 1477.6–11.
9. *Iliad* 5.905; *Odyssey* 10.361, 8.426–468, and 19.386–507.
10. Dalby, "The *Iliad*, the *Odyssey*."
11. See the detailed overview by Ian Morris in Morris and Powell, *A New Companion*, pp. 534–559.
12. Penelope and her two maids: *Odyssey* 1.331.
13. On colonization in the poems, see Graham, "The *Odyssey*, History, and Women."
14. Finley, *World of Odysseus*, p. 34.

15. Alkaios fragment 130, Lobel and Page, *Poetarum Lesbiorum Fragmenta*; see the translation and commentary of Burnett, *Three Archaic Poets*, pp. 176–180. The poem survives on a papyrus from Egypt, not quite complete.

16. *Odyssey* 24.294.

17. Compare Milich, *Stranger's Supper*, p. 18.

18. See Chadwick and Chadwick, *Growth*, vol. 2, p. 230, citing work by Rybnikov.

19. Wace and Stubbings, *A Companion*, p. 441; Stanford, *The Odyssey*, vol. 1, p. xliii.

20. See Amory, "The Reunion"; Foley, "Penelope as Moral Agent."

4. THE MAKING OF THE *Iliad*

1. Hesiod, *Works and Days* 25–26.

2. Murko, *Poésie populaire*, p. 21.

3. Hesiod, *Theogony* 22–32.

4. Apollodoros, *Library* 1.3.3; *Scholia on Iliad* 2.595.

5. Hesiod, *Theogony* 43–50.

6. Hesiod, *Works and Days* 650–662. See West, ed., *Theogony*, pp. 43–46.

7. Stanford, *The Odyssey*, vol. 1, p. 230.

8. Hesiod, *Theogony* 98–103.

9. The argument outlined in these three paragraphs is made with great clarity by Lord, *Singer of Tales*, and by Morris, "Use and Abuse" (though they would not agree with all of my conclusions). Many scholars do not accept it, notably Gregory Nagy; see, for example, Nagy, *Homeric Questions*.

10. Xenophanes fragment 6, West, *Iambi*.

11. Griffin, *Homer*, p. 57.

12. This is controversial. Robert Fowler (*Cambridge Companion*, p. 227) is among recent scholars who believe the poet envisages "a pan-Hellenic and future readership."

13. For opinions of this cup and its relation to the *Iliad*, see Snodgrass, *Homer and the Artists*, p. 53 (distant relationship), and Graham, "The *Odyssey*, History, and Women," p. 7 (direct dependence).

5. FROM *Iliad* TO *Odyssey*

1. Hesiod, *Theogony* 340–345. See Hainsworth, *The Iliad*, pp. 318–320; West, ed., *Theogony*, pp. 259–263.
2. The seven cities near Pylos: *Iliad* 9.149–156.
3. *Odyssey* 4.351–434.
4. For Odysseus's voyages, see Bérard, *Les navigations*. For trading voyages in the epics, see Graham, "The *Odyssey*, History, and Women."
5. Baedeker, *Greece*, p. 10.
6. The quotation is from Marlowe, *Doctor Faustus*, line 1354.
7. See Farron, "The *Odyssey* as Anti-Aristocratic Statement."
8. Hesiod, *Works and Days* 10.
9. Solon fragment 29, West, *Iambi*; Aristotle, *Metaphysics* 983a2; Plutarch, *How to Listen to Poets* 16a.
10. Xenophanes fragment 1, West, *Iambi*. The preceding quotation is fragment 6.
11. Xenophanes fragment 2, West, *Iambi*.
12. For another discussion of the issues raised in this section, see Doherty, "Sirens, Muses" and *Siren Songs*.
13. *Odyssey* 22.462–464; Heubeck et al., *Commentary*, vol. 3, p. 297; Stanford, *The Odyssey*, vol. 2, p. 388.
14. Rieu, *The Odyssey*, p. xii.

6. IDENTIFYING THE POET

1. Watkins, "The Language of the Trojans"; Latacz, *Troy and Homer*, pp. 49–72.
2. *Iliad* 4.433–438.
3. *Iliad* 2.867.
4. Bowra, *Tradition and Design*, p. 152.
5. *Iliad* 1.403, 2.812–813, 20.74, 14.291.
6. Bowra, *Tradition and Design*, p. 154.
7. Hipponax fragment 61, West, *Iambi*.
8. *Odyssey* 10.305, 12.61.

9. Watkins, "Language of Gods." See also West, ed., *Theogony*, pp. 386–388.

10. For discussion and references, see Dalby, *Language in Danger*, pp. 78–80.

11. Herodotus, *Histories* 1.146.2–3; see Graham, "The *Odyssey*, History, and Women" on this passage.

12. Stanford, *The Odyssey*, pp. lix–xciv.

13. For Hesiod's dialect, see West, ed., *Theogony*, pp. 72–91. For the Homeric dialect, see Janko, *The Iliad*, pp. 8–19.

14. See pages 225–227 and Janko, *Homer, Hesiod, and the Hymns*.

15. See Burkert, "Das hunderttorige Theben"; S. West in Heubeck et al., *Commentary*, vol. 1, pp. 33–34; Graham, "The *Odyssey*, History, and Women," p. 5.

16. *Iliad* 13.126–154, 16.211–217. See Janko, *The Iliad*, pp. 59–64, for a brief discussion and references.

17. *Odyssey* 9.39–46; cf. Archilochos fragment 2, West, *Iambi*; Hipponax fragment 4, ibid.

18. Alkman fragment 5, Page, *Poetae melici Graeci* [Athenaios 416c].

19. Cicero, *On the Orator* 3.12.45. For further discussion and references, see Dalby, *Language in Danger*, pp. 76–81.

20. Percy, *Reliques*, "Essay on ancient minstrels," note AA.

21. Smith, *Epic of Pājūbī*, p. 14; *Huon de Bordeaux* 5510–5519.

22. *Beowulf* 3150–3155.

23. Chadwick and Chadwick, *Growth of Literature*, vol. 2, p. 229.

24. Ibid., vol. 2, p. 187 for the *kaleki*; vol. 3, pp. 515, 553, 663, 668 for women poets in Ethiopia and Algeria.

25. Ibid., vol. 1, pp. 536–543. See page 222.

26. Ovid, *Metamorphoses* 5.250–679.

27. Ní Uallacháin, *Hidden Ulster*; Chadwick and Chadwick, *Growth of Literature*, vol. 2, pp. 252–255, vol. 3, pp. 894–895; Phillips, *Sijobang*.

28. Nagy, "An Evolutionary Model," p. 171.

29. Merolla, *Gender and Community*, p. 130, note 26; Doherty, *Siren Songs*, p. 5.

30. Flueckiger, "Caste and Regional Variants," p. 40; Nagy, "An Evolutionary Model," pp. 170–171.

31. On Sappho and oral poetry, see Segal, "Eros and Incantation,"

and Nagy's own full exploration of the Sappho poem and its epic contacts, *Comparative Studies*, pp. 118–139.

32. Merolla, *Gender and Community*.
33. Philippi, *Songs of Gods*, p. 45. Philippi builds on the work of Japanese anthropologists and collectors, which I cannot read.
34. Percy, *Reliques*; Ní Uallacháin, *Hidden Ulster*.

7. FROM ORAL EPIC TO WRITTEN CLASSIC

1. Bentley, *Remarks*.
2. Snodgrass, *Homer and the Artists*, pp. 89–98.
3. For this painting, on a Corinthian *krater* (wine-mixing bowl) of the early sixth century, see ibid., pp. 135–136 and fig. 53.
4. Sappho fragment 44, Lobel and Page, *Poetarum Lesbiorum Fragmenta*; Alkaios fragment 44, ibid.; see West, "The Date," pp. 206–207.
5. Josephus, *Against Apion* 1.12.
6. Xenophanes fragments 9 and 10, Diehl, *Anthologia*.
7. Simonides fragment 59, Page, *Poetae melici Graeci*.
8. Simonides fragment 19, West, *Iambi*, quoting *Iliad* 6.146. It has been argued that this text is not by Simonides.
9. Herakleitos 104, 56, Diels and Kranz, *Die Fragmente*.
10. Ibid., 42. The information on false starts in athletic contests comes from Herodotos, *Histories* 8.59.
11. Pindar, *Isthmian Odes* 4.37–43.
12. Pindar, *Nemean Odes* 7.20–23.
13. Pindar, *Pythian Odes* 4.277–9.
14. Athenaios, *Deipnosophists* 347e; Aristotle, *Art of Poetry* 1409b2–7.
15. *Iliad* 14.245–246; Herodotos, *Histories* 2.23.
16. Herodotos, *Histories* 2.53.
17. Pindar, *Nemean Odes* 2.1–5.
18. Plato, *Ion* 530d; *Republic* 599d.
19. Plato, *Phaidros* 252b.
20. Isokrates, *Praise of Helen* 28. On the biographies, see Lefkowitz, *Lives*.
21. Hesiod, *Works and Days* 654–659; *Homeric Hymn to Apollo* 147–150.

22. On Hesiod's professional status, see West, ed., *Theogony*, p. 48, with my comments on page 224.

23. *Scholia on Pindar, Nemean Odes* 2.1. On this text, see Burkert, "Kynaithos."

24. Herodotos, *Histories* 2.116–117.

25. *Thebais* fragment 1, West, ed., *Greek Epic Fragments* [*Contest of Homer and Hesiod* 15]; Herodotos, *Histories* 5.67.

26. Thoukydides, *Histories* 3.104.

27. Ibid., quoting *Homeric Hymn to Apollo* 165–172.

28. *Homeric Hymn to Apollo* 173.

29. Hesiod fragment 360, Merkelbach and West, *Fragmenta Hesiodea* [*Scholia on Pindar, Nemean Odes* 2.1].

30. Janko, *Homer, Hesiod, and the Hymns.*

31. Burkert, "Making of Homer" [p. 112 of the 2001 version]; cf. West, "Invention of Homer," pp. 368–372.

32. Herodotos, *Histories* 7.6; *Hipparchos* attributed to Plato, 228b. This dialogue was not written by Plato but by some other, perhaps contemporary admirer of Sokrates.

33. Isokrates, *Panegyric* 159; Lykourgos, *Against Leokrates* 102; Xenophon, *Memoirs of Sokrates* 4.2, *Symposion* 3.6; Aristophanes, *Frogs* 1034–1035.

34. Pausanias, *Guide to Greece* 7.5.13; Pseudo-Herodotos, *Life of Homer; Contest of Homer and Hesiod.*

8. THE REDISCOVERY OF ORALITY

1. Newman, *The Iliad.*

2. Lord, *Singer of Tales*, pp. 11–12.

3. Meillet, *Les origines*, p. 61.

4. For further discussion, see Martin, *Language of Heroes*, pp. 146–152; Foley, "What's in a Sign?"

5. See Martin's exploration (*Language of Heroes*, pp. 159–205) of Achilles' reply to the embassy (*Iliad* 9.307–429), especially the list of new formulas (pp. 181–182). Cf. Parry, "Language of Achilles."

6. Lord, *Singer of Tales*, p. 26.

7. Ibid., pp. 27–28.

8. B. L. Whorf, quoted in Carroll, *Language*, p. 21.
9. Chadwick and Chadwick, *Growth of Literature*, vol. 2, pp. 245, 437.
10. Lord, "Avdo Meteđovic," and Lord, tr., *The Wedding*.
11. Bowra, *Tradition and Design*, p. 45.
12. Lord, *Singer of Tales*, pp. 8–10.

9. READING THE *Iliad* AND THE *Odyssey* AFRESH

1. *Iliad* 9.413; Sappho fragment 44.4, Lobel and Page, *Poetarum Lesbiorum Fragmenta*; *Rigveda* 1.9.7. The link was first noted by the German scholar Adalbert Kuhn in the mid-nineteenth century. See West, "Rise of the Greek Epic," pp. 152–153; Watkins, *How to Kill a Dragon*.
2. On Penelope's chamber, there is one page by J. J. Russo in Heubeck et al., *Commentary*, vol. 3, pp. 42–43, and many more pages in Bérard, *Les navigations*.
3. Janko, *The Iliad*, p. 4, with references.
4. Griffin, *Homer*, p. 42.
5. Byock, "Saga Form"; Taplin, *Homeric Soundings*, p. 63.

GUIDE TO
FURTHER READING

Details of books mentioned here and in the notes can be found in the bibliography.

TRANSLATIONS OF THE *ILIAD* AND THE *ODYSSEY*

The first full English translations of the *Iliad* and the *Odyssey* were by the Elizabethan playwright and poet George Chapman. Two hundred years later these lively translations inspired Keats's famous sonnet "On First Looking into Chapman's Homer"; after almost four hundred years they remain readable in small doses, although most readers prefer to choose a modern translation. Alexander Pope completed his *Iliad* in

1720 and his *Odyssey* in 1726. The *Iliad* was greeted with widespread praise, although the classical scholar Richard Bentley commented, "It is a pretty poem, Mr. Pope, but you must not call it Homer." Bentley was right: Pope tells the story of the *Iliad* with just as much verve as the original poet, but with a classical, Augustan, eighteenth-century feel. Although Pope's use of formulaic phrases is not like that of an oral poet, he still employs them fluently and convincingly, so their effect on the reader is similar, working alongside the narrative to build the heroic world of Greece and Troy as imagined by a great poet.

Matthew Arnold's famous essay *On Translating Homer* was published in 1861, with a continuation in 1862. Arnold comments briefly on Chapman's *Odyssey* and at some length on Pope's *Iliad*. He reserves most of his criticism for a just-published translation of the *Iliad* into a ballad-like meter by Francis Newman. This and other Victorian translations he reviewed are now deservedly forgotten, but the essay remains a pleasure to read. It is included in R. H. Super's edition of Arnold's prose works.

Arnold never translated the whole *Iliad* himself. Perhaps this is just as well. The brief translations of his own that he inserts in the essay are excellent, but they are in hexameter (the original Greek meter), which is very hard to maintain in English for more than a few lines of verse. Longfellow tried it, but few followed his example, and it's difficult to believe that even Arnold could have succeeded in converting the whole *Iliad* or *Odyssey* into good English hexameters.

Among prose translations, people still sometimes refer to the Victorian pair, the *Odyssey* by S. H. Butcher and Andrew Lang and the *Iliad* by Lang, Leaf, and Myers. They are very accurate, in a way that verse translations can never be, but their language is irritatingly archaic. Millions of copies exist of the Penguin translations by E. V. Rieu; his *Odyssey* launched the Penguin Classics, and his *Iliad* followed soon after. They are easy to read but give a false impression of the original poems: repetitions are carefully concealed, and the formulas are translated differently at each occurrence. Much closer to the originals are the *Iliad* and *Odyssey* by Martin Hammond and the *Odyssey* by Walter Shewring. These are the best translations to use if you want to know what the *Iliad* and the *Odyssey* say.

The tradition of verse translations begun by Chapman continues four hundred years later. I find those by Richmond Lattimore somewhat hard going—the heavy rhythm makes them slow to read—but they are far closer to the original epics than any other verse translation. Robert Fitzgerald's translations flow much more smoothly. If you want to experience the *Iliad* and the *Odyssey* as English poetry, try these, or the more recent translations by Robert Fagles.

GREEK LITERATURE

Hesiod, who composed his poems around 700 B.C., is the earliest Greek poet according to the chronology adopted in this book. His *Theogony* and *Works and Days* are available in English translation by Martin West. West's scholarly editions of the two poems are packed with interest but can be fully used only by readers who know Greek.

The *Homeric Hymns,* along with fragments of other poems that were sometimes claimed to be Homer's, are in Hugh Evelyn-White's translation. After Hesiod and the Homeric poems, Greek literature down to the time of Pindar and Aischylos survives only in short poems and fragments of longer ones. Fragments of other epics (including *Kypria*) appear in Greek and English in Martin West's *Greek Epic Fragments from the Seventh to the Fifth Centuries B.C.* Fragments of lyric poets, including Alkaios, Alkman, Sappho, and Stesichoros, are in D. A. Campbell's *Greek Lyric;* fragment numbering follows that of the standard Greek editions by Lobel and Page, Page, and Davies. Fragments of elegiac and iambic poets, including Archilochos, Hipponax, and Simonides, are in Gerber's two volumes; fragment numbering follows that of the standard Greek edition by West.

Several translations of the classical Greek authors mentioned in this book—Pindar, Aischylos, Herodotos, Thoukydides, and Plato— are easily available. For works by Isokrates, including his *Praise of Helen*, see the bilingual edition by Norlin and van Hook; for Strabo's *Geography*, see the bilingual edition by Jones. For Pausanias's *Guide to Greece*, see Levi.

Two English translations exist of the medieval Greek epic *Digenis Akritas*. One, useful though pedestrian, by John Mavrogordato, is based on the fourteenth-century Grottaferrata manuscript. The other, by

David Ricks, is based on the sixteenth-century Escorial manuscript, but its text is rearranged by Ricks into five poems. There is a collected edition of the different manuscript versions, in Greek only, by Kalonaros.

OTHER TEXTS AND LITERARY TRADITIONS

Of the several general surveys of oral poetry, the biggest is a three-volume manual by H. M. Chadwick and N. K. Chadwick, which appeared too early to take account of Parry's work. The Chadwicks believed in a "heroic age" through which human cultures progress only once; this heroic age would be the subject of epic and also the period when epic traditions were created. Medieval Spanish and French epics did not fit the theory and are omitted from the Chadwicks' survey. Maurice Bowra's one-volume survey *Heroic Poetry* shares some of these beliefs. Albert Lord's major work, published only eight years later, in 1960, marks a huge change in approach; he had been Milman Parry's research assistant. Later, A. T. Hatto and J. B. Hainsworth edited a two-volume collective survey of epic traditions. On the social or anthropological functions of epic, see Byock, "Saga Form," and Duggan, "Social Functions."

It is clear that there are links between the meters and the formulas of poetry in several early Indo-European languages, and these links show that some poetry, in some analogous meters, must have existed in proto-Indo-European, which is reconstructed as the ancestor of these languages. The fullest explorations of the subject are by Calvert Watkins (*How to Kill a Dragon*) and Gregory Nagy (*Comparative Studies*); see also the section "Age of the Oral Tradition" on page 223. Among literatures mentioned separately below, Indo-European links have been demonstrated in Hittite, Latin, Irish, Anglo-Saxon, Norse, and Sanskrit.

This book says little about ancient Near Eastern and Egyptian literatures, because surviving texts did not influence the poet of the *Iliad* and the *Odyssey* strongly or directly. Major work on the influence of Near Eastern cultures on early Greece has been done by Walter Burkert, Martin West, and Sarah Morris, who also contributed a chapter, "Homer and the Near East" to I. Morris and Powell's *A New Companion to Homer*. I referred to the Egyptian praise poet Pentauor and his *Song of the Battle of Qadesh*; for this, see Lichtheim, vol. 2, pp. 62–72. For the work of the Sumerian woman poet and priestess Enheduanna, see Pritchard, pp. 579–582. Translations of the Hittite historical documents mentioned can be found in Latacz's *Troy and Homer*.

Latin literature, like Greek, spans the ancient and medieval periods. Oral narrative no doubt existed in early Latin, but it does not survive, except as adapted into historical prose in Livy's *History of Rome* and into classical hexameters in Ovid's *Fasti*. Ovid's *Metamorphoses* and Virgil's *Aeneid* are literary epics drawing on Greek rather than Latin models. Translations of these texts of the first centuries B.C. and A.D. are easy to find (for the *Fasti*, see Frazer).

Geoffrey of Monmouth's *History of the Kings of Britain* is a legendary history written in the twelfth century that claims a Trojan origin for the kings of pre-Roman Britain; see the translation by Lewis Thorpe. Finally, *Waltharius* is a medieval Latin epic poem telling the legendary story of Waltharius and Hiltgunt, their escape from the court of Attila, and the heroic single combat between Waltharius and Hagano, son of Guntharius. The historical setting is central Europe in the fourth century A.D. The poem derives from a widespread oral tradition, also recorded in very different forms in Anglo-Saxon, German, and other literatures. It was written around 930 by Ekkehard of the monastery of St. Gall, perhaps on the basis of a German oral epic familiar to him. There is a translation by Dennis Kratz.

Irish is the oldest European literature after Greek and Latin. *Táin Bó Cuailnge*, "The Cattle Raid of Cooley," is the greatest of early Irish epics; it is in prose with verse passages. It was perhaps first written down in the eighth century but continued circulating orally for several hundred years. There are translations of different versions by Thomas Kinsella and Cecile O'Rahilly.

Although not closely based on authentic Gaelic texts, *Ossian's Poems* (by James Macpherson) are important for their place in the rediscovery of oral literature in modern times. The recent collection of Irish oral poetry from Ulster by Pádraigín Ní Uallacháin is important to the argument of this book because it shows the contribution made by women to the transmission of oral poetry.

The Anglo-Saxon epic *Beowulf*, written down around A.D. 1000, tells of legendary events around five hundred years before. The Anglo-Saxon catalogue poem *Widsith*, probably written in the late seventh century, takes the form of a memoir by the singer "Widsith" listing his travels and encounters. *Waldere* is a fragment of an epic that must have told a story very like that of the Latin *Waltharius*. There are translations of all three texts by S. A. J. Bradley; other translations of *Beowulf* are easily found.

The first serious collection of English ballads, based largely on manuscript sources but with some use of oral tradition, was Thomas Percy's *Reliques of Ancient English Poetry*, which includes two versions of the famous ballad *Chevy Chase*.

One of the greatest of Icelandic sagas is *Laxdaela Saga*, a prose narrative written about 1245, of which there is a translation by Magnus Magnusson and Hermann Pálsson. The saga has sometimes been attributed to Ari the Learned, who was certainly the author of *Íslendingabók*, or "Book of the Icelanders" (Ellwood). The two major narratives of the Norse discovery of America are *Groenlendinga Saga* and *Thorfinns Saga Karlsefnis*, or the Saga of Eric the Red (for translations of both, see Magnusson and Pálsson). A very different version of the story told in the Anglo-Saxon *Beowulf* is found in a fourteenth-century Icelandic text, the *Saga of King Hrolf Kraki* (Byock). The thirteenth-century *Thidrekssaga* (Buck) includes a version of the story also known from the Latin *Waltharius* and the Anglo-Saxon *Waldere*. The best-known medieval German epic is the *Nibelungenlied*, which has connections with the same tradition; see the translation by A. T. Hatto, and, on this tradition in its oral context, Haymes.

The French epic tradition seems to have begun with the story told in the *Chanson de Roland*, or "Song of Roland," of which the oldest and best-known version was written about 1080; see Brault and the study by Duggan. The *Pèlerinage de Charlemagne*, or "Pilgrimage of Charlemagne," and *Huon de Bordeaux* were among many legendary tales of Charlemagne and his knights composed during the following two centuries. There is a translation of the "Pilgrimage" by Glyn Burgess and Anne Cobby.

A survey of oral epic traditions in Indian languages appears in Blackburn et al., including a paper by Joyce Flueckiger on the story of *Candainī*. For the *Epic of Pābūjī*, see the bilingual edition by John Smith. Our knowledge of Indian orality begins with the Sanskrit *Rigveda*, a collection of religious lyrics that is probably at least three thousand years old. There is no reliable complete translation; see the selection in English by Wendy Doniger.

I have referred to several classic collections of Serbian and Bosnian oral epics, by Andrija Kačić-Miošić, Vuk Stefanović Karadžić, and Mathias Murko. These are not available in English. *The Wedding of Smailagić Meho*, collected by Milman Parry, exists in a bilingual edition (Lord).

Elias Lönnrot's *Kalevala* was a reworking of Finnish oral narratives into the form of a long epic. There is a very full survey of Russian oral traditions in the Chadwicks' three volumes. Ainu epics have been published in translation by Donald Philippi. For Kabyle (Algeria) oral narratives, see the study by Daniel Merolla. Epics in Minangkabau (western Sumatra) are the subject of Nigel Phillips's work. The epics of *Sunjata* or *Sonjara* belong to a widespread tradition known in Mandinka and related Mande languages of West Africa, telling the exploits of the founder of the Mali empire in the thirteenth century. Published versions have been tape-recorded from performances by the Gambian griots Bamba Suso and Banna Kanute (Innes et al.) and the Malian Fa-Digi Sisoko (Johnson). Also see Austen.

HOMERIC STUDIES AND CONTROVERSIES

The fullest commentaries in English are the six-volume Cambridge *Iliad* commentary edited by G. S. Kirk and the three-volume Oxford *Odyssey* commentary by Heubeck et al.

Useful one-volume introductions to Homer and to one or both epics include Camps, Griffin, Silk, and Powell; more specialized in their approach are Nagy, Martin, Taplin, Latacz, and the papers collected in Crielaard and Cairns. The *Companion to Homer* (Wace and Stubbings) may still be handy but is outdated in many details; the *New Companion to Homer* (Morris and Powell) aims to replace it.

Age of the oral tradition: There are two great differences between Homeric Greek and any everyday language: the poet habitually uses forms of the same word that come from different dialects and forms of the same word that were current at different periods. These traits are most evident when the word is part of a formula, and if it were to be modernized or adjusted to the expected date and dialect, the formula would no longer fit its place in the line. (See also the section on the digamma, page 227). Some linguistic details can be shown to date from Mycenaean times, six hundred years before the epics were written; others were already obsolete then and must be at least eight hundred years old (see West, "Greek Poetry" and West, "The Rise of Greek Epic"). Some linguistic features linked with the meter and style of the poems are much older still (Watkins; West, "Indo-European Metre").

Additionally, some details of everyday life described in the epics clearly descend from Mycenaean times: they made sense then and not later. One such is the *tower-like shield*, a special attribute of the Greek warrior Aias, which sounds just like the shields seen on Mycenaean paintings of the sixteenth and fifteenth centuries B.C., which were not in use afterward. The formulas that specify this shield had at least an eight-hundred-year history by the time they were used in the *Iliad* (7.219, 11.485).

Aoidoi and rhapsodoi: A great many scholars believe that *aoidos* was the technical term for a poet who specialized in creating oral epics; this is why the term "aoidean poetry" is used for "Greek oral epic" by the English translators in Latacz, *Troy and Homer.*

Many scholars (but by no means all) additionally believe that creative *aoidoi* were very soon supplanted, as performers of epic, by a new profession of *rhapsodoi*, who recited a fixed text (Burkert, followed by Graziosi, Powell). Accepting this hypothesis entails believing that knowledge of the epics spread widely in writing at an early date (otherwise there would be no fixed texts, and the *rhapsodoi* would have nothing to recite), and Burkert argues this case, but on shaky grounds. This common view of *rhapsodoi* has not been adopted by West, was demonstrated to be erroneous by Ford, and is characterized by Nagy as simplistic and even misleading.

As I read ancient Greek usage *aoidoi* seems to be the set of singers or poets, *rhapsodoi* the subset who usually performed hexameter narratives, and *Homeridai* a subset of the latter, members of a lineage that they believed to go back to Homer. I note West's view that there was a set of "trained rhapsodes" to which Hesiod did not belong, assuming, I think, that one could not be a farmer and a rhapsode at the same time; but we do not know how exclusive the profession of oral poet might have been or whether the way it was learned could be described as "training." In modern times, the most Homeric of the oral singers of Bosnia, Avdo Međedović, was a farmer, like Hesiod, and there was really no training (though Lord himself confusingly entitles the relevant chapter of his work "Singers: Performance and Training"). A youngster decided, more or less consciously, to learn to sing, and did so by listening to and imitating a skilled singer. In West Africa some epic singers are now able to make a living entirely by singing, thanks to radio and television, but others live mainly by farming (Conrad).

Audience: Richard Bentley theorizes that the *Iliad* was for an audience of men, the *Odyssey* for women; Jasper Griffin, perhaps responding to the same perceptions, suggests that the *Iliad* was performed to an aristocratic audience, the *Odyssey* not.

Bentley also saw that early Greek lyric poetry was essentially aristocratic while epic was performed for a wider and more popular audience. A similar relationship holds good in several other traditions, notably that of medieval France (some classicists, as ignorant of medieval French literature as was the young Maurice Bowra, have this wrong). In the mid- to late twentieth century, it was commonly said that the Homeric epics were aristocratic propaganda (for an earlier view, see Calhoun; references and brief comment can be found in Dalby, "The *Iliad*, the *Odyssey*" and "Homer's Enemies").

Catalogue of Ships: For studies, see Page; Simpson and Lazenby; and Kirk.

Some used to argue that Boiotia comes first and bulks large because the Trojan expedition set off from Aulis in Boiotia; some argued that it was because Boiotia was the home of catalogue poetry, the home of Hesiod in particular. New evidence of the Mycenaean importance of Thebes and of the Mycenaean pedigree of some previously obscure Boiotian names makes such theories less convincing (Latacz). It now seems more likely that Thebes was really dominant at the period at which a war might have taken place, although the rest of the *Iliad* does not reflect the fact.

Joachim Latacz assumes, with little question, that the catalogue was always part of the tradition that led to the *Iliad*. This helps him to argue the general historicity of the *Iliad*, but it downplays the inconsistencies between the catalogue and the rest.

Date: For the date of Hesiod's work, see West, *Theogony,* pp.

40–48; his dating is adopted in this book. West considers that the *Iliad* and the *Odyssey* are significantly later than Hesiod; his views on the date of the epics (mid-seventh century for the *Iliad*, 625–600 or even later for the *Odyssey*; see *Theogony*, p. 46; "The Date of the *Iliad*," and "Iliad and Aethiopis") are close to those adopted here. It should be understood that these are minority views.

Barry Powell has boldly argued that the Greek alphabet was invented to write the *Iliad* and the *Odyssey*; this, if accepted, dates them sometime before 750 B.C. Anthony Snodgrass, having carefully marshaled the artistic evidence, likewise concludes that the writing of the *Iliad* took place around 750, but there is an apparent conflict between Snodgrass's dating of the poems and his evidence, which does not show that these particular poems were known at an early date (though the Troy and Odysseus stories certainly were). Among others writing recently on the subject, A. J. Graham concludes for the "second half of the eighth century BC"; see also Crielaard.

The fullest statistical study of the linguistic evidence is by Richard Janko. Janko tries to calculate the relative date of the *Iliad*, the *Odyssey*, the poems of Hesiod, the *Catalogue of Women*, and some of the *Homeric Hymns*. His various measures, taken individually, tend to give similar results, which makes the result more convincing.

What does the method show? Janko himself is careful to acknowledge that it cannot give an absolute date to any of the poems, because there is no handy external evidence to provide calibration and because in any case, even in everyday spoken language, language changes are not susceptible to absolute dating. He believes that it can give a relative dating. The fact that digamma (the lost *w* sound of prehistoric Greek) is treated as if it were present in a gradually decreasing proportion of lines in the *Iliad*, the *Odyssey*, the *Works and Days*, the *Theogony* (with the *Catalogue of Women*), and the *Hymn to Aphrodite*, and that a comparable progress can be observed when other measures are applied, suggests to Janko that the poems were composed in this order.

If we actually were observing a series of language changes, and particularly if each of the poems recorded the speech of a different speaker of the same dialect, this could be valid. But if only three or four poets are involved (if, as is usually agreed, the *Works and Days* and *Theogony* are both by Hesiod, and if the *Iliad* and the *Odyssey* are both by one poet), the application of the method already becomes complicated, because the speech of a single individual, growing older, does not change at the same rate as the speech of a dialect community. And if, as is generally assumed, "Homer" and Hesiod represent two different schools or traditions, from two different parts of Greece where different everyday dialects were spoken, applying the method becomes more difficult still. But there is another and greater problem. The result of the count of observed digamma (for example) does not show how often digamma was pronounced; it had certainly ceased to be pronounced by speakers of Ionic Greek before any of these poems were made. We are not observing a series of language changes but a gradual decline in the resistance to those changes in a special poetic language as used by particular singers in different genres.

Difference between the written epics and their oral analogues: This is seldom discussed seriously. The various performances of Demodokos and Phemios in the *Odyssey* are often assumed to be just like the performance of the two extremely long surviving epics (see Dalby, "The *Iliad*, the *Odyssey*," for references).

Jasper Griffin suggests that on the two occasions that produced the *Iliad* and the *Odyssey*, the poet imposed a very long poem on his hearers instead of complying with their natural demand for something that could be heard complete in one or two sittings. In other words, the poet and not the audience was in control on this occasion. Griffin also suggests that the *Iliad* was performed to an aristocratic audience, the *Odyssey* not, but it is not easy to see how these two unpopular performances to different audiences would have resulted in written poems.

Gregory Nagy highlights the evidence that in later Athens the *Iliad* and the *Odyssey* were performed at a quadrennial festival in a sort of relay by successive performers; aiming to show that this tradition had a long history, which may explain the origin of such long poems in oral performance, he bravely suggests that the poet has a relay performance in mind in the *Iliad* scene of Achilles' singing, and that Patroklos is waiting to take a turn when Achilles is done.

Digamma: In most of the dialects of Greek, the sound *w*, known to Greek specialists as *digamma*, disappeared (ceased to be used) sometime before the beginning of written literature. Once this sound had become a thing of the past, there would normally be no reason for any evidence of it to be seen in later texts. In the language of Greek epic, however, there is plenty of evidence of digamma. In Greek verse, syllables are counted, and a consonant, including *w*, makes a division between two syllables. If a word ending in a vowel is followed by a word beginning with a vowel, the first vowel is elided, with the result that two syllables count as one. Therefore, if a word formerly beginning with digamma now begins with a vowel and if it follows another vowel in a formula or in a commonly repeated line, the formula no longer fits its place or the rhythm of the resulting line becomes incorrect. One line of the *Iliad* provides a case of the strange effect of the disappearing digamma. In the Catalogue of Ships, the leader from Syme, Nireus, is described as *Nireus, the handsomest man who ever went to Ilios/Nireus, hos kallistos aner hypo Ilion elthe* (*Iliad* 2.673). These last three words ought to make six syllables, but the rhythm requires seven. This is how it is known that *Ilios*, the usual name of Troy in the *Iliad*, used to begin with digamma (and therefore matches the Hittite name for the city, *Wilusa*): earlier singers must have said *hypo Wilion elthe*, "went to Wilios." Once digamma had disappeared, the same phrase in current Ionic Greek would have had six syllables (*hyp' Ilion elthe*), but wherever it occurs in the *Iliad* it still has to be spoken with seven (*hypo Ilion elthe*) to maintain the rhythm. It is possible to survey the *Iliad* and other early epics in order to count the places in which digamma is "observed," as in this line, and the places where it is not. (Why not in those places? Because no older formula is involved and the poet, or a recent predecessor, has devised a line afresh.) The importance of the digamma was first recognized, with remarkable insight, by Richard Bentley in the early eighteenth century. Richard Janko's study makes use of this, among other linguistic traits, in estimating the date of the early epics (see *Date*).

Formulas, repeated scenes, and oral composition: Chadwick and Chadwick saw dimly what Parry was meanwhile demonstrating: that formulas assist the oral poet. The work of Mark Edwards is the place to begin when studying the repeated scenes in the *Iliad* and the *Odyssey*.

Most readers have found that the repetitions of lines and phrases contribute to the literary quality of these as of other epics. Few scholars have understood this; W. A. Camps is one who has. Some have characterized the formulaic style with words such as "primitive" (Bowra), and some translators, such as Rieu, attempt to disguise it.

The problem whether formulaic poems can show originality was rightly dismissed by Maurice Bowra, who saw that as much originality can be shown by an oral poet in the choice of formulas as by a literary poet in the choice of words.

Gender and the poet: Samuel Butler startled late Victorian England with his argument that the poet of the *Odyssey* was a woman. Gregory Nagy is one of the very few modern scholars who have considered the question. The collection of papers edited by Cohen deals with other gender issues but not with this one.

Papers by Lillian Doherty and Helene P. Foley in Cohen's 1995 volume are especially relevant to the status of women and gender relationships in the *Odyssey*. Foley writes on the position of Penelope in the *Odyssey* (see also Amory). Lillian Doherty, in this and another paper, discusses the issue of truth in epic and how the *Odyssey* throws doubt on it, with a focus on the episode of the Sirens.

There is a tendency to downplay the extent to which women are the cause and pretext of the fights and arguments among men in the *Iliad*. It's hard to overlook Helen, but some plot outlines of the *Iliad* state that Agamemnon and Achilles are at odds over "honor" or the "distribution of booty" (both true) while omitting to mention that the booty is Briseis. The film *Troy*, open to criticism on other counts, was unfairly criticized for exaggerating the role of women in the story.

Historical references in the poems: Joachim Latacz provides a very up-to-date survey of the historical and archaeological background to the Troy story, with discussion of Troy's regional and trade importance. On these matters Latacz largely supersedes Denys Page's long-influential work. Boedeker is also useful. On the historical and geographical background, see also Dickie, Mellink, Winter, Latacz, and the section on the Catalogue of Ships above.

For general approaches to the question of history in oral tradition, see Henige and Vansina. Moses Finley and Geoffrey Kirk discussed the possible historical bases of the Troy story. Kirk disputes Finley's analogy with medieval European epics on Attila, Theoderic, and other late antique figures (an analogy that tends to show that oral epics may combine historical details from different periods), flatly asserting that medieval epics are influenced by written texts. If Kirk were right, one might suppose that the written texts would have helped, rather than

hindered, medieval epic poets in dealing with their chronological difficulties. I accept that Finley's analogy remains a useful one.

On the linguistic background to the story told in the epics, there has
been relatively little discussion, but Latacz gives a lot of space to the late
Hittite seal recently found at Troy and its language (compare Watkins).

A. J. Graham corrects Walter Burkert on the *Iliad* reference to
Egyptian Thebes: Graham is surely right to doubt that Upper Egypt, as a
separate state under a Nubian dynasty (c. 715–663 B.C.), would have
been familiar to many Greeks. Graham's conclusion (differing from mine,
page 138) is that the *Iliad* reference is a survival from the Bronze Age.

Identifying the poet: Some modern scholars believe that the two
poems are to be attributed to different poets; the differences between
the two poems are well brought out by Jasper Griffin. Others believe
that one poet was responsible for both (e.g., Janko). Many acquiesce in
naming this one poet Homer, if not wholeheartedly.

Hasty reading has led some to say, wrongly, that ancient sources
describe Homer as a writer. Albert Lord, for example, misreading the historian Josephus (*Against Apion* 1.12) and others, states that Josephus
puts forward a view of Homer as oral poet to oppose a general assumption among his predecessors that Homer used writing. Josephus's predecessors generally describe Homer as "making" or "composing" or
"singing" his poems, not writing them; what's more, Josephus makes it
clear that he is restating the common view (*phasin*, "they say").

Pausanias (in the *Guide to Greece*, written about A.D. 170) says that
Homer "made" or "composed" his poems in the cave near Smyrna, but
Peter Levi's usually excellent translation says instead that Homer
"wrote" his poems. In her *Lives of the Greek Poets*, Mary Lefkowitz provides a translation of the anonymous *Life of Homer* and surveys the biographical traditions about the legendary singer. Her translation is accurate,
but in her survey she makes the same mistake as Levi, often attributing to
ancient authors the statement that Homer "wrote" his poems.

For the ancient biographical traditions on Homer, see also West,
"The Invention of Homer."

Orality: Albert Lord made a lifelong attempt to reserve the term
"oral" to traditional formulaic narrative poetry; in other words, if it was
nonformulaic, or lyric, or prose, it couldn't be oral. Lord's highly confusing usage contributed, I think, to the misconception by certain scholars,

against the contemporary evidence, that epic was at first the only significant literary form in early Greece (Redfield). I have not adopted Lord's
usage in this book: I need a general word for all kinds of poetry and
prose that people might have enjoyed before they became familiar with
written literature, and I call them oral. On this and related issues in studies of oral literature, see also Finnegan; Bynum; Foley; and Russo.

Social, economic and literary context: For economics, Moses
Finley's highly readable *The World of Odysseus* can serve as the starting
point. See also A. J. Graham's 1995 paper surveying references to
seaborne trading and colonization in the epics. There are fewer discussions of the poems in their literary context, owing to the general
assumption that we know no other literature contemporary with the
epics (see Dalby, "Homer's Enemies"). On the artistic context of the
poems, see the excellent illustrated survey by Snodgrass, and on images
of Greek oral poets, see Padgett.

Finley found no trace in the two epics of the classical Greek *polis*,
"city-state." Kurt Raaflaub (in Morris and Powell) discussed the issue
more recently, suggesting that the *polis* seen in the epics is a loose
agglomeration of largely autonomous households rather than a community of citizens; see also Nagy, "Shield of Achilles," and my comments
on page 79.

The most recent description of Homeric society as a working system is by Hans van Wees; see also Kurt Raaflaub, cited above. The dubious nature of such reconstructions is betrayed by the term "fairy tale,"
repeatedly used of Scherie by Raaflaub, apparently because he prefers
not to use the Scherie episode as a source. Ian Morris shows that the
society depicted in the *Iliad* and the *Odyssey*, so far as it relates to any
reality, must relate to the poet's own time (though with reminiscences of
earlier periods). The nature of the relationship is often discussed (e.g.,
Dalby, "The *Iliad*, the *Odyssey*," and Raaflaub).

Writing and the Iliad *and the* Odyssey: F. A. Wolf argues (in spite of
the Bellerophontes episode; see page 100) that the poet of the *Iliad* and
the *Odyssey* knew nothing about writing. Long afterward, Milman
Parry and Albert Lord showed that this could not be so. Lord demonstrated from comparative evidence that each performance of an oral
epic is new. Thus the writing down of the poems must be the crucial
event for us; previous oral epics in the tradition cannot have been the

Iliad or the *Odyssey* and in any case are inaccessible to us. Even if unable personally to write, the poet whose work we are reading must have been aware of writing.

Gregory Nagy is notable among recent scholars who do not accept Lord's view, preferring to suppose that the poems existed for a long period in oral transmission and were written down as late as the sixth century. On this issue Lord is assumed in this book to have proved his point.

Lord argues, on comparative evidence, that the epics known to us were dictated to a scribe by an illiterate poet. The comparative evidence is weaker than he thinks. The text variants in French medieval epics, including the *Song of Roland*, and in the Greek medieval epic *Digenis Akritas* are best explained on the basis that both orality and literacy were involved at an early stage in spreading knowledge of these individual texts, and this is actually demonstrated in some detail by Lord's evidence. Yet he assumes without question that the multiple versions of medieval epics came into existence on different occasions when illiterate *jongleurs* dictated their texts to scribes, because "oral dictated texts" are his universal explanation for the existence of written texts of premodern poems of oral origin. He ignores the evidence that some *jongleurs* could write and read.

In this book, Lord's view is accepted as probable but unprovable. Many scholars prefer to suppose that the poet worked in writing.

On the early reception of the poems once written, see Graziosi. For the later iconography of the Troy and Odysseus stories, with a focus on images of women, see Cohen. The transmission of the texts of the epics by ancient and medieval scribes is not dealt with in this book; the most innovative recent study is Gregory Nagy, *Homeric Questions*.

BIBLIOGRAPHY

Alexiou, Margaret. *The Ritual Lament in Greek Tradition.* Cambridge: Cambridge University Press, 1974.

Amory, Anne. "The Reunion of Odysseus and Penelope." In *Essays on the Odyssey.* Charles H. Taylor, ed. Bloomington: Indiana University Press, 1963.

Arnold, Matthew. *On Translating Homer.* London: Longman, 1861.

———. *On Translating Homer: Last Words.* London: Longman, 1862.

Austen, Ralph, ed. *In Search of Sunjata: The Mande Oral Epic as History, Literature, and Performance.* Bloomington: Indiana University Press, 1999.

Baedeker, Karl. *Greece.* 2d ed. Leipzig: Baedeker, 1894.

Bentley, Richard. *Remarks upon a Late Discourse of Free-Thinking.* London: John Morphew, 1713.

Bérard, Victor. *Les navigations d'Ulysse.* 4 vols. Paris: Colin, 1927–1929.

———. "Le plan du palais d'Ulysse." *Revue des Études Grecques* 67 (1954): 1–34.

Blackburn, Stuart H., Peter J. Claus, Joyce B. Flueckiger, and Susan S. Wadley, eds. *Oral Epics in India.* Berkeley: University of California Press, 1989.

Blegen, Carl, et al. *Troy: Excavations Conducted by the University of Cincinnati, 1932–1938.* Princeton: Princeton University Press, 1950–1958.

Boedeker, Deborah, ed. *The World of Troy: Homer, Schliemann, and the Treasures of Priam.* Washington, D.C.: Society for the Preservation of the Greek Heritage, 1997.

Bowra, C. M. *Heroic Poetry.* London: Macmillan, 1952.

———. *Homer.* London: Duckworth, 1972.

———. *Tradition and Design in the Iliad.* Oxford: Clarendon Press, 1930.

Bradley, S. A. J., trans. *Anglo-Saxon Poetry: An Anthology of Old English Poems.* London: Dent, 1982.

Brault, Gerard J., ed. and trans. 2 vols. *The Song of Roland.* University Park: Pennsylvania State University Press, 1978.

Breasted, J. H. *Ancient Records of Egypt.* 5 vols. Chicago: University of Chicago Press, 1906–1907.

Buck, Katherine Margaret, trans. *The Wayland-Dietrich Saga: The Saga of Dietrich of Bern and His Companions.* London: A. H. Mayhew, 1924–1929.

Burgess, Glyn S., Anne Elizabeth Cobby, trans. *The pilgrimage of Charlemagne.* New York: Garland, 1988.

Burkert, Walter. "Das hunderttorige Theben und die Datierung des Ilias." *Wiener Studien* 89 (1976): 5–21.

———. "Kynaithos, Polycrates and the Homeric Hymn to Apollo." In *Arktouros: Hellenic Studies Presented to B.M.W. Knox.* G. W. Bowersock, W. Burkert, and M.C.J. Putnam, eds. Berlin: De Gruyter, 1979, pp. 53–62.

———. "The Making of Homer in the 6th Century B.C.: Rhapsodes versus Stesichorus." In *Papers on the Amasis Painter and His World.* Malibu: Getty Museum, 1987, pp. 43–62. Corrected reprint in Cairns, ed., *Oxford Readings in Homer's Iliad,* pp. 92–116.

―――. *The Orientalizing Revolution: Near Eastern Influence on Greek Culture in the Early Archaic Age.* Rev. ed., Margaret E. Pinder and W. Burkert, trans. Cambridge, Mass.: Harvard University Press, 1992.

Burnett, Anne Pippin. *Three Archaic Poets: Archilochus, Alcaeus, Sappho.* London: Duckworth, 1983.

Butcher, S. H., and A. Lang, trans. *The Odyssey of Homer.* London: Macmillan, 1879.

Butler, Samuel. *The Authoress of the Odyssey.* London: Longmans, 1897.

Bynum, David. "The Generic Nature of Oral Epic Poetry." In *Folklore Genres.* Daniel Ben-Amos, ed. Austin: University of Texas Press, 1976, pp. 35–58.

Byock, Jesse L. "Saga Form, Oral Prehistory, and the Icelandic Social Context." In *New Literary History* 16 (1984–1985): 153–173.

―――, trans. *The Saga of King Hrolf Kraki.* London: Penguin, 1998.

Cairns, Douglas L., ed. *Oxford Readings in Homer's Iliad.* Oxford: Oxford University Press, 2001.

Calhoun, G. M. "Classes and Masses in Homer." *Classical Philology* 29 (1934): 192–208, 301–316.

Campbell, D. A., ed. and trans. *Greek Lyric.* 5 vols. Cambridge, Mass.: Harvard University Press, 1988–1993.

Camps, W. A. *An Introduction to Homer.* Oxford: Clarendon Press, 1980.

Carroll, John B., ed. *Language, Thought, and Reality: Selected Writings of Benjamin Lee Whorf.* New York: Technology Press, 1956.

Castro, Jovita Ventura, et al., eds. *Philippines,* vol. 1A, *Anthology of ASEAN Literatures. Epics of the Philippines.* Quezon City: ASEAN Committee on Culture and Information, 1983.

Chadwick, H. Munro, and N. Kershaw Chadwick. *The Growth of Literature.* 3 vols. Cambridge: Cambridge University Press, 1932–1940.

Chapman, George, trans. *Homer's Odysses.* London: Nathaniell Butter, 1616.

————. *The Iliads of Homer, Prince of Poets.* London: Nathaniell Butter, 1611.

Charlesworth, James H., ed. *The Old Testament Pseudepigrapha.* 2 vols. London: Darton, Longman and Todd, 1983–1985.

Cohen, Beth, ed. *The Distaff Side: Representing the Female in Homer's Odyssey.* New York: Oxford University Press, 1995.

Conrad, David C., ed. *A State of Intrigue: The Epic of Bamana Segu According to Tayiru Banbera.* Oxford: Oxford University Press, 1990.

Crielaard, Jan Paul, ed. *Homeric Questions.* Amsterdam: Gieben, 1995. See J. P. Crielaard, "Homer, History, and Archaeology: Some Remarks on the Date of the Homeric World," pp. 201–288.

Dalby, Andrew. "Homer's Enemies: Lyric and Epic in the Seventh Century." In *Archaic Greece: New Approaches and New Evidence.* Nick Fisher and Hans van Wees, eds. London: Duckworth, 1998, pp. 195–211.

————. "The *Iliad,* the *Odyssey,* and Their Audiences." *Classical Quarterly* 45 (1995): 269–279.

————. *Language in Danger: How Language Loss Threatens Our Future.* London: Allen Lane, 2002.

Davies, Malcolm. "Euripides' *Telephus* fr. 149 Austin and the Folk-Tale Origins of the Teuthranian Expedition." *Zeitschrift für Papyrologie und Epigraphik* 133 (2000): 7–10.

————, ed. *Poetarum Melicorum Graecorum Fragmenta.* Vol. 1. Oxford: Clarendon Press, 1991.

Dickie, M. "The Geography of Homer's World." In *Homer's World: Fiction, Tradition, Reality.* O. Andersen and M. Dickie, eds. Bergen: Norwegian Institute at Athens, 1995, pp. 29–56.

Diehl, Ernestus, ed. *Anthologia Lyrica Graeca.* 6 parts. Leipzig: Teubner, 1923–1952.

Diels, H., and W. Kranz, eds. *Die Fragmente der Vorsokratiker.* 5th ed. Berlin, 1934–1935.

Doherty, Lillian Eileen. *Siren Songs: Gender, Audiences, and Narrators in the Odyssey.* Ann Arbor: University of Michigan Press, 1995.

————. "Sirens, Muses, and Female Narrators in the Odyssey." In *The Distaff Side: Representing the Female in Homer's Odyssey.* Beth Cohen, ed. New York: Oxford University Press, 1995, pp. 81–92.

Doniger O'Flaherty, Wendy, trans. *The Rig Veda: An Anthology.* Harmondsworth, England: Penguin, 1981.

Duggan, J. J. "Social Functions of the Medieval Epic in the Romance Literatures." *Oral Tradition* 1 (1986): 728–766.

————. *The Song of Roland: Formulaic Style and Poetic Craft.* Berkeley: University of California Press, 1973.

Easton, D. F., J. D. Hawkins, A. G. Sherratt, and E. S. Sherratt. "Troy in Recent Perspective." *Anatolian Studies* 52 (2002): 75–109.

Edwards, M. W. "Homer and Oral Tradition: The Type-Scene." *Oral Tradition* 7 (1992): 284–330.

————. *The Iliad: A Commentary.* Vol. 5: Books 17–20. Cambridge: Cambridge University Press, 1991.

Ellwood, T., trans. Ari the Learned. *The Book of the Settlement of Iceland.* Kendal, England: T. Wilson, 1898.

Evelyn-White, Hugh G., ed. and trans. *Hesiod, the Homeric Hymns, and Homerica.* Cambridge, Mass.: Harvard University Press, 1914.

Fagles, Robert, trans. Homer. *The Iliad.* New York: Viking, 1990.

————. Homer. *The Odyssey.* New York: Viking, 1996.

Farron, S. G. "The Odyssey as Anti-Aristocratic Statement." *Studies in Antiquity* 1 (1979–1980): 50–101.

Finley, M. I. *The World of Odysseus.* New York, 1978.

Finnegan, Ruth. *Literacy and Orality.* Oxford: Oxford University Press, 1988.

————. *Oral Poetry: Its Nature, Significance, and Social Context.* Cambridge: Cambridge University Press, 1977.

Fitzgerald, Robert, trans. Homer. *The Iliad.* Garden City, N.Y.: Anchor, 1974.

————. Homer. *The Odyssey.* Garden City, N.Y.: Anchor, 1961.

Flueckiger, Joyce Burkhalter. "Caste and Regional Variants in an Oral Epic Tradition." In *Oral Epics in India.* Stuart H. Blackburn et al., eds. Berkeley: University of California Press, 1989, pp. 33–54.

Foley, Helene P. "Penelope as Moral Agent." In *The Distaff Side: Representing the Female in Homer's Odyssey.* Beth Cohen, ed. New York: Oxford University Press, 1995, pp. 93–115.

Foley, John Miles. *Immanent Art: From Structure to Meaning in Traditional Oral Epic.* Bloomington: Indiana University Press, 1991.

——. *The Theory of Oral Composition. History and methodology.* Bloomington: Indiana University Press, 1988.

——. "What's in a Sign?" In *Signs of Orality: The Oral Tradition and Its Influence in the Greek and Roman World.* E. Anne Mackay, ed. Leiden: Brill, 1999, pp. 1–27.

Ford, A. L. "The Classical Definition of Rhapsodia." *Classical Philology* 83 (1988): 300–307.

Fowler, Robert, ed. *The Cambridge Companion to Homer.* Cambridge: Cambridge University Press, 2004.

Frazer, J. G., ed. and trans. *Publii Ovidii Nasonis Fastorum Libri Sex.* 5 vols. London: Macmillan, 1929.

Garstang, J., and O. R. Gurney. *The Geography of the Hittite Empire.* London: British Institute of Archaeology at Ankara, 1959.

Gerber, Douglas E., ed. and trans. *Greek Elegiac Poetry from the Seventh to the Fifth Centuries B.C.* Cambridge, Mass.: Harvard University Press, 1999.

——. *Greek Iambic Poetry from the Seventh to the Fifth Centuries B.C.* Cambridge, Mass.: Harvard University Press, 1999.

Giovannini, A. *Etude historique sur les origines du catalogue des vaisseaux.* Berne: Francke, 1969.

Graham, A. J. "The *Odyssey*, History, and Women." In *The Distaff Side: Representing the Female in Homer's Odyssey.* Beth Cohen, ed. New York: Oxford University Press, 1995, pp. 3–16.

Graziosi, Barbara. *Inventing Homer: The Early Reception of Epic.* Cambridge: Cambridge University Press, 2002.

Griffin, Jasper. "The Epic Cycle and the Uniqueness of Homer." *Journal of Hellenic Studies* 97 (1977): 39–53.

——. *Homer.* Oxford: Oxford University Press, 1980.

——. "Homer and Excess." In *Homer: Beyond Oral Poetry. Recent Trends in Homeric Interpretation,* V. M. Bremer et al., eds. Amsterdam: Grüner, 1987, pp. 85–104.

——. "Homeric Words and Speakers." *Journal of Hellenic Studies* 106 (1986): 36–57.

Güterbock, H. G. "Troy in Hittite Texts? Wilusa, Ahhiyawa, and Hittite History." In *Troy and the Trojan War: A symposium held at Bryn Mawr College, October 1984.* M. J. Mellink, ed. Bryn Mawr: Bryn Mawr College, 1986, pp. 33–44.

Hainsworth, J. B. *The Iliad: A Commentary.* Vol. 3: Books 9–12. Cambridge: Cambridge University Press, 1993.

Hammond, Martin, trans. Homer. *The Iliad.* Harmondsworth, England: Penguin, 1987.

———. Homer. *The Odyssey.* London: Duckworth, 2000.

Hatto, A. T., trans. *The Nibelungenlied.* Harmondsworth, England: Penguin, 1965.

———, and J. B. Hainsworth, eds. 2 vols. *Traditions of Heroic and Epic Poetry.* London: Modern Humanities Research Association, 1980–1989.

Haymes, E. R. "Ez wart ein buoch funden: oral and written in Middle High German heroic epic." In *Comparative Research on Oral Traditions: A Memorial for Milman Parry.* J. M. Foley, ed. Columbus, Ohio: Slavica, 1987, pp. 235–244.

Henige, David P. *The Chronology of Oral Tradition.* Oxford: Clarendon Press, 1974.

Heubeck, A., S. West, et al. *A Commentary on Homer's Odyssey.* 3 vols. Oxford: Oxford University Press, 1988–1992.

Holst-Warhaft, Gail. *Dangerous Voices: Women's Laments and Greek Literature.* London: Routledge, 1992.

Hood, Sinclair. "The Bronze Age Context of Homer." In *The Ages of Homer: A Tribute to Emily Townsend Vermeule.* Jane B. Carter and Sarah P. Morris, eds. Austin: University of Texas Press, 1995, pp. 25–32.

Innes, Gordon, trans. Bamba Suso and Banna Kanute. *Sunjata: Gambian Versions of the Mande Epic.* Lucy Durán and Graham Furniss, eds. London: Penguin, 1999.

Janko, Richard. *Homer, Hesiod, and the Hymns: Diachronic Development in Epic Diction.* Cambridge: Cambridge University Press, 1982.

———. *The Iliad: A Commentary.* Vol. 4: Books 13–16. Cambridge: Cambridge University Press, 1992.

Johnson, John William, ed. and trans. Fa-Digi Sisoko. *The Epic of Son-Jara: A West African Tradition.* Bloomington: Indiana University Press, 1986.

Jones, H. L., ed. *The Geography of Strabo.* 8 vols. Cambridge, Mass.: Harvard University Press, 1917–1932.

Kalonaros, P. P., ed. *Vasilios Digenis Akritas*. 2 vols. Athens: Papadima, 1941–1942.

Kinsella, Thomas, trans. *The Táin*. Dublin: Dolmen, 1969.

Kirk, G. S., ed. *Homer. The Iliad: A Commentary*. Cambridge: Cambridge University Press, 1985–1994.

———. *The Iliad: A Commentary*. Vol. 1: Books 1–4. Cambridge: Cambridge University Press, 1985.

———. *The Iliad: A Commentary*. Vol. 2: Books 5–8. Cambridge: Cambridge University Press, 1991.

Korfmann, Manfred. "Troia, an Ancient Anatolian Palatial and Trading Center." In *The World of Troy: Homer, Schliemann, and the Treasures of Priam*. Deborah Boedeker, ed. Washington, D.C.: Society for the Preservation of the Greek Heritage, 1997, pp. 53–74.

Kratz, Dennis M., trans. *Waltharius and Ruodlieb*. New York: Garland, 1984.

Lang, Andrew, Walter Leaf, and S. H. Myers, trans. *The Iliad of Homer*. London: Macmillan, 1883.

Latacz, Joachim. *Homer: His Art and His World*. Ann Arbor: University of Michigan Press, 1996.

———. *Troy and Homer: Towards a Solution of an Old Mystery*. Oxford: Oxford University Press, 2004.

———. "Wilusa, Wilios, Troia: Zentrum eines hethitischen Gliedstaats in Nordwest-Kleinasien." In *Die Hethiter und ihr Reich*. Stuttgart: Theiss, 2002, pp. 196–203. English translation available at www.uni-tuebingen.de/troia/eng/wilusaengplus.pdf.

Lattimore, Richmond, trans. Homer. *The Iliad*. Chicago: University of Chicago Press, 1951.

———. *The Odyssey of Homer*. New York: Harper and Row, 1967.

Lefkowitz, Mary R. *The Lives of the Greek Poets*. London: Duckworth, 1981.

Levi, Peter, trans. Pausanias. *Guide to Greece*. Harmondsworth, England: Penguin, 1971.

Lichtheim, M. *Ancient Egyptian Literature*. 3 vols. Berkeley: University of California Press, 1973–1980.

Lobel, E., and D. Page, eds. *Poetarum Lesbiorum Fragmenta*. Oxford: Clarendon Press, 1968.

Lord, Albert Bates. "Avdo Međedović, Guslar." *Journal of American Folklore* 69 (1956): 320–330.

————. "Homer's Originality: Oral Dictated Texts." *Transactions and Proceedings of the American Philological Association* 84 (1953): 124–134.

————. *The Singer of Tales.* Cambridge, Mass.: Harvard University Press, 1960.

————, trans. Avdo Međedović. *The Wedding of Smailagić Meho.* Cambridge, Mass.: Harvard University Press, 1974.

Lorimer, H. L. *Homer and the Monuments.* London: Macmillan, 1950.

Lyons, M. *The Arabian Epic.* Cambridge: Cambridge University Press, 1995.

Macpherson, James, trans. *The Poems of Ossian.* London: Strahan and Becket, 1773.

Magnusson, M., and H. Pálsson, trans. *Laxdaela Saga.* Harmondsworth, England: Penguin, 1969.

————. *The Vinland Sagas: The Norse Discovery of America.* Harmondsworth, England: Penguin, 1965.

Martin, Richard P. *The Language of Heroes: Speech and Performance in the Iliad.* Ithaca: Cornell University Press, 1989.

Mavrogordato, John, ed. and trans. *Digenes Akrites.* Oxford: Clarendon Press, 1956.

Meillet, A. *Les origines indo-européennes des mètres grecs.* Paris: Presses Universitaires de France, 1923.

Mellink, Machteld J. "Homer, Lycia, and Lukka." In *The Ages of Homer: A Tribute to Emily Townsend Vermeule.* Jane B. Carter and Sarah P. Morris, eds. Austin: University of Texas Press, 1995, pp. 33–43.

Merkelbach, R., and M. L. West, eds. *Fragmenta Hesiodea.* Oxford: Clarendon Press, 1967.

Merolla, Daniela. *Gender and Community in the Kabyle Literary Space: Cultural Strategies in the Oral and in the Written.* Leiden: Research School CNWS, School of Asian, African and Amerindian Studies, 1996.

Milich, Zorka. *A Stranger's Supper: An Oral History of Centenarian Women in Montenegro.* New York: Twayne, 1995.

Morris, I. "The Use and Abuse of Homer." In *Oxford Readings in Homer's Iliad.* Douglas L. Cairns, ed. Oxford: Oxford University Press, 2001, pp. 57–91.

Morris, Ian, and Barry Powell, eds. *A New Companion to Homer*. Leiden: Brill, 1997.

Morris, S. P. "Greek and Near Eastern Art in the Age of Homer." In *New Light on a Dark Age: Exploring the Culture of Geometric Greece*. S. Langdon, ed. Columbia: University of Missouri Press, 1997, pp. 56–71.

Murko, Mathias. *La poésie populaire épique en Yougoslavie au début du XXe siècle*. Paris: Champion, 1929.

Nagy, Gregory. *The Best of the Achaeans: Concepts of the Hero in Archaic Greek Poetry*. Baltimore: Johns Hopkins University Press, 1979.

———. *Comparative Studies in Greek and Indic Meter*. Cambridge, Mass.: Harvard University Press, 1974.

———. "An Evolutionary Model for the Making of Homeric Poetry: Comparative Perspectives." In *The Ages of Homer: A Tribute to Emily Townsend Vermeule*. Jane B. Carter and Sarah P. Morris, eds. Austin: University of Texas Press, 1994, pp. 163–179.

———. *Greek Mythology and Poetics*. Ithaca: Cornell University Press, 1990.

———. *Homeric Questions*. Austin: University of Texas Press, 1996.

———. *Poetry as Performance: Homer and Beyond*. Cambridge: Cambridge University Press, 1996.

———. "The Shield of Achilles: Ends of the *Iliad* and Beginnings of the Polis." In *New Light on a Dark Age: Exploring the Culture of Geometric Greece*. S. Langdon, ed. Columbia: University of Missouri Press, 1997, pp. 194–207.

Newman, F. W., trans. *The Iliad of Homer*. London: Walton and Maberly, 1856.

Ní Uallacháin, Pádraigín. *A Hidden Ulster: People, Songs, and Traditions of Oriel*. Dublin: Four Courts Press, 2003.

Norlin, George, and LaRue van Hook, trans. *Isocrates*. 3 vols. Cambridge, Mass.: Harvard University Press, 1928–1945.

O'Rahilly, Cecile, ed. and trans. *Táin Bó Cúalnge*. Dublin: Dublin Institute for Advanced Studies, 1967.

Padgett, J. Michael. "A Geometric Bard." In *The Ages of Homer: A Tribute to Emily Townsend Vermeule*. Jane B. Carter and Sarah P. Morris, eds. Austin: University of Texas Press, 1995, pp. 389–405.

Page, Denys L. *History and the Homeric Iliad*. Berkeley: University of California Press, 1959.

———. *Poetae melici Graeci*. Oxford: Clarendon Press, 1962.

Parry, Adam. "The Language of Achilles." *Transactions and Proceedings of the American Philological Association* 87 (1956): 1–7. Reprinted in *The Language and Background of Homer*, G. S. Kirk, ed. Cambridge: Heffer, 1964, pp. 48–54; also reprinted in Adam Parry, *The Language of Achilles and Other Papers*. Oxford: Clarendon Press, 1990.

———, ed. *The Making of Homeric Verse. The collected papers of Milman Parry*. Oxford: Clarendon Press, 1971.

Parry, Milman. "Studies in the Epic Technique of Oral Verse-Making, 1. Homer and Homeric Style." *Harvard Studies in Classical Philology* 41 (1930): 73–147.

———. *L'épithète traditionnelle dans Homère: Essai sur un problème de style homérique*. Paris, 1928. English version: "The Traditional Epithet in Homer." In *The Making of Homeric Verse. The Collected Papers of Milman Parry*. A. Parry, ed. Oxford: Clarendon Press, 1971, pp. 1–190.

Percy, Thomas. *Reliques of Ancient English Poetry*. 5th ed. 3 vols. London, 1812.

Philippi, Donald L. *Songs of Gods, Songs of Humans: The Epic Tradition of the Ainu*. Tokyo: Tokyo University Press, 1979.

Phillips, Nigel. *Sijobang: Sung Narrative Poetry of West Sumatra*. Cambridge: Cambridge University Press, 1981.

Pope, Alexander, trans. *The Iliad of Homer*. 6 vols. London: Bernard Lintott, 1715–1720.

———. *The Odyssey of Homer*. 6 vols. London: Bernard Lintott, 1725–1726.

Powell, Barry B. *Homer*. Malden, Mass.: Blackwell, 2004.

———. *Homer and the Origin of the Greek Alphabet*. Cambridge: Cambridge University Press, 1991.

———. "Why Was the Greek Alphabet Invented? The Epigraphical Evidence." *Classical Antiquity* 8 (1989): 321–350.

Pritchard, James B. *Ancient Near Eastern Texts Relating to the Old Testament*. 3d ed. Princeton: Princeton University Press, 1969.

Raaflaub, Kurt A. "A Historian's Headache: How to Read 'Homeric Society'?" In *Archaic Greece: New Approaches and New Evidence*.

Nick Fisher and Hans van Wees, eds. London: Duckworth, 1998, pp. 169–193.

Redfield, J. M. *Nature and Culture in the Iliad: The Tragedy of Hektor.* Chicago: University of Chicago Press, 1975.

Reece, Steve. *The Stranger's Welcome: Oral Theory and the Aesthetics of the Homeric Hospitality Scene.* Ann Arbor: University of Michigan Press, 1993.

Richardson, N. *The Iliad: A Commentary.* Vol. 6: Books 21–24. Cambridge: Cambridge University Press, 1993.

Ricks, David, ed. and trans. *Byzantine Heroic Poetry.* Bristol, England: Bristol Classical Press, 1990.

Rieu, E. V., trans. Homer. *The Iliad.* Harmondsworth, England: Penguin, 1950.

———. Homer. *The Odyssey.* Harmondsworth, England: Penguin, 1945.

Ruskin, John. *Modern Painters.* London: Smith, Elder, 1856.

Russo, Joseph A. "Oral Theory: Its Development in Homeric Studies and Applicability to Other Literatures." In *Mesopotamian Epic Literature: Oral or Aural?* Marianna E. Vogelzang and Herman L. J. Vanstiphout, eds. Lewiston, Maine: Edwin Mellen Press, 1992, pp. 7–21.

Segal, Charles. "Bard and Audience in Homer." In *Homer's Ancient Readers.* Robert Lamberton and John J. Keaney, eds. Princeton: Princeton University Press, 1992, pp. 3–29.

———. "Eros and Incantation: Sappho and Oral Poetry." In *Reading Sappho: Contemporary Approaches.* Ellen Greene, ed. Berkeley: University of California Press, 1996, pp. 58–75.

Shelmerdine, Cynthia W. "Shining and Fragrant Cloth in Homeric Epic." In *The Ages of Homer: A Tribute to Emily Townsend Vermeule.* Jane B. Carter and Sarah P. Morris, eds. Austin: University of Texas Press, 1995, pp. 99–107.

Shewring, Walter, trans. Homer. *The Odyssey.* Oxford: Oxford University Press, 1980.

Shipley, Graham, and Lin Foxhall, eds. *Cambridge Guide to Classical Civilization.* Cambridge: Cambridge University Press, forthcoming.

Silk, Michael. *The Iliad.* Cambridge: Cambridge University Press, 1987.

Simpson, R. Hope, and J. F. Lazenby. *The Catalogue of Ships in Homer's Iliad*. Oxford: Clarendon Press, 1970.

Smith, John D. *The Epic of Pābūjī*. Cambridge: Cambridge University Press, 1991.

Snodgrass, Anthony. *Homer and the Artists: Text and Picture in Early Greek Art*. Cambridge: Cambridge University Press, 1998.

Stanford, W. B., ed. *The Odyssey of Homer*. 2 vols. 2d ed. London: Macmillan, 1958.

Super, R. H., ed. Matthew Arnold. *On the Classical Tradition*. Ann Arbor: University of Michigan Press, 1960.

Taplin, Oliver. *Homeric Soundings: The Shaping of the Iliad*. Oxford: Clarendon Press, 1992.

Thorpe, Lewis, trans. Geoffrey of Monmouth. *The History of the Kings of Britain*. Harmondsworth, England: Penguin, 1966.

van Wees, Hans. "Princes at Dinner: Social Event and Social Structure in Homer." In *Homeric Questions*. Jan Paul Crielaard, ed. Amsterdam: Gieben, 1995, pp. 147–182.

———. *Status Warriors: War, Violence, and Society in Homer and History*. Amsterdam: J. C. Gieben, 1992.

Vansina, Jan. *Oral Tradition as History*. Rev. ed. London: James Currey, 1985.

Wace, A.J.B., and F. H. Stubbings, eds. *A Companion to Homer*. London: Macmillan, 1962.

Watkins, Calvert. *How to Kill a Dragon: Aspects of Indo-European Poetics*. New York: Oxford University Press, 1995.

———. "Language of Gods and Language of Men: Remarks on Some Indo-European Meta-linguistic Traditions." In *Myth and Law Among the Indo-Europeans*. Jaan Puhvel, ed. Berkeley: University of California Press, 1970, pp. 1–17.

———. "The Language of the Trojans." In *Troy and the Trojan War: A Symposium Held at Bryn Mawr College, October 1984*. M. J. Mellink, ed. Bryn Mawr: Bryn Mawr College, 1986, pp. 1–19.

West, Martin L. "The Date of the Iliad." *Museum Helveticum* 52 (1995): 203–219.

———. *The East Face of Helicon: West Asiatic Elements in Greek Poetry and Myth*. Oxford: Clarendon Press, 1997.

————. "Greek Poetry 2000–700 B.C." *Classical Quarterly* 23 (1973): 179–192.

————. "Iliad and Aethiopis." *Classical Quarterly* 53 (2003): 1–14.

————. "Indo-European Metre." *Glotta* 51 (1973): 161–188.

————. "The Invention of Homer." *Classical Quarterly* 49 (1999): 364–382.

————. "The Rise of the Greek Epic." *Journal of Hellenic Studies* 108 (1988): 151–172.

————. *Studies in Greek Elegy and Iambus.* Berlin: De Gruyter, 1974.

————, ed. and trans. *Greek Epic Fragments from the Seventh to the Fifth Centuries B.C.* Cambridge, Mass.: Harvard University Press, 2003.

————, ed. Hesiod. *Theogony.* Oxford: Clarendon Press, 1966.

————, ed. Hesiod. *Works and Days.* Oxford: Clarendon Press, 1978.

————, ed. *Iambi et elegi Graeci.* 2d ed. Oxford: Clarendon Press, 1989–1992.

————, trans. Hesiod. *Theogony and Works and Days.* Oxford: Oxford University Press, 1999.

Winter, Irene J. "Homer's Phoenicians: History, Ethnography, or Literary Trope?" In *The Ages of Homer: A Tribute to Emily Townsend Vermeule.* Jane B. Carter and Sarah P. Morris, eds. Austin: University of Texas Press, 1995, pp. 247–271.

Wolf, F. A. *Prolegomena ad Homerum.* Halle: Libraria Orphanotrophei, 1795.

Ziegler, Konrat, and Walther Sontheimer, eds. *Der kleine Pauly.* Munich: Artemis, 1975.

INDEX

ABOUT THE AUTHOR

Andrew Dalby is a historian and linguist with a long-standing interest in oral literature. He is best known for his writings about food, wine, and pleasure in the ancient world: *Siren Feasts, Empire of Pleasures, Dangerous Tastes, Food in the Ancient World from A to Z, Flavours of Byzantium*, and, with Sally Grainger, *The Classical Cookbook*. He has also written on the languages of the world (*Dictionary of Languages*) and on the past and the likely future of world languages (*Language in Danger*). His books have been translated into ten languages. An escaped librarian, he now lives by writing. He lives in France, grows fruit, and makes hard cider.